LET TRUMP
BE TRUMP

LET TRUMP BE TRUMP

THE INSIDE STORY *of*
HIS RISE *to the* PRESIDENCY

COREY R. LEWANDOWSKI
AND DAVID N. BOSSIE

CENTER
STREET®

NEW YORK   NASHVILLE

Center Street
Hachette Book Group
1290 Avenue of the Americas, New York, NY 10104
centerstreet.com
twitter.com/centerstreet

First Edition: December 2017

Center Street is a division of Hachette Book Group, Inc. The Center Street
name and logo are trademarks of Hachette Book Group, Inc.

The publisher is not responsible for websites (or their content)
that are not owned by the publisher.

The Hachette Speakers Bureau provides a wide range of authors for
speaking events. To find out more, go to www.HachetteSpeakersBureau.com
or call (866) 376-6591.

Print book interior design by Timothy Shaner, NightAndDayDesign.biz

Library of Congress Cataloging-in-Publication Data has been applied for.

ISBNs: 978-1-5460-8330-6 (hardcover), 978-1-5460-8329-0 (ebook)

Printed in the United States of America

LSC-C

10 9 8 7 6 5 4 3 2 1

TO PRESIDENT DONALD J. TRUMP
AND FIRST LADY MELANIA TRUMP
AND THE ENTIRE TRUMP FAMILY FOR
MAKING AMERICA GREAT AGAIN.

COREY R. LEWANDOWSKI
To my wife, Alison, and our kids, Abigail, Alex,
Owen, and Reagan. I could not have embarked
on this amazing journey without your help and support.
Because of your resolve we have helped to change
the world. Thank you for everything!

And to Mom, you never let me quit anything.
I owe you so much. I love you all!

DAVID N. BOSSIE
To my wonderful wife, Susan, and our beautiful
children, Isabella, Griffin, Lily, and Maggie.
Your love and laughter continue to inspire me
on our incredible journey together.

And to my parents, Norm and Marie. Thank you for
instilling in me a strong work ethic and a love
of country. I love you all very much.

CONTENTS

LET TRUMP BE TRUMP

I pledge to every citizen of our land that I will be president for all Americans, and this is so important to me. For those who have chosen not to support me in the past, of which there were a few people . . . [*laughter*] I'm reaching out to you for your guidance and your help so that we can work together and unify our great country.

—DONALD J. TRUMP, VICTORY SPEECH,
NOVEMBER 8, 2016

CHAPTER 1

ELECTION NIGHT

Donald Trump's chances of winning are approaching zero.
—*Washington Post,* October 24, 2016

Donald Trump Stands a Real Chance of Being the Biggest
Loser in Modern Elections
—*Huffington Post*, October 27, 2016

Our final map has Clinton winning with 352 electoral votes.
—*Los Angeles Times*, November 6, 2016

DONALD J. TRUMP couldn't have struck a more perfect tone in acknowledging his victory on election night. It's hard to imagine what one might say in accepting a job at which so many were counting on you to succeed and so many others never wanted you to have in the first place. We'd like to think Americans of all political beliefs felt a little bit of optimism for our great country after President-elect Trump made his acceptance speech. In part because of the media coverage, it was one of the most bitter, contentious presidential elections in recent memory.

Yes, Donald Trump had said things typical politicians would never have said, but what needed to be said about the Washington establishment's failure to stand up for the people they were elected to represent. He certainly hadn't minced any words about his opponent, Hillary Clinton, just as she hadn't about him. But that night, at that moment, it was important to the country to see Mr. Trump the same way we had seen him for the last two years: gracious, respectful, and speaking to and for all Americans, Republican, Democrat, and Independent—the Americas who have been forgotten for too long. President-elect Trump was gracious in thanking Hillary Clinton for her service to our country and asking Republicans and Democrats for their help and guidance.

Anyone who knows Donald Trump the way we do knows he was sincere during those few moments onstage, and even his critics praised his acceptance speech. Even the self-deprecating part about the "few people" who didn't support him was pure Trump. But more than anything else, he was at that moment humbled by the honor that had been bestowed on him by a country he truly loves, confident in his abilities and the miracles possible when the free men and women of this great land work together to achieve greatness.

That was the Donald Trump America saw in the first hours of November 9, 2016, after Hillary Clinton had conceded the election. The twenty-four hours leading up to that moment were another story altogether.

At around one o'clock in the afternoon on Election Day, Dave Bossie left the campaign's war room in Trump Tower and made the five-minute walk to 30 Rock to do an interview with Hallie Jackson on MSNBC. Jackson had asked him where he was most concerned. "It's not a concern," he said. "We just have our path to 270." Over and over he had told interviewers that week that Trump's gateway to the presidency ran through

North Carolina, Ohio, Iowa, and Florida. On Jackson's show he sounded knowledgeable, confident.

But on his way back to Trump Tower he was just trying to keep straight the thoughts that flared in his mind. He had been talking to the campaign's state directors all day, people like Mike Rubino in Virginia, Scott Hagerstrom in Michigan, Eric Branstad in Iowa, Bob Paduchik in Ohio, Susie Wiles in Florida, and David Urban in Pennsylvania. All key battleground states. All giving him anecdotal reports like, "It's raining in Cleveland" or, "The turnout is low in these precincts" or, "They have machine problems in Philly" (no surprise there).

In one moment he was sure Trump would win. In the next, he thought we didn't have a chance.

By late afternoon, it looked like the latter. In the war room, on the fourteenth floor of Trump Tower, a space that had once housed the set for *The Apprentice*, it was all hands on deck. Ivanka, Don Jr., Don Jr.'s wife, Vanessa, Eric, and Eric's wife, Lara, were working the phones. Our communications team, led by Hope Hicks, Jason Miller, Jessica Ditto, and Boris Epshteyn was heroic. People such as Bryan Lanza, Kaelan Dorr, Clay Shoemaker, Chris Byrne, Steven Chung, Andy Surabian, Cliff Sims, and others, some of whom had been with the campaign since the beginning, were calling top-five radio shows in key markets such as North Carolina, Florida, and Ohio. During the campaign, the Trump children did scores and scores of interviews, and on Election Day they did one right after the other.

"Go out and vote for my father," they said.

"Hurry, before the polls close!"

The truth was, some on the campaign were already jumping ship. The Friday before the election, Sean Spicer, then the chief strategist for the Republican National Committee and a campaign adviser, called a meeting at RNC headquarters in which his team gave tier-one network reporters its predicted totals for the Electoral College vote. The information was strictly on background and under embargo. In that meeting, the Republican data team said that Donald Trump would get no more than 204 electoral votes, and that he had little chance of winning any of the battleground states, and that even dead-red Georgia was a toss-up. On the record, Spicer and the RNC's chief of staff, Katie Walsh, did several network and newspaper briefings just before the election in which they downplayed the race at the top of the ticket and instead talked about the importance of down-ballot races and the improvement in the RNC's ground game. But Spicer was so convinced of a Trump loss that he was actively petitioning networks for a job the week before the election. In the coming months, a lack of loyalty would split the new administration in two. The actions of Spicer and other RNC staff helped widen that divide.

Because of these actions, Mr. Trump never fully trusted the RNC team.

By five o'clock on election night, though, something close to panic had set in in the war room. That's when the candidate himself took to the phone. When Jason Miller joined the campaign as communications adviser, and Paul Manafort was still the campaign's chairman, the two would come up with lengthy briefing notes for Trump's radio interviews containing information like "This guy's located in X city or market and has been the show's host for X number of years, and he has an X-thousand-person listenership." Trump would look at the paper and say, "What the fuck is this? I don't need all this. Just give me a phone number and tell me who to call."

In any traditional campaign, with any traditional candidate, a staffer would call the radio producer and say something like,

"Hold on for Mrs. Clinton in three minutes." But not with our candidate.

"Hi, this is Donald Trump," he said into the receiver. "Let me speak to the host." And that's what he did in the war room, call after call. Some of the producers didn't believe him. "No, you're not," they said. "Yes, I am," Trump would say. It would have been hysterical if the presidency of the United States hadn't been on the line. Things were upside down. And they only got worse.

Meanwhile, in Washington, DC, Donald Trump's first campaign manager was steaming. It was the last place Corey R. Lewandowski wanted to be. For the first time in living memory, both presidential candidates were spending election night in New York City. Hillary Clinton's campaign was headquartered at the Jacob K. Javits Convention Center on the far west side of Manhattan, while Donald Trump's campaign war room was in Trump Tower. The Trump campaign had booked the New York Hilton Midtown on Sixth Avenue for its after-party, while Hillary and Bill took a suite at the Peninsula Hotel, just a little over a block away. But CNN, in its infinite wisdom (as Corey likes to say), had decided the best place for Donald Trump's former campaign manager to broadcast his election-night commentary from was the CNN studio in Washington.

Corey Lewandowski's relationship with Jeff Zucker, the president of CNN, was good but colorful. And though CNN and Zucker feigned outrage at some of the things Corey did while he was working for the network, including catching a ride on Trump Force One, the 757 with TRUMP emblazoned on the fuselage, while the rest of the press corps languished behind, they were mostly thrilled with the information that only he had or could share with their viewers. That access had helped provide Anderson Cooper with an interview with Melania Trump days after the *Access Hollywood* tape turned the Trump campaign upside down.

But on election night, of all nights, Zucker wouldn't let Corey go to New York, where he longed to be more than anywhere in the world. He wanted to be with the team, his team, which he never really left.

In the CNN studio, when the early numbers indicated that the election was going to go as the mainstream media predicted, the cable news anchors and commentators were having a good time at Corey's expense, both on camera and off. No matter how much the Wolf Blitzers, the John Kings, the Jake Tappers, and the scores of reporters from other networks professed their even-handedness and their unbiased approach to covering the election, the truth was they almost unanimously wanted Trump to lose. Some disliked the candidate intensely. Many disliked Corey because he worked for Trump. Later in the evening, the political commentator Van Jones would call Corey "a horrible person."

Corey, however, didn't give a fuck what they thought.

All he cared about were the returns and winning.

At exactly 5:01 p.m., Dave was in his office when his BlackBerry rang. On the line was Chris Vlasto, a senior producer at ABC. Dave and Vlasto's relationship went back over twenty years. They knew each other from the Clintons' Whitewater and campaign-finance investigations, when Vlasto was the producer of an investigative news team and Dave was the chief investigator for the House Committee on Government Reform and Oversight.

"Are you sitting down?" Vlasto asked.

"Oh boy," Dave said. "This can't be good."

"No, it's not. You guys are in for a long night."

Vlasto had the early exit numbers that the consortium of news networks—the Associated Press, ABC News, CBS News, CNN, Fox News, and NBC News—had collected. The consortium followed eleven battleground states, including Ohio, Florida, and Pennsylvania. Trump was down in eight of the eleven states by five to eight points. The news was devastating. A kill shot.

You just don't come back from spreads like that, Dave thought. There just weren't enough votes out there to come back from five to eight points down.

Dave wrote the numbers Vlasto gave him on a piece of copy paper on which he had previously scribbled some precinct turnout numbers from Cuyahoga County, Ohio. He then left his office and walked down the internal staircase to the fifth floor, where the campaign's Election Day war room was located. In Trump Tower, going from the fourteenth floor to the fifth floor means traveling only one level. The missing numbers have something to do with either the height of the lobby or real estate value—take your pick. On five, he ran into Stephen K. Bannon, the campaign's CEO and strategist, who had just come out of the inner war room, a smaller, private data and troubleshooting office for senior campaign staff.

"What's up?" Bannon asked.

Dave had just finished reading Bannon the numbers when Mr. Trump's son-in-law Jared Kushner walked over to them. Dave started from the beginning and began reading the numbers to Jared. Then Reince Priebus, the Republican National Committee's chairman, joined the huddle. For privacy, the group went out to the balcony that overlooked Fifth Avenue. There, Dave began to read the dismal numbers for the fourth time, but this time something struck him as odd. According to the consortium's exit poll numbers, Trump was down seven points in Colorado.

Jared called his father-in-law in the residence and tried to soft-pedal Vlasto's numbers.

"Melania," Mr. Trump called to his wife, "Jared says we're going to lose."

Mr. Trump then snapped his flip phone closed and tossed it across the room and onto the bed. "What a waste of time and money," he said.

At 5:34, Dave received an email from Vlasto with the early exits he had requested. He scrolled down to the bottom of the page where there were two footnotes describing what the asterisks next to some of the numbers meant. One asterisk signified a "partial phone and exit poll." Two asterisks meant "all phone and no exit poll." Colorado was one of the states marked with two asterisks. Colorado votes 100 percent by mail-in ballot. There was no way to have accurately polled people who mailed in their ballots over the previous days or weeks.

Dave took the sheet and found Jared, Bannon, and Priebus.

"I think these numbers are bad," he told them.

At around nine o'clock, the boss arrived in the war room on the fourteenth floor and stood in front of a wall mounted with six seventy-five-inch TVs, all showing different networks. The number of people in the room had somehow swelled. There were dozens of pizza boxes piled on the tables. Melania Trump was there, as were the Trump kids. Governor Mike Pence, his wife, Karen, and their daughter, Charlotte, were there. New Jersey Governor Chris Christie was there, as was Dr. Ben Carson. Bob Mercer, the reclusive conservative billionaire, was dressed in a dapper three-piece gray suit. Bannon said he looked like Rich Uncle Pennybags, the Monopoly man. Dave's wife, Susan, and his son Griffin, his nephew Daniel, and his brother-in-law, Scott Hall, were there. They had gotten separated from the rest of Dave's family, who were over at the Hilton with everyone else. They all closed in around Governor Pence and Donald Trump.

Election Day is the worst day of any campaign. It's the day when you let go of the steering wheel and leave your destination up to fate. Most people in politics don't do well when it's fate's turn to drive, especially when the car you're in seems to be headed off a cliff.

The team led by Dave and scheduler Caroline Wiles had the gas pedal to the floor during the last days on the road. From the Phoenix "Trumpmania" event in July 2015 to Grand Rapids on Election Day morning, Donald Trump's rallies were the driving force of the campaign. But the final swing Dave had built was just a stone killer, three days of crisscrossing the country, doing six events a day, and finally landing in Michigan after midnight on Election Day.

As the boss watched the TVs in the war room, his hopes were falling apart. We were down in Ohio, down in Florida, and down in North Carolina.

"Hey geniuses," the boss said to no one in particular, "how's this working for us?"

Dave went over and tried to reassure him, echoing the same things that Jared, Steve, and Kellyanne Conway had said. "It's the early vote and absentee ballots," he said. The Democrats put all their emphasis there and ignored Election Day. "They cannibalized their Election Day vote." Though Trump was down significantly in absentee and early voting in North Carolina, the spread wasn't as much as Romney's four years earlier. Romney made up the difference on Election Day and came back to win his only battleground state victory. The team was positive that the Trump campaign would do the same, if for no other reason than Hillary's numbers in the urban areas weren't nearly as strong as Obama's. The team had made the same argument to several networks and newspapers over the previous few days. Fox's political editor Chris Stirewalt was pointedly skeptical. Still, the team was able to convince the network to change its prediction for North Carolina from leaning toward Clinton to a toss-up—or at least it did for a little while. We took it as a small victory, but Fox changed the forecast back to leaning toward Hillary before Election Day.

The boss wasn't convinced. "Look at the numbers, genius," he said.

But the numbers had already started to turn. The undercover Trump voters, as Kellyanne Conway called them, the ones who didn't believe the Left's propaganda against Trump but who felt isolated by it, were streaming to the polls and finally got their say.

The shift in momentum began as a feeling. Dave called Susie Wiles, Trump's state campaign manager in Florida, for the twenty-fifth time, or so it seemed. She had overseen setting up a state war room in which every possible outcome could be calculated, based on absentee ballots and early voting. Susie and her team knew the numbers they had to hit in each of the state's sixty-seven counties. And, going into the election, she was confident that candidate Trump was going to win the state. Vlasto's numbers had Trump down by five in Florida. As the polls closed, with data collection and analysis, her confidence hadn't wavered. The margins in the southernmost "D counties," or Democratic counties, told the story. The narrow spreads in those counties boded well for Trump's chances.

Dave took the internal staircase to Bill Stepien on the fifth floor. Stepien had been New Jersey Governor Chris Christie's top political aide before Christie fired him over the Bridgegate scandal. He had joined Trump's team in August as the campaign's national field director. Along with his deputy Justin Clark and their team, Stepien had worked feverishly on the absentee and early voting results for weeks leading up to Election Day. On Election Day, it was his job to keep track of the results down to the county and precinct level. Jared and Bannon asked Stepien to do a deep dive county by county in Florida. He used the official election results map from the Florida secretary of state and, starting with Key West and Monroe County, began his way north. By the time he and his team reached Hillsborough and Pinellas Counties, on the I-4 corridor in the Tampa area, they knew Florida was in Trump's column.

At the same time, Dave was on the phone with Eric Branstad, the state director in Iowa. With 25 percent of the vote in, Trump was down by forty thousand votes. Branstad ensured him they were right where they wanted to be. "It's all the early urban and Des Moines area," he said. "Don't worry; we're not going to have a problem." Dave then called Mike Rubino in Virginia, and the state directors in North Carolina, Michigan, Wisconsin, and Ohio.

The flip seemed to happen in minutes; Trump went from forty thousand down in Iowa to up the same number in the blink of an eye. When he did, the bedrock under Manhattan began to tremble. At 10:21 p.m., the networks called Ohio for Trump and the famous skyline began to shake and sway. At 11:07, North Carolina fell. The island split wide open when Florida tumbled at 11:30.

It was then we sent everyone, except senior staff, to the Hilton.

* * *

Around midnight about a dozen or so of us, including Governor Mike Pence, his wife, and their daughter; Kellyanne Conway, the campaign manager; Hope Hicks, communications expert; Stephen Miller, Trump's speechwriter and policy adviser; Chris Christie; Bannon; Brad Parscale, the campaign digital director; the Trump children and their spouses; and the candidate went along with Dave up to the residence on the sixty-sixth floor of Trump Tower. Crammed into the kitchen, many of us watched the results on a tiny TV. We all thought we were going to win but were waiting for Pennsylvania, Michigan, and Wisconsin to be called. It seemed like an eternity. About one o'clock, Mr. Trump walked into the kitchen.

"Dave, can you believe this?" he said. "We just started this to have some fun."

"We had some of that, too, sir," Dave replied.

About two fifteen, we'd moved to the front foyer. It was there at 2:20 when Kellyanne's phone rang.

"What state are you calling?" she asked the AP editor.

"We're not calling a state," he said. "We're calling the race."

Dave had the privilege of informing Governor Pence, who was in the living room with Karen and Charlotte, that he was now the vice president elect of the United States.

It took the president-elect, the vice president elect, their families, and the senior campaign staff less than ten minutes to get from the foyer of the residence at the top of Trump Tower to backstage at the Hilton a few blocks away. The Secret Service and the NYPD had the streets blocked off.

Earlier in the week, Robby Mook, Hillary Clinton's campaign manager, perhaps with the thought of the Al Gore's loss to George W. Bush in 2000 in mind, had emailed and issued what was essentially an ultimatum. Mook said that if they lost, which of course they didn't expect to do, they would call and concede within fifteen minutes after the AP called the race. But, he said, she would also wait only fifteen minutes for Trump's campaign to phone before she gave a victory speech. To Hillary's credit Huma Abedin called Kellyanne just as we arrived backstage at the Hilton.

"Is Mr. Trump available to talk with Hillary?" Huma asked.

"Oh yes," Kellyanne answered. "He's very available."

The concession call was a gracious exchange, Kellyanne told interviewers. Mrs. Clinton was cordial and warm. At 3:00 a.m., the vice president elect and his family took the stage. Mr. Pence thanked the wildly cheering crowd and then announced the president-elect. George Gigicos, the campaign's advance director, cued the stirring music, and after waiting a few moments to build the drama, President-Elect Trump, his wife, Melania, and the Trump children walked down a staircase and around a long catwalk, a route George had arranged to be reminiscent of Mr. Trump's escalator ride when he launched his campaign back in June of 2015, and onto the stage. The expression on the face of President-elect Trump was one of pure gratitude. It had always been his connection with the people that fueled him and us during the campaign. Mr. Trump had invited the senior staff to join him. He hadn't allowed anyone to begin drafting an acceptance speech until we knew victory was assured. He didn't want to jinx himself. Jared, Ivanka, Stephen Miller, Steve Bannon, and Kellyanne huddled over Miller's computer and fashioned a speech just in the nick of time.

As he delivered it, surrounded by family and staff, Donald J. Trump stepped into the history books as the next president of the United States of America.

At four o'clock in the morning, after being onstage for the acceptance speech, Dave walked back with the president-elect and his family to the Hilton's service elevator, which was big enough to haul grain. At street level, they walked back to the loading dock and to the waiting motorcade.

Instead of riding back to Trump Tower with the boss, Dave wanted to find Susan and his kids. During the campaign, he'd missed the birthday of his daughter Maggie Reagan, and had missed Maggie's first day of kindergarten. He'd missed his daughter Lily's field hockey season, Griffin's fall baseball season, and all of his daughter Isabella's softball season. He'd missed watching SEC football with his son. He missed Halloween. Now, more than anything, he wanted to kiss his wife and hug his kids. As the motorcade pulled away, Dave stood in the street alone.

The victory party was winding down, and Trump fans in various states of intoxication and euphoria spilled into the street. He found Susan and the kids in front of the hotel on Sixth Avenue. Together they walked a deserted Fifty-Fourth Street toward the apartment Dave had taken for the campaign. Steam rose from the manhole covers. The smell of hotel trash filled their nostrils. A man sprayed the sidewalk with a hose. The scene was like something out of a film noir. For the last ten weeks, Dave had been at the center of a political tornado. It had taken all he was able to give. Now, walking with his family on the desolate street, he took a deep breath that felt to him like his first in months.

It would have been impossible then for Dave, or Corey, to step away from the intensity of election night and see the moment for what it was: the culmination of the greatest political event in the history of our republic. It was certainly the story of the most talented and unique candidate ever. A political phenomenon, Donald Trump was elected president of the United States without having ever run for public office or having even served in government in any capacity. He captured the imagination of a country, dominated news cycles for eighteen months straight, and led a movement like none that had been seen before. If it hadn't happened before their own eyes, Donald J. Trump's ride to the White House would have been a story hard for them to believe.

In the pages ahead, you'll find out why. You'll be backstage at Trump's rallies. You'll fly with us on Trump Force One, and ride along with us in motorcades. You'll be in the minds and hearts of those who played supporting roles, and you'll come to see the star of the show in a completely different light. This book is also the personal journey of two ordinary guys thrust into the most extraordinary of circumstances. We tell this story without restraint. Loyalty and the unvarnished truth can coexist. In fact, one doesn't survive without the other. We speak in one voice, and for no one but ourselves. This story isn't about us; however, it's about a candidate like no other and the team that helped propel him to the White House.

And it's a story that begins where the best long shots are born.

CHAPTER 2

HOUSE MONEY

The word "luck" is a very important word—very important.
There's no more important word than "luck."
But you can help create your own luck.
—Donald J. Trump, April 24, 1988

YOU MIGHT NOT KNOW IT from looking at him, but Donald Trump is one of the most superstitious men that most people have ever met. Sometimes, he'll throw salt over his shoulder before he eats. He called *Fox and Friends* every Monday morning during the primaries because he didn't want to change a winning routine. And he believes that some people, usually ones with low energy, carry bad luck and need to be avoided at all cost.

If you worked for Mr. Trump, you knew there were certain rules.

We were never allowed to celebrate before a win was certain, and we always had to take our losses with grace. Anything else and you'd invite in some bad juju. It's the reason that come election night we didn't have a victory speech—or a concession speech—written ahead of time.

"Don't jinx me," Mr. Trump would say.

Who knows? Maybe it's adhering to all these little rules and rituals that's kept Donald J. Trump in such good standing with the universe all these years. Like Midas, he's turned everything he's touched into gold: real estate, hotels, publishing, television, and now politics. Still, sometimes it astounds us both—the way it baffled the media and half the American electorate for so long—that Donald Trump and this ragtag band of outsiders, misfits, and political neophytes was able to pull off the biggest electoral upset in American political history. Then again, as the boss always reminded us, we had the best candidate to ever put his name on a ballot.

Still, considering how our story turns out, the backdrop of Las Vegas is a pretty good place for it to start.

It was sometime in 2010 when Dave picked up his BlackBerry, the retro phone he still refuses to part with, and dialed his friend in Vegas. Three-quarters of the way across the country, Steve Wynn took the call in his casino-floor office in "The Wynn," as they call his five-star hotel and casino, the one with the stunning seventy-foot waterfall that tumbles into a three-acre man-made lake.

The call had little to do with politics. Dave was going to try to ply some swag out of Mr. Wynn for an auction held at the annual golf tournament he ran. "Ply" isn't the right word. The tournament raised money for the Children's National Medical Center in Washington, DC, a hospital that Dave knew the inner workings of intimately. Surgeons there had operated on his son, Griffin, when he was just three years old to fix holes in his heart. You see, Griffin was a miracle baby. He had already had a heart surgery at two days old to fix the descending aorta of his heart, which was too narrow to get blood out to his body. Though it was successful, Griffin would have five more major surgeries: one on his heart and four on his brain. Through all of them, Dave and Susan sat anxiously in hospital waiting rooms and on hard benches outside cardiac or neurology operating rooms, waiting for the results. During Griffin's brain surgery, doctors suggested that Dave and Susan go out and spend a day together in New York City, where they'd gone for a specialist. This might be a long one, they said. Could be up to eighteen hours long. Instead, Dave and Susan stayed near the operating room, knowing the odds of their son surviving were almost unbearably low. The hospital had made them sign papers acknowledging it.

Inside, the team of neurological interventionists took turns going through the veins in Griffin's brain—his head, because of significant hydrocephalus, was nearly the size of an adult male's, though his body stayed as small as a toddler's—and watching it the whole time on multiple high-definition screens above their heads.

Then, just a couple of hours in, something happened. Just as the doctors were getting at the area near his vein of Galen aneurism that they'd gone in to seal up, the blood vessel sealed on its own. The doctors watched on the screen, amazed. They cut the surgery short and paged Dave and Susan, who were getting breakfast with Susan's sister, Nathalie, who had flown in from Denver to help out. They thought the worst because only a short time had passed.

"Your son's a miracle," Dr. Alejandro Berenstein, the lead surgeon, said. "I've never heard of anything like that happening, let alone seen it."

And just like that, in a few hours, Susan and Dave saw hope. Even with three more brain surgeries and one open-heart surgery, Griffin had a future.

So Dave and a buddy, Mike Murray, who would later become one of Ben Carson's campaign managers, decided to run a golf tournament for the renowned DC children's hospital, and their friends were always happy to support it. And Steve Wynn, though he was a relatively new friend, was no exception.

Frank Luntz, the coarchitect of Newt Gingrich's Contract with America, had introduced Dave to Steve Wynn in early 2010. Later, Dave flew out to Vegas and had dinner with Wynn in the steak house in his casino. Dave, the president of a nonprofit conservative political organization, had recently won a lawsuit against the Federal Election Commission in a First Amendment case you might have heard of. The Supreme Court's *Citizens United* decision in January 2010 would rewrite US campaign finance laws, ensuring that money spent for political purposes was protected as free speech under the Constitution and couldn't be regulated by the government. As a businessman and a frequent political donor, Wynn was someone Luntz thought Dave should know. He also thought the two would get along. He was right. They did.

Wynn promised Dave several great prizes for his tournament, including room comps and a foursome at his beautiful Wynn Golf Club, a par-70 course right by his casino in Vegas. Had the phone call ended after Steve Wynn's display of generosity, Dave would have been perfectly content. But luckily, for our sake, the conversation continued, and that's when Lady Luck began to smile on our story. Dave mentioned that he held the tournament at what was then known as the Loews Island resort golf club in DC.

"My friend Donald Trump just bought that golf course," Wynn told him.

Dave doesn't like to brag, but since we're writing this book together, he doesn't have to. He is good at what he does, and you don't become a political operative of Dave Bossie's magnitude without recognizing an opportunity when you hear one. He stored the information about Trump and a month or so later called Wynn back.

"You think you could introduce me to Donald Trump?" he asked. Although he didn't know exactly what Trump would do for him, he figured getting to know the owner of the course where he held the tournament could only have an upside. On this crap table, he saw no harm in throwing the dice.

There wasn't any harm. Without missing a beat, Wynn called out to his assistant.

"Cindy, get the Donald on the phone for me, please."

And just like that, Dave was on a conference call with two billionaires.

"Any friend of Steve's is a friend of mine," Trump would say after the introductions. "Next time you're in New York, come see me."

"Funny," Dave said, "I'm scheduled to be in New York City in the next couple of weeks."

As there was no such scheduled trip, Dave made a mental note to make the reservations as soon as he hung up.

When Trump got off the line, Steve Wynn had some parting advice.

"Ask Donald to waive the fee for the course," he told Dave.

I'm on a roll, Dave thought as he hung up the phone.

The next week he walked into Trump Tower for the first time in his life with a wish list of auction prizes in his head. In the elevator up to the twenty-sixth floor, where Donald Trump had his fantastic office, Dave started to have second thoughts about this plan he had hatched. Sure, it was for a good cause, but he was about to walk in to see Donald Trump, whom he knew only about as well as you could know anybody from television and a five-minute phone conversation, and ask for stuff. Besides, he was Donald Trump. *The Apprentice. The Art of the Deal.* Trump had succeeded spectacularly in the world of Manhattan real estate. There are no waters more dark and shark infested.

As it would turn out, Trump was easy to talk to and incredibly generous. He would say yes to every single item on Dave's list, which, by the end of the meeting, had grown to include foursomes at his Trump National Bedminster, Trump National Westchester, Trump International West Palm Beach, a day on the set of *The Apprentice* for four people, a dinner for six with the Donald himself at Jean-Georges, the famous Manhattan restaurant, and a $5,000 donation from Mr. Trump to Children's National Medical Center.

Over the years, Mr. Trump has also been more than gracious to Griffin, who has grown into a healthy, grand slam–slugging fourteen-year-old golf enthusiast. Whenever the two of them see each other, they talk golf and baseball. Not many people know this, but Trump was a pretty good ballplayer himself back in high school. Sometimes during the campaign to come, Dave would hear him talk about it, usually during long rides in the car or the private airplane. But hardly ever to a crowd. Mr. Trump was also thoughtful and gracious to Dave's girls. He knew they played tennis and one day he called Dave and said Serena Williams was going to be at Trump National to open his tennis facility. He told Dave to bring the girls.

Still, there was a point in that first meeting when Dave thought he might have ruined the whole deal.

"Steve Wynn suggested that I ask you for the golf course for free," he said.

Trump's benevolent smile faded.

"Oh, Steve's a good friend," Trump muttered finally. The real estate mogul's eyes began to narrow. In the coming years, Dave would grow to know that look well. It was his "tough as nails" look, a New York real estate killer look. Sometimes, before Trump did interviews on shows like O'Reilly or Hannity, he'd turn to Hope Hicks or Keith Schiller, his longtime body-guard, Jason Miller, or Corey or Dave to ask if the stare was up to par that day.

"How's the look?" he'd say, looking straight through the camera.

But this was the first time that Dave had ever seen the iron girder stare. Behind it, he could practically see Mr. Trump imag-ining Steve Wynn chuckling, feet up on his desk in Sin City. He could also see Trump plotting how he was going to get even.

But just as fast as "the look" came, it disappeared. Trump explained to Dave that he had golf courses all over the world, and had friends who ran fantastic charity tournaments on just about every one of them.

"If I set a precedent with you, then how could I say no to anyone else?" he asked. "My manager wouldn't be able to make it work. But I will do something nice for you. Don't worry, you'll love it."

He then invited Dave to lunch at the Trump Grill in the atrium of Trump Tower. At the table, Trump began to take his end of the deal.

Though Dave knew the topic of politics would come up, he didn't go to see Trump with any other motive besides mak-ing a connection for his golf tournament. In fact, he was hop-ing to sidestep an in-depth political discussion. Like everyone else, he knew Trump's reputation for false political starts. Donald Trump had been considering running for president as far back as 1987, when a "Draft Trump" movement caught fire and blazed through the press. It was way back then when he gave perhaps his first political speech at a restaurant in Portsmouth, New Hampshire. His appearance packed the place and cameras televised the event. It was a harbinger of things to come.

After lunch, Trump told Dave that he would be in touch. It was a promise he kept. The day of the tournament, Dave kept his phone on in case anyone had a problem. It rang when he was playing the sixth hole. Mr. Trump wanted to know how he liked the golf course, the food, and the staff.

During 2011, Dave and Trump spoke on the phone often. In June 2011 in New Hampshire, Mitt Romney announced he was running for the presidency in 2012, and soon Trump was telling Dave that Mitt was a terrible candidate, an opinion that was widely shared among Republican political pros and, ultimately, with good old Republican voters alike. Finally, during one conversation, Dave asked the question that had been hanging in the air.

"Do you want to run?"

"I don't know," Trump said. "I want to, but . . ."

Despite Donald Trump's past political performance, it was a substantial enough maybe for Dave to put in some work on a little exploratory operation.

"Let's see what we come up with," he said.

That year, Dave commissioned a poll, just to test the waters, with questions like: "Would you like to see Donald Trump get in the race?" "Do you think Donald Trump would make a good president?" and "Do we need a businessperson as president?"

When the numbers came in, they showed that Trump's name recognition was off the charts, but Dave already knew that. They also revealed that Mr. Trump's business credentials registered higher with prospective voters than Romney's did. But that wasn't such big news. What did surprise Dave was that the poll said that Trump would beat Romney head-to-head in some important primary states.

There was only one real negative, but it was a big one. The prospective voters didn't believe he would run. Still, the poll was perhaps the first documented evidence that Donald J. Trump would be a formidable candidate for the Republican nomination.

Trump ended up endorsing Romney on February 2, 2012, from the event stage of the Trump International Hotel in Las Vegas, just a few hundred feet from the floor of Steve Wynn's casino.

"There are some things that you can't imagine happening in your life," Romney said, standing next to Trump the day he received his support. "And this is one of them."

There's no way for us to know for sure if Mitt was trying to be sarcastic or not. If he was, he changed his tune when the endorsement began to translate to votes in Michigan, Ohio, and other prominent Republican states. Just after he endorsed Romney, during the tight final weeks of the election, Trump recorded a few robocalls—political-speak for those prerecorded phone messages that always seem to come as you're sitting down to dinner—raving about Mitt Romney and running down some of the other candidates. Just about every night, voters in individual battleground towns would get a one-minute phone call from Donald Trump himself, all smooth and earnest and fired up about Mitt.

"I support Mitt Romney because he's the outsider in the race," he'd say. "He's a good man; he's working hard. We've gotta get him elected because he's the one man who'll beat President Obama. He will win. You've gotta give him that chance."

Friendly, casual, and honest—just like the straight-to-camera Facebook monologues that'd go viral in 2016 and help him win his campaign.

Unfortunately, Mitt didn't end up being very lucky. Yet his loss to Barack Obama in 2012 turned out to be most fortunate for the billionaire builder and Vegas casino owner who had endorsed him. In hindsight, the turn of events shouldn't have been much of a surprise. Ask any seasoned gambler on the Strip, and they'll tell you.

The house always wins.

CHAPTER 3

NEW HAMPSHIRE

While I won't be running for Governor of New York State, a
race I would have won, I have much bigger plans in mind—stay
tuned, will happen!
—@realDonaldTrump, March 14, 2014, 5:27 p.m.

Stop pretending—Donald Trump is not running for president.
—Kyle Smith, *New York Post*, May 30, 2015

IT'S HARD TO SAY what makes a person want to run for president. All the scrutiny, the travel, the time and money you have
to spend—it's a physical, mental, and emotional gauntlet. Some
people do it because others want them to, and some run just to
spite the ones who don't. The press came up with all sorts of rea-
sons why Donald Trump was running: "He's just building his
brand," they wrote. "He's got a new TV deal," they said. "It's all
ego-driven," they opined.

But it wasn't ego, because it was never about him. One night,
he was talking to Keith Schiller, a guy who's known him longer
than any of us. Before he had signed on as Mr. Trump's body-
guard in 1999, Keith had been an NYPD narcotics detective in
the Thirty-Fourth Precinct in Manhattan, an area then known

for intense drug trafficking. During drug raids, it was Keith's job to break down the doors with a battering ram. Fiercely loyal, once Keith started working for Mr. Trump he wanted no other job. Whether the boss was doing a quality check on a new property or making his way through a throng of fans who wouldn't stop pawing at him, Keith was there. Keith has been such a constant in Mr. Trump's life, the Trump kids think of him as an uncle—an uncle who would take a bullet for their father. On this night, early in the campaign, they were in the limo, looking out at a crowd that had gathered in the street.

"You and me, Keith, we're hotter than we've ever been," Trump said. "This is big shit."

"Yes, sir," Keith said. "Running for president of the United States, sir. Leader of the free world, sir."

"Yep, you and me."

By 2013, Dave started working with a young lawyer named Sam Nunberg who was helping Trump with scheduling, writing some political speeches, and navigating the political landscape. Roger Stone, a longtime Trump associate, had introduced Nunberg to Trump. Still, it seemed that whenever Trump had a question about politics, whether it be new poll numbers or policy positions, one of the people he would call was Dave. In time, Dave learned to stick close to the phone; calls from Trump could come at any time.

That February, Donald Trump—at that time, a very famous TV star but still something of a political unknown—attended the annual Conservative Political Action Conference (CPAC) with Dave. There, Trump opened the second day with a speech that received mixed reviews from the audience. Though always self-confident, the future president wasn't nearly as persuasive from the podium as he would become. Maybe with a trained eye one would recognize the sparks of electricity he generated then weren't all that different from the nova he would become in front of fan-filled stadiums two years later. But there weren't many eyes trained on Donald Trump in those days—not the right eyes, anyway.

"You have to start donating to the Republicans," Dave told him one day. "You can't be Republican nominee if the only people you give to are Chuck Schumer, Harry Reid, and Nancy Pelosi."

Trump bristled. "I'm a businessman," he said. "I give to everyone."

But Dave had done the research. "Yes, you're a businessman," he said. "But no, you're not giving to everyone. You're giving to mostly Democrats."

Dave made a list of Republican members of Congress and senators running campaigns across the country, and then suggested a budget of $500,000. He recommended that he start writing checks for each of the names on his list for the maximum allowed by the FEC—$2,600 per election, and he began introducing Trump to some of the bigger names to whom he donated. Rick Santorum, the winner of the 2012 Iowa caucuses, visited Trump's office with his daughter, Sarah Maria, to express his thanks.

Once Mr. Trump aligned his political donations with his politics, Dave set out to see how the candidate would do on the road.

Around this time, Dave and J. T. Mastanadi, Citizens United's political director, came up with an idea of putting together events that would host presidential hopefuls in the first primary states: New Hampshire, Iowa, and South Carolina. These events would be a who's who of conservative politics, all-day-long political

events held for die-hard conservative and libertarian audiences—
people who lived for politics. The "Freedom Summits," as Dave
and the Citizens United team had decided to call them, would
be the earliest events in the presidential election cycle. And they
would set the stage for the stampede of Republican presidential
contenders that would follow.

While Dave was busy refining the concept for the first
Freedom Summit, to be held in New Hampshire in April
2014, Corey Lewandowski was working as the national director of voter registration for Americans for Prosperity (AFP).
The advocacy group was part of the vast network of David and
Charles Koch, the two richest and most politically active libertarians in the country.

Corey's role at AFP required him to oversee all voter registration efforts throughout the country and to run recruitment
campaigns that would champion certain conservative and libertarian causes. He and his wife, Alison, then had four kids,
one girl and three boys. After a few years running several hectic
statewide campaigns, Corey seemed to have finally settled into a
calm, structured job in an office.

The office happened to be in Londonderry, New Hampshire,
a quiet town on the state's southern border that consisted mostly
of apple orchards and small, tight-knit neighborhoods. It was
located just a few miles down the road from the Courtyard
Manchester, the hotel where it was decided to hold the first
Freedom Summit. Locals just called the hotel "the Yard."

We knew each other only by reputation. At least mostly.
We had met briefly and had talked on the phone. But Dave had
heard plenty about Donald Trump's future campaign manager.

On National Tax Day in 2010, Corey had helped organize a Tea Party tax revolt on the lawn of the New Hampshire State House in Concord, and managed to draw thousands of people to the event. Later that day, he took to the stage in Manchester and debated a life-size cardboard cutout of New Hampshire's Democratic governor, John Lynch. He took a few swings at Lynch for being a short guy, then slapped a "big spender" sticker right on his flat cardboard lapel. The crowd, mostly angry, tax-loathing conservatives, laughed and cheered. Two weeks later, with his wife, Alison, about to give birth, Corey hosted the presidential hopefuls Mitt Romney, Tim Pawlenty, Michele Bachmann, and Herman Cain at a dinner held by Americans for Prosperity—no small feat, considering it was nine months until the beginning of the primary season, a long way out for most big-name candidates.

It was clear that Corey knew New Hampshire politics cold. If there was anyone with whom Dave could partner to stage a Freedom Summit there, it was Corey.

It was September 2013 when the communications director of Citizens United introduced us. Jeff Marschner had worked for Dave for four years by then and had known Corey when they both worked in the US Senate in the early 2000s. They both used to work for the senator of New Hampshire, Bob Smith; Marschner as the senator's deputy press secretary, and Corey as his campaign manager. Right off the bat, we formed a strong team.

Around this time, Dave commissioned a poll by Kellyanne Conway testing Mr. Trump in an election for the governor of New York against the incumbent, Andrew Cuomo. Dave, JT, and Jeff traveled to Trump Tower to review the first night's results with Mr. Trump. Trump suggested that we add this question to the poll: "Would you rather see Donald J. Trump run for governor of New York or president of the United States?"

The New Hampshire Freedom Summit was an unqualified success. Dave was able to lure big Republican names such as former Speaker Newt Gingrich, Governor Mike Huckabee, Senator Ted Cruz, and Senator Rand Paul, while Corey brought in New Hampshire senator Kelly Ayotte; Arthur C. Brooks, a leading conservative voice and the president of the American Enterprise Institute; New Hampshire House Speaker Bill O'Brien; and tax fighter Tom Thomson, the son of the famous New Hampshire governor Meldrim "Ax the Tax" Thomson. The event also drew Tennessee congresswoman Marsha Blackburn, Utah senator Mike Lee, the radio host Laura Ingraham, and the Iowa Republican heavyweight congressman Steve King. The speakers needed no introduction for the Freedom Summit crowd. It was an all-star cast playing before a full house.

Going into the event, Paul and Cruz were the biggest stars, and both delivered strong speeches. In that faraway time, Rand Paul was the early front-runner for the nomination, and he roused the crowd with signature issues such as civil liberties and pushing back against the National Security Administration and the blanket surveillance of everyday Americans by the Obama administration.

Cruz displayed his talent as an orator by talking about growing the Republican brand and reaching out to Hispanics and others most affected by the stagnant economy.

But as good as Cruz and Paul were, the event was Trump's.

A crowd of about a thousand packed the conference center at the Yard. These were limited-government conservatives and libertarians. Mr. Trump walked out onto the stage with Frank Sinatra's "New York, New York" playing on the sound system. He talked off the cuff about things like trade and the economy— not quite the orthodoxy to which the room typically ascribed. But he had them in the palm of his hand. The biggest applause line was for what he was then calling the border fence.

Then he indulged in a half hilarious, half serious, eight-minute riff on why politicians shouldn't be allowed to use teleprompters. But the most memorable thing he said that day went almost unnoticed. Though he had used the phrase before, it was the first time he had used the words as a rallying cry.

"There is something we have to do, and we have to do it fast," he said. "We have to make America great again."

Only looking back can we see the moment for what it was: a turning point in American campaigning. From a messenger, the likes of which had never appeared in American politics, came a complete repudiation of the status quo. Donald Trump was about to start throwing lightning bolts at the ruling elite. And no one—not the government, the media, the Catholic Church or the Republican Party (never mind the Democrats)—would be safe.

Hunter S. Thompson once wrote, "Probably the rarest form of life in American politics is the man who can turn on a crowd and still keep his head straight." Onstage, Donald Trump was like a machine that learns as it goes. As his audiences grew, he seemed to grow with them, feeding off their energy. Manchester that day might not have been the first time Mr. Trump showed such talent in a political setting populated with serious presidential candidates. He had spoken at CPAC all the way back in 2013. But at the Freedom Summit in Manchester, he showed a glimpse of what he would perfect on the campaign trail, a combination of Teddy Roosevelt's love of verbal combat, the charm and celebrity of Ronald Reagan, and the pure brashness of Donald J. Trump. In Manchester, Trump the candidate began to emerge. Even at that early moment, he was head and shoulders above any of the other speakers. He went way beyond his allotted time to speak. Nothing new. We had to cancel a video that was supposed to play during lunch. But we didn't care, nor did the people in the audience; nearly all of them had their cell phones out, recording the speech in photographs and on video—a phenomenon that would continue at events throughout his campaign. Nor did the press, which included a live feed by C-SPAN. They were all under Trump's spell.

From that night on, campaign politics would never be the same—not that anybody knew it then, not even those of us who are supposed to know what we're doing in the business. Heck, we still didn't believe he would run.

Even though he'd beguiled the press, the mainstream reporters were reluctant to interview Donald Trump after the event for fear of being laughed off the phone by their editors. That wasn't the case with Bannon, then the host of Breitbart on Sirius Radio. Bannon couldn't wait to get Trump on the air.

It was Dave who introduced Bannon to Trump back in August 2010. Dave and Bannon have been friends and business partners since 2006, churning out documentary films including *Fire from the Heartland*, which chronicled Tea Party women, including Ann Coulter and Michele Bachmann, and *Generation Zero*, about the global roots of the financial meltdown. Dave was the producer on the films, which Steve wrote and directed. One morning, Dave asked Bannon if he'd be interested in meeting Donald Trump.

"Why?" Bannon asked. He was swamped with movies and running Breitbart full time.

"He's thinking of running for president," Dave said.

Steve let out a short laugh. "Yeah? Of what country?"

Though his answer was glib, Bannon did not think of Trump as the lightweight that most people in politics then did. He'd be willing to meet him, so long as he was serious.

They met in Trump's office on the twenty-sixth floor of Trump Tower. Dave had prepared a presentation and went over every single aspect of a presidential primary campaign for Trump. In extensive detail, he walked him through what he would need to do for each of the first three primary states: Iowa, New Hampshire, and South Carolina. Dave compared an early campaign for president to running for governor in three states. He told Trump whom he would have to hire, and what each hire's job would be. He went over the field that Trump would be up against and the issues that would matter in the race. He told him how much it would cost. It was a master class in primary politics, and Trump was enthusiastically engaged. Bannon, who at the time was the executive chairman of Breitbart News, was impressed with Trump's mastery of the Socratic method of learning.

As they walked out of Trump Tower that day, Dave asked Bannon what he thought the chances were of Trump running for president in 2012.

"It's amazing how quickly he picks up on stuff," Steve said. "But he's got a zero chance. Less than zero."

But that was then. By 2014, Bannon had completely rethought his assessment. By 2016, he would be helping to steer Trump's campaign.

* * *

It was after Trump's interview with Bannon at the New Hampshire Freedom Summit that Dave introduced Corey to his future boss. Trump was there with Keith Schiller and Sam Nunberg. They chatted with us for a few minutes. We had our hands full. We had handled, line-by-line, the travel arrangements for all of the speakers and were then dealing with the logistics of getting everyone home. We didn't have to worry about getting Donald Trump home, who seemed in no hurry to leave. Instead, he asked Dave if his son liked helicopters.

A short while later, Dave and Griffin, along with Dave's friend Matt Palumbo and his son Dean piled into Trump's SUV and headed to the nearby airfield. There the Sikorsky S-76, the one with kid leather seats and 24-karat plate gold fixtures, lifted off, tilted north, and headed for a quick, ten-minute spin over the White Mountains. When we landed, Mr. Trump told Griffin that the ride just cost him $5,000. "That's how much I like your dad," he said. It wouldn't be the last time Donald Trump gave kids helicopter rides. And the next time would prove to be one of the greatest campaign spectacles ever.

Corey was impressed by Trump. The thought of working for him, however, never entered his mind. But Fate and Dave had already begun to conspire to align the two men's paths. The next step that brought Corey closer to Trump came a few weeks later.

Dave was in Virginia watching his daughter Isabella play softball in a tournament when his phone rang. Mr. Trump was on his way to the 2014 White House Correspondents Association Dinner, held at the Washington Hilton.

"Are you going to the dinner?" Trump asked.

Dave wasn't going anywhere. Isabella was playing her third of four games that day. Besides, he'd already been to his fill of correspondents dinners. He also didn't get why Trump was going. Year after year, it seemed, he ended up the butt of the jokes. In 2011, Seth Myers torched him, and then Obama took his shots.

"I don't have a tux," Dave said.

"Come on," Trump insisted. "We need to talk."

"We can talk on the phone," Dave said

"You're missing the game!" Susan said to him.

"You have to get me a campaign manager," Trump said. "You promised to get me one, now let's get it done."

The call, covering a broad range of issues and topics, lasted nearly an hour. By the time Dave hung up, he knew that he had better find Trump a campaign manager.

Over the next few months, Trump and Sam Nunberg called Dave regularly. There might have been only a handful of people in Washington with more connections and political knowledge than Dave. He could come up with a list of names and phone numbers right off the top of his head. That wasn't the problem. The problem was twofold: One, finding someone who believed that Donald Trump would run for president. It was a significant risk, and the people Dave knew were already working in jobs and had families and mortgages. Those who were looking for jobs with campaigns were looking for candidates with stable political operations. Few would be willing to take a chance on something that might dry up in a few weeks or months.

The second reason might have been even more challenging. And that was finding someone with the right personality to work with Trump. The boss, as we would come to call him, was someone who liked to call the shots and wouldn't stand for anything less than all you had. Though he knew him to be incredibly loyal and generous, Dave also knew he could be abrasive, to say the least. The big thing was, however, that Dave knew that Trump would not fit into a traditional campaign strategy or get along with a traditional political handler.

That's when Corey Lewandowski came to mind.

Dave was aware that Corey had been involved in a bunch of statewide campaigns. He also knew he was running a division of the Koch Brothers' Americans for Prosperity, which had cohosted the Freedom Summit without a hitch. Dave knew Corey had the temperament, personality, and character to handle Trump. But mostly he believed Corey was tough enough to work for the boss.

Corey grew up in Lowell, Massachusetts, a blue-collar old mill city of about 100,000. He lived in a small home on Coburn Street right next to a low-cost housing development, which, during the late 1980s, was overrun with crack cocaine and crime. One night, the police conducted surveillance of a drug operation right in his kitchen, watching through the window at the apartment complex next door. His parents separated early in his life, and his father died when he was in high school. His role model was his maternal grandfather, a union printer and World War II veteran, who lived with Corey's grandmother about three city blocks away. It was his grandfather who instilled in Corey the value of hard work. From a paper route when he was nine, to working at Dunkin' Donuts, to driving a forklift at Somerville Lumber, to his time in politics, Corey had been working hard his whole life.

He attended college at the University of Massachusetts Lowell. The only reason he could afford it was because his mother worked in the financial aid office. Still, at first, his college career looked like it was going to end before it got started. The core undergraduate courses—psychology, sociology, and English 101—bored him to tears, so he spent more time attending parties and chasing girls than he did in class. At the end of the first semester he was given a choice: go on academic probation or take a semester off. He opted for option number two. He was friendly with a girl whose family owned a dairy farm in upstate New York. He thought it would be an adventure. It turned out to be the hardest work he ever did—that is, until he became Donald Trump's campaign manager. All day long, he was hauling hay and cleaning barns. The cows had to be milked twice a day, every day, in rain and snow and cold. In upstate New York, it snows a lot. His experience on the farm taught him two things. One was respect for farmers and the hard work they do—because of them you can just waltz into a store and pick up a container of milk. And two was that he'd better take school more seriously, because he sure didn't want to be a farmer the rest of his life.

Back in school, he took all the core classes over again and aced all of them, doing especially well in the writing course. He would end up graduating cum laude from UMass and being accepted into graduate school at American University in Washington, DC, where he obtained his master's degree in American Government and Public Policy.

In the fall of 1997, he applied to the Republican National Committee's campaign management college.

Soon after graduating from the course, he researched every incumbent Republican member of congress who had received less than 55 percent of the vote in his or her last election. He then sent a résumé and followed up with a phone call to every one of them. His efforts paid off. Dave DiStefano, the chief of staff to Congressman Robert W. Ney (R-OH) called back and asked Corey if he would come to Ohio to discuss the congressman's upcoming reelection effort.

Corey stayed with Ney through two successful campaign cycles, during which time he forged a close relationship with the congressman. In 2000, Corey went to work at the Republican National Committee as the Northeast's legislative political director, a position in which he raised funds, recruited candidates, and served as the liaison to the national committee. Though he loved building resources for Republican campaigns, he longed for one of his own.

He got his chance in 2002, but it was short lived. After Smith lost the primary to John E. Sununu Jr., who had the full backing of the Bush family, Corey turned his attention to matters outside of politics. He married Alison and started a family. He sold real estate for a while and worked for a PR firm. He then considered a career as a police officer. He enrolled in the New Hampshire police academy and graduated in 2006, a week before his daughter, Abigail, was born. Still, round-the-clock tours and small paychecks were hard to manage for a guy with a growing family. Besides, there was something else calling him away from any other career.

By 2008 he was back in politics, where he belonged, taking the job with the Kochs' Americans for Prosperity.

It was in October 2014 when Dave first approached Corey with the idea to work for Trump. It was just before the midterm elections, and Corey was overseeing voter registration for the whole country. By that time, Corey had been with Americans for Prosperity for seven years. The organization had opened an office for him one exit from his home in Windham, New Hampshire. In addition to the importance of his position, which

Corey took very seriously, he was in a pretty good situation. He liked what he was doing and where he was doing it. That said, Corey will always consider an opportunity when presented with one. So when Dave said, "Hey, Trump may be running. Do you have any interest in speaking to him?" Corey answered, "Sure."

And with that one small word, his life changed forever.

CHAPTER 4

YOU'RE HIRED

When I have a meeting, I don't waste time. It's quick,
short, and to the point.
—DONALD J. TRUMP, FROM *THE APPRENTICE*, NOVEMBER 4, 2005

THE MEDIA TALKED almost exclusively about Donald Trump's most controversial statements and never about what he said and did the other 99 percent of the time. But we both knew, long before we became involved with Donald Trump as a political candidate, that there was a lot more to him than sound bites or what anyone saw on *The Apprentice* or during his other public appearances. The Donald Trump we came to know was the incredibly generous one who built a multibillion-dollar corporation and employed thousands of people over the years. That takes a lot more brains, dedication, and hard work than any television audience will ever see.

The boss was interviewed about his hiring strategy back in 2014. He surprised the guy interviewing him with his answer, but it wouldn't surprise anyone who has worked for Mr. Trump. When asked what he valued in an employee, Mr. Trump gave the interviewer a one-word answer: loyalty. It was something the boss had for everyone on his team and required from everyone in return. Corey used to tell the staff all the time that the campaign was about two things: the staff's loyalty to Donald J. Trump and Donald J. Trump's loyalty to the staff. Although he demanded excellence from us and could be very rough when he didn't get it, Trump always stood by us when we were under fire from the outside.

The other value high on the boss's list was work ethic. He got that from his father, Fred Trump, himself a successful businessman, who worked seven days a week. Mr. Trump once said his father used to go to church on Sunday and then right out to check on a building or to attend to some other part of his business. Fred Trump worked right up to the day he died at ninety-three years old. "I have a lot of friends, they take vacations for six weeks and eight weeks and three months and they're never happy. So, I watched my father. So, I like to work," Mr. Trump once told Steve Forbes.

There are a lot of people in politics with fancy degrees and long, impressive résumés, but not quite so many with that kind of work ethic. There are even fewer with loyalty. Donald Trump happened to have all of the above. He was looking for people who'd be as loyal and hardworking as he was. Dave knew Corey Lewandowski was one of them.

At noon, on Monday, January 5, 2015, Corey sat alone in the Starbucks in the atrium of Trump Tower wearing his best suit, a crisply ironed shirt, and shoes he had shined the night before. He'd used hair spray that morning, which, when you consider he's from Lowell, is hilarious. The town Corey grew up in isn't a guys-use-hair-spray kind of place. And besides, he didn't need it. Corey wears his hair the length of a drill sergeant's.

At 12:15 p.m., a man in his early thirties with a receding hair-line and wearing an expensive suit with a pocket square walked into the coffee shop. Corey had met Sam Nunberg briefly at the Freedom Summit in New Hampshire. Sam had also emailed Corey a couple of times since then, including that morning to tell him he'd meet him at the Starbucks at noon. Corey had been in Manhattan since eight o'clock that morning. He'd left his home in Windham at three thirty just in case there was traffic. Nunberg being fifteen minutes late bothered him.

I drive from New Hampshire, and I'm four hours early, he thought, *and this guy only has to ride down in an elevator, and he's late.*

The relationship hadn't gotten off on the best foot.

After the requisite greetings, Nunberg led Corey back up to the office on the twenty-fourth floor. There he asked Corey if he minded if he vaped.

"Knock yourself out," Corey said. *Strike two,* he thought.

In between drags on his vape pen, Nunberg told Corey about some of the things he'd done on Donald Trump's political behalf, including writing the early political speeches. Although Nunberg had some good points, he also could be blind to the deceptiveness of the press.

A few months before the Freedom Summit, Nunberg arranged for a one-on-one interview with Trump for a writer from the tabloid website *Buzzfeed*. The boss didn't want to do the interview; he knew the website trafficked in junk journalism, especially when it came to covering him. But Nunberg prom-ised that the writer would be fair. Mckay Coppins, the writer, was a friend of his, he said. Inaccuracies, sarcasm, and "wise guy," remarks, as Mr. Trump would call them, filled the piece. The title told the whole story: "36 Hours on the Fake Campaign Trail with Donald Trump." Trump fired Nunberg immediately but then hired him back. That wouldn't be Nunberg's last whirl through the revolving doors of Trump Tower.

When it came to his relationship with Trump, Nunberg had nine lives.

By the time they left to go to Trump's office, the whole interaction with Sam on the twenty-fourth-floor office hadn't impressed Corey at all—not Nunberg himself, and certainly not Trump's political operation. Corey couldn't believe that Donald Trump, one of the biggest brands in the world, had a political team that consisted of one guy, a desk, and practically nothing else.

However lacking the political apparatus around him was, Donald Trump himself was everything Corey had imagined.

When Corey first walked into his office, Mr. Trump was on the phone—no surprise there. Magazines, folders, newspapers, and photocopies of news stories, mostly about him, and marked up with a black pen in a handwriting Corey would become intimately familiar with, filled the desk in front of him. During the campaign, the amount of mail he received was insane—banker's boxes filled with notes, photos, letters, magazines, news articles, items both small and large. Mr. Trump would go through every piece of mail. Behind Trump was just glass, through which was the most spectacular New York City view Corey had ever seen. The Plaza Hotel and Central Park looked like miniature models of themselves. Awards and plaques filled the shelf under the windows. Plaques like a humanitarian award from the Jewish National Fund, and photos with famous people, like a young Donald shaking hands with Ronald Reagan, filled the walls. He'd collected hundreds of them over the years. To his right was a bench seat filled with sports memorabilia that was a collector's

dream: Shaq's shoe, a Jeter-signed bat, Mike Tyson's champion-
ship belt, a Tom Brady Super Bowl–worn helmet.

"Look at you! Right out of Central Casting," Trump said to
Corey as Nunberg introduced them. "A good-looking guy."

There were three red velvet chairs facing the desk. Trump
motioned for Corey and Nunberg to sit, and they did—Corey in
the middle, Nunberg to his right.

"I want you to know I have the greatest air force in the
world," Trump began, unprompted.

"I've got a 757, I've got a Citation X. And I've got three
helicopters."

Corey sat there with a half smile on his face, not knowing
quite how to respond.

"I've also have a bunch of houses and seventeen golf courses."

The whole scene was surreal. It felt like something out of the
opening of *The Apprentice*.

Though the air force thing sounded like gratuitous boasting
or a non sequitur, Corey would come to find in the months and
years that followed that Donald Trump's mind works differently
than most. His thoughts sometimes come out like pieces of a
puzzle. It's only later when you put the pieces together that you
realize how much they're worth. Sometimes the puzzle pieces
form a masterpiece.

Corey was still wondering why Trump was telling him what
he owned when the mogul began to list the prospective campaign managers with whom he'd already met.

"Are you better than them?" he asked.

"I don't know, I think so," Corey answered. "But I know I'll
work harder."

Trump nodded.

He then asked Corey how much it would cost to run a presidential campaign in the first three states: Iowa, New Hampshire,

and South Carolina, a question for which Corey was ready. On the phone the night before, he and Dave had discussed what Trump might ask.

"Twenty-five million," he said.

If the number bothered the real estate mogul, he didn't show it.

"I'll spend your money like it was my own," Corey added, just to be sure.

Trump nodded again. "What's my chances of winning the Iowa caucuses?" he said.

"You've been divorced twice, and Iowa is a very conservative state," Corey said carefully.

This time Trump didn't nod. Instead, he shrugged.

"I'd like you to run my New Hampshire operations for me."

Corey had no interest in running one state campaign, but before he could tell Trump, Nunberg jumped in.

"He wants to run the whole thing, sir."

Trump looked at Nunberg, and then back to Corey. "You want me to give you the keys to the whole place?"

"Yes sir," Corey said.

"What do you think my odds of winning are?"

"Five percent."

"I think it's ten percent," Trump said. "Let's split the difference. Seven and a half."

"Sounds good to me," Corey said, smiling.

"How much money do you need to make?"

"Twenty thousand a month."

"How'd you come up with that number?" Trump shot back.

Corey told him that Matt Rhodes, Mitt Romney's campaign manager, made fifteen thousand a month, and he reminded him of his promise to work harder.

"Plus, I think I should make a bonus if we finish in first or second place in Iowa, New Hampshire, or South Carolina," Corey said. "So our incentives are aligned."

Mr. Trump is a world-renowned negotiator, but Corey knew the basics. One of the fundamental ingredients to a successful negotiation, he knew, is leverage. Corey had plenty. He already had a job, a good one. And, despite what Trump said about the other campaign managers that he talked to, Corey knew that the established ones weren't knocking down Trump's door. *If he wants me*, Corey thought, *then he's going to have to make it worth my time.* As confident as Corey was, what Trump said next still shocked him.

"You're hired," the boss said dismissively. "You start tomorrow. All right, get out and get to work."

It was 9:00 p.m. when Corey got his car out of the garage and headed back to New Hampshire. After his meeting with Trump, he'd met with Michael Cohen, Trump's lawyer, and then accompanied Sam Nunberg to an Irish bar on Fifty-Seventh Street for drinks. Well, Sam had drinks. Corey had just one: a Heineken. He knew he had a long drive ahead of him. When it got to be around seven, Sam told Corey he had someone he wanted him to meet.

Roger Stone sat at a table in the nearby restaurant with his wife and granddaughter. He wore an immaculate dark suit, his white hair slicked back, and a tan that might have come from a can. Thanks to a couple of straight-up martinis, he was gracious and talkative. Corey knew Stone only by reputation, one that was murky at best. Still, he was happy to listen. At this point, he was glad to hear from anyone who could shed some light on the personality of his new boss. Stone and Trump had known each other for thirty years. Still, looking back, Corey would remember the meeting with Stone as strange. For one thing, it would be the last time he'd see him until Trump was the front-runner for the nomination. Stone didn't even come to Trump Tower the day his friend announced his run for the presidency. Then there was the remark by Nunberg on the way to the restaurant.

"The only reason you have the job with Trump is that Roger Stone said you could," he'd said.

On its face, the statement sounded ridiculous to Corey. But he had just entered the world of Donald Trump, and there was much he didn't know.

As Corey navigated the city traffic to the FDR Drive and then onto the Triborough Bridge, the events of the day spun in his mind. He still didn't believe a campaign would happen. He was glad that he had insisted on a contract, one with a ninety-day out clause and a three-month severance, something that is unheard of in the business of politics. Still, he had just taken a big gamble.

He was heading north on the New York State Thruway when he tapped Alison's number on his cell.

"It looks like I just took a job with Donald Trump," he told his wife.

"What does that mean?" she said.

"I'm not sure," he answered. "Let's talk when I get home."

Corey met Alison when he was a freshman at a small Catholic high school in Massachusetts. It was the end of the school year, and his class attended a fair held at Alison's Catholic grammar school. She was twelve. He was thirteen. He had known her older sister, who was a year ahead of him in high school. The next fall, Alison enrolled as a freshman in Corey's high school. Pretty soon after that, they were dating, an on-again, off-again relationship that was on at the time Corey graduated. They went to his senior prom together. The romance continued when Alison went away to college at Bridgewater State. Corey would make the hour drive from Lowell to Alison's school often. But when Corey graduated from UMass in December 1995 and moved to Washington, DC, to attend graduate school at American University, the relationship began to fade. The truth was, the political bug had bitten him, which is something like what sailors in the old days must have felt when they realized that their first true love was the sea.

He might have had second thoughts, though. In 1997, he called Alison out of the blue. It was during that conversation when she told him she was getting married. Corey knew Alison's fiancé. They had both wanted to be electrical engineers and were in all the same classes the first semester in college. He liked Brian Kinney and admired him for his work ethic. His family had owned a Texaco gas station in Lowell for a couple of generations and, when he wasn't in class, Brian was pumping gas. The gas station was right around the corner from Alison's family home; her brothers worked there for years.

But if Corey pined over a missed opportunity, the feeling didn't last for long, at least on the surface.

By 2001, Corey was working for the RNC as the Northeast political director. At the time, he was living in Old Saybrook, Connecticut, and working in Trenton, New Jersey, which is about a four-hour commute. He spent most nights during the week in a Marriott in Princeton, New Jersey. But on the night of September 10, 2001, he slept in Old Saybrook and left for work early the morning of the eleventh. Corey was a fan of Howard Stern and had the show on the car radio when Stern began talking about a small plane hitting the World Trade Center. Like many people, the radio host didn't realize the significance of what was happening. But as the events that morning unfolded, Stern went from shock jock to newsman. When Corey crossed the Tappan Zee Bridge over the Hudson River, he had a clear view of Manhattan. It was only then that he could put a visual to Stern's words. From midspan, he could see the Twin Towers burning.

It was the next morning that an old high school classmate called Corey to tell him that Brian Kinney, Alison's husband, had been on flight 175, the one that slammed into the South Tower. He was killed.

Corey came back to Lowell to attend Brian's funeral. After the service, he went to a restaurant where there was a small reception attended by family and close friends. Corey knew everyone in the room; he had grown up with most of them in Lowell. There, he talked to Alison for the first time in four years.

As fate would have it, two months later Corey took a job managing the reelection campaign of Bob Smith, the senator from New Hampshire. He left Old Saybrook and moved to Manchester, New Hampshire, about a thirty-five-minute drive from Lowell, where Alison still lived. Soon they reconnected.

Corey married Alison in December 2005. Abigail, their first child, was born in October 2006, the twins, Alex and Owen, in February 2009, and Reagan during the Americans for Prosperity dinner in April 2011. He considers Brian Kinney an American hero, one who died for his country, and believes that his sacrifice is no less important than those killed on the battlefield.

* * *

Alison was still up when the headlights of Corey's car flashed across the front windows as he pulled into the driveway. It was one o'clock in the morning. As they sat in the kitchen, Corey filled Alison in on the juicy details.

It all sounded fascinating. After all, you don't get a chance to work for a big celebrity every day. Corey told her about the contract and promised her that they would be okay. Mr. Trump seemed excited, he told her. And Trump did call Dave while Corey was on the phone with him after the meeting. It was a leap of faith, for sure, but it wasn't the first leap Alison had taken with her husband. Corey's wife is Lowell born and bred. She's one of eight siblings, and the only one who doesn't still live within four miles of the others. When Corey first approached her with the idea of moving to New Hampshire, he might as well have said they were going to live on the moon. But that was nine years earlier, and things had worked out just fine. She had no reason to believe that her husband's new job was anything other than a great opportunity.

"Don't sweat it too much," Corey said to her.

Though Alison had left Lowell, she still had plenty of Lowell's toughness left in her. She wasn't going to sweat it, at least not right away.

But the truth of it was that Corey didn't know how long the new job was going to last, or what it would entail. The whole thing could evaporate like Sam Nunberg's vape mist at any moment.

CHAPTER 5

THE ISLAND OF THE MISFIT TOYS

What separates the winners from the losers is
how a person reacts to each new twist of fate.
—@realDonaldTrump, September 20, 2014, 2:03 a.m.

Government will become lean and mean, except it
will have a big, fat, beautiful heart.
—Donald J. Trump, 2016

ONE OF THE THINGS the media harped on during the campaign
was the supposed "lack of organization" due to the boss's refusal
to hire an army of politicos who make a living off campaign
contributions. Yes, we ran "lean and mean," but that's because
Donald Trump understood why his businesses made billions in
profits and the government is $20 trillion in debt. Mr. Trump
doesn't believe that throwing more money at a problem is the
answer.

In business, controlling costs has a lot to do with success or
failure. Like Mr. Trump always said, "To bring in a building on
time and under budget, you have to manage dozens of vendors

selling hundreds of goods or services. And you have to make sure you are getting the best price on every single one of them, while also ensuring that what they're selling you meets the specifications for safety and quality."

The boss knew from experience that success wasn't a matter of spending lavishly or cutting corners. It was a matter of spending wisely. So we ran very lean at first and spent the money we needed to, when we needed to, to win. Just as he didn't waste money on a building but also didn't go cheap on what was important to make it safe and valuable, Mr. Trump didn't waste money or go cheap on the campaign. On the contrary—and the media always got this wrong—Donald J. Trump never said no to a spending request. At the end of the day, however, Hillary Clinton spent twice as much money and lost. Donald Trump brought his campaign in on time, under budget, and into the White House. But it all started smaller than most people would believe.

D onald Trump's first campaign office was just a little bigger than a cubicle. The tiny space on the twenty-fourth floor of Trump Tower contained two desks next to each other, separated by a credenza. For the first six months, Corey kept his expectations similarly small, calling himself, "Donald Trump's senior political adviser" instead of his campaign manager. When Dave called the office, he'd often ask for the "very senior adviser." Corey was never hard to find, given that he was pretty much the only guy in the office, which until then had been the modest lair of Sam Nunberg alone.

As with every job he'd ever had, however, Corey showed up on day one ready to work.

One of Corey's and Dave's heroes is Lee Atwater, the

game-changing political icon, and the coarchitect of the modern Republican party. Throughout his career, Atwater rubbed shoulders with all the guys Corey would come to admire, working his way up from congressional campaigns and other small races to the Reagan White House, until finally becoming the mastermind behind George H. W. Bush's winning presidential campaign in 1988.

From the moment he started with Trump, Corey had a biography of Atwater on his desk, a book called *Bad Boy* by John Brady, which he tried to keep within reach at all times, right next to Sun-tzu's *The Art of War*. It had always been easy for Corey to see a bit of himself in Atwater, to use Lee's career as a kind of rough blueprint for his own. Both men came from outside the DC scene and shared a mild disdain for all the glitz and Ivy League glamour that came with it; and yet, as Brady puts it in the book, they both "learned things that they didn't teach at Harvard's Kennedy School of Government."

Oddly enough, Corey would come to share a few of Atwater's anxieties about rolling with the political and economic elite. Brady writes in places about an uneasy friendship that Atwater had with Roger Stone writing that Atwater was uncomfortable with the way Stone "liked expensive suits, palled around with Donald Trump and the jet set."

Most important, though, Corey admired Atwater's ability to, as he often put it, "see around corners"—in other words, the talent to anticipate whatever unlikely circumstance might happen next, subtle shifts in public opinion, a kink in some polling models, even a sudden rainstorm on Election Day. Working for Donald Trump, Corey would become adept at the art of anticipation; there was no other way to survive. But it also helped, especially in his early months on the job, that he had another set of eyes. Even better, eyes that were attached to a guy who'd come around these particular corners a few hundred times himself.

Dave, sensing that it might take his first pick for campaign manager a little time to get acclimated, called Corey almost every morning at 8:00 a.m. sharp, dialing from the car after he dropped his kids off at school. In the beginning, Corey didn't know if he should be hiding in the tiny campaign office, sitting by Trump's side upstairs, or some combination of the two. He couldn't tell if the boss liked his space, wanted frequent updates, or even how much of his attention the boss could afford to spend on the campaign at all. After all, he was still running the Trump Organization then, which employed thousands of people around the country and saw billions in revenue every year.

Dave had a few ideas about that. For Dave, it all boiled down to a simple piece of advice: Make sure you have things buttoned up. And that's what he told Corey to do before he saw Trump.

In those early days, Corey would prioritize two or three bullet points to bring up to the twenty-sixth floor, then run through them in a few tight sentences, not unlike a proposal or a sales pitch. In those days, it wasn't uncommon for Trump to have mere minutes—sometimes seconds—to sign off on big decisions regarding the campaign. He had new hotels to build, checks to cut, and, most important, a multibillion-dollar business to run, the future of which he needed to secure if he had any hope of seeing it grow while he was out campaigning. If Corey could get him for a few minutes in the office to plan a campaign stop, he'd consider it a good day. Donald J. Trump never cared about the schedule. Corey would work with Rhona Graff, Donald Trump's longtime personal assistant and senior vice president of the Trump Organization, to arrange all of that.

The first big lesson that Corey learned about his new boss was that Donald Trump practically lived on his phone, a big black landline at the left-hand corner of his desk. In the early days, every time Corey walked into Trump's office, he seemed to be on the phone with some titan of industry or celebrity. One day early on when he walked in, Trump was on the phone with former president Bill Clinton, having a lengthy conversation with him.

Trump also used the phone to manage his organization. The lesson was that if you worked for Donald Trump, you better have your phone on, because he was going to call.

Then there was the internal politics within Trump Tower, that Dave and Corey discussed.

Along with frequent phone calls from Mr. Trump, and a short meeting that they had every morning on the twenty-sixth floor of Trump Tower, Corey could count on seeing his boss at least twice a day.

Though all the windows look identical from the outside, Trump Tower is actually divided in half—twenty-six floors on the lower half, for commercial use, and twenty-six more at the top that are exclusively residential. The twenty-fourth floor, where Corey and Sam Nunberg shared their little half room of an office, was what people who spent time in both halves of the tower called the "cut-through" floor. Because each half had its own dedicated elevator, you couldn't get from the commercial section to the residential—or the other way around.

So, when he wanted to get from the top-floor, where he lived, to his office on the twenty-sixth, Mr. Trump would have to take the elevator down from his 15,000-square-foot triplex penthouse to twenty-four, walk past Corey's office, then take the commercial elevator up two floors to his office.

More often than not, the boss would stop in to see what was going on with the political operation. When he did, he'd usually see a couple of staff members, some papers, maybe a few notes on strategy. Corey was laying the groundwork for the campaign but didn't have anything to show yet. Beginning a habit that he'd keep until election night, Corey had already begun to tack up pictures and notes that arrived at the office to the wall. Looking back, he realizes that the room must have looked more like a college dorm room than a campaign office, as there were so many odds and ends lying around. Whatever it looked like, it bore little resemblance to the free-balling, cartwheeling road show that the campaign would become.

The first campaign hires Corey made were state campaign directors in the first three primary states: Jim Merrill, Ed McMullen, and Geri McDaniel in South Carolina; Matt Cipielowski in New Hampshire; and Chuck Laudner in Iowa. These were the people who'd be in charge of setting up small Trump headquarters in their home states, then reporting back to home base in New York. Corey made sure that they knew the voters and districts of their states inside out, the same way he knew the local climate of New Hampshire. Because of that, Matt Cipielowski was an easy choice—local boy, Polish, and Corey's former right-hand man at Americans for Prosperity, where Cipielowski had worked as a field director.

As a member of the South Carolina House of Representatives since 2000, Jim Merrill was an easy choice, too. At the time, he was the majority leader of the state House. He also owned a public relations and marketing firm in South Carolina. McMullen had been in South Carolina politics and business for twenty-five years. He had also been the president of the South Carolina

Policy Council, a conservative think tank, through 2007. Those two were a perfect team in the state.

Chuck Laudner, who had been the chief of staff for Representative Steve King, served as the executive director of the Iowa Republican Party, and helped guide Rick Santorum in a successful Iowa Caucus campaign in 2012, was an obvious pick. Corey hired him immediately on the emphatic recommendation from Dave.

Laudner knew Iowa Republican politics maybe better than anyone and had a proven track record of winning. He also knew which events a candidate absolutely had to attend—just to "check the box," as he put it—and which ones could suck up too much of a campaign's energy without translating to votes.

Early in 2015, Trump and Corey flew to Iowa, where Trump spoke at an event called the Land Investment Expo, an agricultural conference in Des Moines hosted by the social conservative Bob Vander Plaats. It was a paid speech for Donald J. Trump. It was on this trip when the boss and Corey met Chuck for the first time. It was also the first time that Corey, Chuck Laudner, or anyone else from the tiny campaign team had ever seen Trump speak in front of such a niche crowd. They had seen him do fine in front of die-hard political crowds, but Iowa farmers? When it came right down to it, Donald Trump knew how to speak to the people, whether they were from the Iowa farmland or Woodside, Queens. There is no better communicator.

Joining the boss and Corey on the trip were Hope Hicks and Amanda Miller, an early campaign staffer, and Keith Schiller. Chuck and his wife, Stephanie, met Mr. Trump's jet at the airport, and they rode with Corey and Trump to the hotel where the event was to be held. During the short ride, Trump peppered Chuck with questions about Iowa. Having been the state director for Santorum and running the shop for Steve King, both of whom are big personalities, he knew the importance of a good, back-and-forth relationship. Moving forward, trust would be important—especially when it came to making decisions.

The trip turned out to be another moment that foretold the campaign's future. Well, almost. Trump, in what by then seemed like an inevitability, was a hit. He donated a weekend at Mar-a-Lago, his Florida club, that raised $40,000. In return, the expo gave him a one-acre deeded parcel of Iowa. Even for a guy with enough acreage to spare, it was pretty cool. Though he spoke about the type of real estate that involved towering buildings, hotels, and golf courses, his language translated to field management and farm investments. He mesmerized the crowd, which numbered a thousand or more. They gave him a thundering, standing ovation.

From the Land Expo, we went right to a Republican dinner, where the boss gave a political speech replete with references to border fences, China, trade, and jobs—using early versions of the lines that he'd soon polish into his greatest hits—and energized the room. Going from one venue to the other we witnessed an incredible display of oratorical versatility. Neither of us knew of anyone who could hop between modalities quite as well, and certainly not as naturally, as Trump had that day. There is very little in politics that Chuck Laudner hasn't seen, but he was impressed. He predicted that Trump would win the Iowa caucuses, though they were still over a year away.

Mr. Trump started to feed off the momentum. You could see it in the eyes of the people who attended his rallies, in the way he stood in front of the audience and invited them, as if he was standing again in front of Griffin and Abigail at the New Hampshire Freedom Summit, keys to his helicopter in hand, to come along on the ride he was offering. The mind-set that would become the hallmark of our campaign had formed thirty years ago in our leader. Now it was time to show it to America.

First, it was Donald Trump against the Establishment; soon, it would become the United States against the World—America First!

The day after the Land Expo, Dave and Citizens United, along with Steve King, hosted the Iowa Freedom Summit at the Hoyt Sherman Place, an old 1,500-seat historic theater with a raised proscenium stage. As at the New Hampshire Freedom Summit we had hosted nearly nine months earlier, twelve presidential hopefuls strode to the stage, one after the other, ready to give their speeches.

In planning for the event, Dave was worried about the crowd. He packed the schedule with military-like precision. Sure, the crowd was big, but as lunchtime approached, Dave began to wonder if people would come back for the second half of the summit after leaving the theater for lunch. If not, nobody would hear Senator Ted Cruz, Governor Scott Walker (who ended up stealing the show), or Donald Trump.

So, as they had in New Hampshire when Trump spoke, Dave and his crew served box lunches right in the theater, just to make sure people would stay in their seats. Dozens of volunteers set everything up on folding tables by the exits, and they told the crowd that lunch would be served in-house. Intermission came and lunches were served, followed by mixed conversation and the sound of just over 1,500 people chomping on sandwiches and chips.

After exactly twenty-two minutes, Dave sent staffers up the aisles with garbage cans to collect any leftover cardboard, then started up again. And it still was a full house.

Seeing around corners, as we would come to find, means more than anticipating a negative ad or seismic shifts in public opinion. For the most part, it's about sweating the small stuff—

phone calls, first names, seating arrangements. Even lunch.

Trump gave a robust speech, as usual. The *Des Moines Register* called him "easily the most brazen speaker to take the stage." But the rest of the media was busy fawning over Scott Walker, claiming that Trump's performance had been a distant second.

Walker had channeled Elmer Gantry and gave the speech of his political life. He strutted the stage with his sleeves rolled up. The spell he cast that day started his presidential aspirations off with a burst and infuriated Trump.

"Who the hell is Scott Walker?" he said later.

Even with the gathering popularity of the campaign and the increasing workload he was taking on, Corey was in no rush to put together a centralized staff. It was nice running things with a small, tight staff for a while.

Looking back, Corey realizes that being virtually alone in the office allowed him to begin building the perfect machine, letting him acquaint himself with all the little pieces and their various functions, ensuring they would run smoothly when he finally decided to bring on more people. In those early days, a large, diversified staff—like the ones that Cruz, Clinton, and Jeb Bush had been building and maintaining for years— would only have clouded his vision.

That, and he had no place to put them.

He was still working out of the twenty-fourth-floor office then, bumping elbows with whoever he had working that day. The only internal hires he had made were Alan Cobb, a lawyer and friend in Kansas who helped with early ballot access and whose last work on a campaign had been on Bob Dole's, and a few interns, who were there to sort through mail and get logistical items in place. They spent a lot of time running into each other, forced to share one of the two desks in the office.

It'd be slow work building a team, Corey thought. But it would also need to be careful work if they were going to have any chance of pulling this off.

When he did start to assemble the core group, it came together like something out of a superhero comic book story—just without the superpowers, or any experience in politics.

For instance, there was Dan Scavino, whose prior political experience was as Mr. Trump's regular caddy at the Briar Hall Country Club in Westchester, New York. In an interview with a Westchester magazine, Dan said that the first time he carried his golf bag, Mr. Trump tipped him with two one-hundred-dollar bills. "I still have those bills," he told the magazine. After attending college in upstate New York and graduating with a degree in communications, Dan bounced around a couple of jobs. When Trump bought the Briar Hall Country Club and renamed it the Trump National Golf Club, he hired Dan as assistant manager. The onetime caddy worked his way up to become the club's executive vice president. He also worked for Joe Torre's Safe at Home Foundation. Just before the boss announced his run for the presidency, Dan was in the process of starting a public relations business. He dropped everything and joined the campaign. He would become Mr. Trump's Twitter lieutenant.

Then there was Hope Hicks. She was already working for the Trumps and had an office one floor above Corey's. At the time, Corey was looking for someone to handle the media for Mr. Trump's nascent campaign, and Hope was doing PR for one of the boss's golf tournaments. He asked Hope if she wanted to come to a rally in South Carolina the following weekend. She was game, but weather grounded her commercial flight, so she didn't make it. The following week, Mr. Trump was headed to Iowa for the Land Expo, and again Corey asked Hope to come along.

"Is there going to be golf?" she asked.

Smart and private, with nearly a photographic memory, Hope had grown up in Greenwich, Connecticut. A talented athlete, she was captain of her lacrosse team at Southern Methodist University. She was also a competitive swimmer and could travel the length of an Olympic-size pool underwater. Along with her sister, Hope was a model for Ralph Lauren when she was eleven. She began at the Trump Organization doing public relations for Ivanka's fashion line and for some Trump resorts, and she served as the director of communications for aspects of the organization.

She didn't have any idea what the job that Corey was offering entailed until Mr. Trump called her into his office.

"I'm going to Iowa this weekend and you're going to be the press secretary for my campaign."

"Which one?" Hope asked. "The Doral marketing campaign?"

"No. My presidential campaign! I'm running for president."

Okay, sure, Hope thought. *Me too.*

Hope had so little knowledge of politics then that when Corey told her he had worked for the Kochs she asked if he knew Danny Masters. "He's worked for Coke for a while," she said.

Along with Hope, there was Keith Schiller, the retired NYPD narcotics cop and Donald Trump's longtime bodyguard. Keith was the head of security for the Trump Organization when the campaign started and then oversaw the boss's private security team when he became a candidate. Our other security guys included Eddie Deck, Gary Uher, and Michael Sharkey, all retired FBI agents; Ron Jurain, an officer in the NYPD; and Burt Mentor, who hadn't any formal security experience but was six four, two hundred and seventy-five pounds, and had been shot a couple of times. As the crowds at the boss's rallies grew, the Trump security team did yeoman's work with crowd control, working out the logistics with local law enforcement and keeping the candidate safe.

We brought on Geri McDaniel from South Carolina to start to build a grassroots campaign in that state. Cassidy Dumbauld came aboard in August 2015, right out of college. Her first job for the campaign was answering mail. Standard operating procedure then (before it became impossible to do so) was to answer every piece of mail Mr. Trump received. Two weeks after she started, Corey called her into his office.

"Why are you here?" he asked.

"Because I want Donald Trump to be president," she answered.

Corey hired her full time on the spot.

John McEntee was another political neophyte. A former walk-on UConn quarterback and YouTube football trickster sensation, he moved on the spur of the moment to New York City from California. In the city, he got a job working for Fox News, where he first learned Donald Trump was running for president. From the moment he found out, he began emailing the campaign asking if he could help. As an intern, he was the first in and the last to leave the campaign's office just about every day. When he came on board officially, he joined the advance team on the road and in the air.

But there was Don McGahn, a partner at Jones Day, the Washington powerhouse law firm, and a former chairman of the Federal Election Commission. McGahn was an expert on campaign finance law. Mr. Trump had asked Dave to recommend the best campaign lawyer in the field, and McGahn's name was the first he thought of. The talented lawyer's move to the Trump team demonstrated a seriousness on the part of the campaign that drew the attention of the Republican establishment. This was a serious move. The white-shoe firm had been involved in presidential campaigns for many years, and had represented candidates such as George W. Bush and Mitt Romney in their presidential runs. No doubt Don had a lot of internal conversations at Jones Day about taking on the new client. He would become the eyes and ears of the Trump campaign in Washington. McGahn, who owns over thirty guitars and plays in a cover band in Ocean City, Maryland, also acted as "Father Confessor" when Corey, usually at night, needed to speak with someone on the team who actually had campaign experience.

The campaign's first national spokesperson was Katrina Pierson. Katrina came aboard shortly after Corey did. As a spokesperson for the Tea Party, a movement she helped found, Katrina was a known commodity on television news shows. Mr. Trump admired her unvarnished honesty on the air and invited her to Trump Tower. There, in the boss's office, they talked for two hours about conservative politics, and at the end of the discussion he offered her the job as his political spokesperson. Katrina flew with us often on Trump Force One. On her first trip, Mr. Trump insisted that she sit up in the jumper seat in the cockpit. Later, when she became inundated with media requests, the boss had the campaign help her build a studio in her home in Dallas. Still, on a busy day—and all the days on the campaign were just that—she'd spend more time in the studio than in any other room in the house. Or so it seemed.

Other members of the team were Campbell Burr, who only worked weekends at first, but soon left her job and came on full-time, and Daniel Gelbinovich, who opened mail for a year. He once bought $2,000 worth of Elvis stamps for the campaign.

Cassidy had to help him return them after he was reminded that they weren't really appropriate for a presidential campaign. Bringing them back wasn't as easy as it sounds. The Postal Service was giving its clerks a bonus for selling the Elvis stamps. They went to several post offices before a clerk in one across from Penn Station agreed to exchange them.

"The only reason I'm taking them back is because I think Trump is going to become president," the clerk said. "If he does, let him know I refunded his money."

We had Meghan Powers, who picked up and moved to Iowa in the middle of December for the primary. There was Thomas Tsveras, our first intern. If you Google the Trump campaign launch announcement you'll see him standing right next to the escalator. We had Thomas Baptiste, who ran the call center, sang in a choir at his church, and addressed everyone by their first and last names. We had Ashley Mocarski, the queen of the late-night press release. There was Robert Gabriel, who was Stephen Miller's assistant and who worked on a plastic desk in a closet-size room with nails coming through the walls. Baylor Myers and Zach McEntee, who was John's cousin, worked on the finance team for Eli Miller, who joined after Marco Rubio faded out, and Steven Mnuchin. There were terrific folks like Jared Smith, Ashton Adams, and Victor Gutierrez and Stephanie Grisham and Ben Weiser, just out of high school, who delayed going to college to work for the campaign.

It's remarkable when you think about it. Donald Trump launched his presidential campaign with a tweet, an escalator ride, and a staff that mostly wouldn't know the difference between a caucus and a cactus.

The only members of Corey's original team who had any political experience, other than him, were Alan Cobb, George Gigicos, and his early advance team, which included Kevin

Chmielewski (whom we beat up a lot—meaning he took a lot of our grief and we ran him ragged—but who was the person who could articulate the type of expectations that the candidate had for these events), Aaron Chang, and Ben Miller, who were with us from the very beginning right until the end, and Don McGahn.

But, even with the additions of McGahn, Cobb, and George, Donald Trump's early campaign team didn't exactly strike fear into the hearts of any other presidential aspirant.

They never saw us coming.

The next big event for Trump was CPAC, which was held in late February 2015 at the National Harbor Hotel in Maryland. There, expectations were low, because Rand Paul, with his Tea Party followers, had been the perennial favorite, due to his father's supporters.

Knowing this, Corey bussed some Trump supporters down from New Hampshire, just to bolster appearances. He also set up a suite in the hotel, and Hope booked a half dozen or so interviews. The small campaign team was working hard, except for Sam Nunberg, who went missing. The night before Trump's speech, Sam went to a karaoke bar that was filled with Rand Paul supporters. The rumor was, he got into a Trump-Paul argument that quickly escalated and ended with a straight right hand to Nunberg's nose. The erstwhile political op walked into the interview room late with a nose that was spread halfway across his face. Trump, who was busy with the media interviews, just glared at him. Later the boss asked Corey if he thought Sam was going to last in his job. "I don't know, boss," Corey said. People who don't know Donald Trump often see him as a cold, calculating mogul bereft of feelings for people. Yes, the boss can certainly be merciless when business is on the line, which for him is almost always. But he sees the humanity in people, and he has a soft spot for those who battle demons.

As the team began slowly expanding, Corey went searching in Trump Tower for more space.

He found it on the fifth floor. It was a raw, empty space—really just one big room. It took up half of the entire floor. The staff of *The Apprentice* had used it to store their camera equipment, and had occasionally set up temporary office space there. The ceilings were unfinished, and fluorescent light bays hung from them, along with exposed pipe and internet wires. The walls to the offices, of which there weren't many, were three-quarters high and made from unfinished plywood. The floor was bare concrete.

Perfect, Corey thought.

He sent interns and staff on a scavenger hunt throughout the building, telling them to grab any unused desks, office chairs, and plastic tables. The interns decorated the walls with letters, photos, American flags, caricatures of Trump and other items, all received through the mail from fans and supporters. Corey took a prefab office with Sheetrock walls and a glass door that opened onto a balcony. He had a clean wooden desk, appropriated from somewhere else in the building, and a big fluffy chair with one haggard rip down the center. There was no heat in the room, so in the winter the campaign bought space heaters that would invariably blow the building's fuses.

When Pope Francis visited New York that June, Mr. Trump and his whole family watched the pontiff ride down Fifth Avenue from Corey's balcony. The interns and Johnny McEntee rode hover boards and skateboards around the room. It looked more like a start-up than a campaign office. There were no pollsters, media coaches, or focus groups. No speechwriter, no "senior strategist" or any of the other types of "professional" political consultants like the ones who had failed for the last eight years to elect a Republican president.

What we did have was a receptionist, Dorothy Blumenthal, who came back to work even after a piece of concrete from the bare walls fell on her.

We were the island of misfit toys.

CHAPTER 6

THE GOLDEN ESCALATOR

The fact is I go down the streets of New York and the people
that really like me are the taxi drivers and the workers, etc. I
mean I really get a better response.
—Donald J. Trump, 1988

ONE THING no one can accuse Donald Trump of is not being
authentic. We should know; we've been in politics for a long
time, and we seen plenty of folks who aren't.

Donald Trump has never changed his message. Just do a Web
search on "Donald Trump 1988," and you'll find him preaching
the same political message he's preaching now: America First.
He appeared on the *Oprah Winfrey Show* in 1988 and said the
same things about our lousy trade policies then that he said
during his 2016 presidential campaign. And that was before
NAFTA.

The boss hasn't been calling out crooked trade deals for
thirty years because it benefits him. He's done it because he cares
about the taxi drivers and the workers running Bobcats and
jackhammers, and they know it. That's why he's always been

well received by regular Americans. That's why we called him "the blue-collar billionaire."

Do you want to know why no politician had a chance against Donald Trump in the primaries? He told it like it was. While other politicians were prepping for debates and drilling talking points, Donald Trump was walking out onto stages and saying what he'd been saying for thirty years. It was like no political campaign ever. They never had a chance.

In any story, but especially one with an outcome as unexpected as ours, there are moments when the course of the plot shifts ever so slightly toward the improbable. The call Corey took in Aruba was one of those moments. Maybe it was the voice of Michael Cohen over the speakerphone telling him when the announcement date would be that lit his fire. Or maybe it was that Corey then learned the most valuable lesson you can learn about working for Donald Trump: Proximity to the boss is power.

On the one hand, you couldn't blame Corey for thinking he could go on vacation without causing too much of a disruption. During that first winter, Trump would fly to Mar-a-Lago just about every weekend, spending time with guests and some old friends who lived full time in Florida, working from an office that he kept at the resort. And Corey was still traveling back and forth to New Hampshire to spend some weekends with his family whenever his schedule would allow. And besides, he'd planned the trip months before he took the job with Trump. The whole family was looking forward to it.

In his bathing suit and flip-flops, with his kids laughing and splashing nearby in the pool, Corey paced the blistering hot cement with his iPhone to his ear. Since Corey had been in Aruba, Trump had probably called him ten times a day. He shuddered to think of his phone bill at the end of the month. This day, the boss had him on speaker, and he could tell a few people were in the room. Then he heard Michael Cohen's voice.

"We've set a date," the boss's lawyer said. "Mr. Trump will announce on a Monday in late May."

It wasn't a surprise that Mr. Trump was going to announce. Corey had been working hard to convince him to enter the presidential race. He had even begun to plan the announcement, partly to help show Mr. Trump he could run a winning campaign. But the date Michael recommended was crazy. Hard as it was to argue while poolside in paradise in a bathing suit, he was going to give it a shot. Though he wasn't dressed the part at that moment, Corey was about to assert himself as Donald Trump's campaign manager.

He told Cohen and the boss, and anyone else who was listening, that a late May announcement date wouldn't work. He needed at least five weeks to plan the event.

"And a Monday wouldn't work either," he said.

Corey explained that Mondays and Fridays are terrible days to try to make news. Monday everyone is still in weekend mode, and Friday is news dump day.

"Tuesday, Wednesday, or Thursday would be best."

Still, on the call, he lowered his iPhone a little to look at it, squinting to make out the screen in the sun. He opened the calendar app. He knew he wanted to hold the event on some date that would amplify the slogan of the campaign—Make America Great Again. Doing that would give the rally what's known in politics as a hook. June 14, which is not only Flag Day but also Mr. Trump's birthday, would've been perfect. Unfortunately, that year it fell on a Sunday.

"June sixteenth," he said. Equidistant from Memorial Day and Fourth of July. Perfect.

The boss agreed with everything Corey said. The next morning, while eating breakfast with the family, Trump called again, this time without anyone else in the room.

"Where are you?" he said.

"I . . . I'm in Aruba, sir," Corey said.

"Get your ass back here," Trump said. Then, *click*.

Leading up to the announcement, the boss did what the boss does best: he built excitement. The press followed him around like a waddle of deranged penguins, just as it had for years. They swallowed his Twitter-announced promises for a "big surprise" the next Tuesday, or Friday, or the week after like they were slurping down pickled herrings, only to see the dates come and go, only to get fooled again. On May 9, Trump participated in the South Carolina Freedom Summit, held at the Peace Center in Greenville and hosted by Dave and Congressman Jeff Duncan of South Carolina—it was a monster. On May 21, Trump took a trip to DC to see the hotel he was building in the Old Post Office building. The press was sure that he would use that property as a backdrop for the announcement. And the boss did little to dissuade that notion. He had banners put up at the construction site that read TRUMP 2016. Once the press was gathered around him, he assured them the date on the banners was when the hotel was going to open, and that it had nothing to do with the presidential race.

Trump campaign attorney, Don McGahn, had his hands full with a candidate that had such vast real estate holdings and was in the middle of a renovation of a GSA building while entertaining a run for the presidency.

Though he was having fun with media, he was also taking some serious steps toward a candidacy. He began to float policy balloons. Recorded radio ads ran in New Hampshire in which he railed against the Trans-Pacific Partnership trade deal. In early May, he told Matthew Boyle at Breitbart News that the trade agreement would be a disaster.

Much was written after the election touting the notion that Trump had gotten his policy ideas during nine interviews he did at early campaign (and precampaign) events with Steve Bannon on Breitbart radio. Trump looked forward to the interviews with Bannon. "Where's my Stevie?" he would ask when he was finished speaking at the events. But Bannon would be the first to tell you that the idea that he, somehow, through some subliminal urging, had placed those ideas in the boss's head is a total fallacy. What the boss learned from his interviews with Bannon was how his policies would play with voters and which ones would reach the most people.

By the way, Mr. Trump learned something from every interview. It didn't matter whether it was Sean Hannity, Bill O'Reilly, Matt Lauer, Don Lemon, the *New York Times*, Michael Savage, or Mark Levin. In each, he would ascertain what was important for him to know by the questions he was being asked. When you look back at his interviews, you can see how they helped him prepare for the debates, both in the primary and the general election. It was political genius and a talent for which he gets very little credit. If anyone but Donald J. Trump showed the same skill, he or she would be called a mastermind. Trump knew what he stood for, but having never run for office, this education helped him craft his message.

Mr. Trump had decided to hold the announcement at Trump Tower. Corey hired union carpenters to build a stage and a three-tier riser for the press. As this was New York, he also had to hire a few friends, cousins, and uncles of people who worked at Trump Tower. Corey had booked the food court on the lower level. Though the space had a few pluses—the famous escalator, for instance—it was rather small. To make room for the stage, they had to turn off the waterfall that was built into a wall.

Matt Calamari, who was chief operating officer of Trump Properties, has been with Donald Trump since 1981. Trump first met Calamari at the US Open tennis tournament, where he was working as a security guard. The story goes that the boss watched him escort a couple of hecklers out of the stadium, which is a nice way of describing what happened that day, and then hired him on the spot to oversee security at Trump Tower. At six foot three, Calamari is a formidable presence. What makes him even more intimidating is that he speaks a little like Joe Pesci from either *My Cousin Vinny* or *Goodfellas*—take your pick—but only if you added about a hundred pounds to the voice and made it a foot taller.

Calamari runs Trump Tower like he owns a piece of the place. He watched Corey's carpenters carry gear and lumber for the stage through the main lobby of the tower like they were conspiring to rob the joint.

"Whoa, Whoa, Whoa!" he yelled at one. "*Don't* put that hammer on my floor! That's *fucking marble!*"

The real owner of the building also had his ideas on how things should work in Trump Tower.

As it would be for the rest of the campaign, Mr. Trump picked the music for the event. He never worried about getting permission to use the songs. He'd say things like, "Use Pavarotti, he loves me!" All he cared about was that the tunes were upbeat and loud—very loud.

Corey had hired Tim Unes, a seasoned pro in the world of political events, to help plan the announcement. Unes then introduced Corey to George Gigicos, who was also an expert at staging—he'd done campaigns for John McCain, Mitt Romney, and George W. Bush. Plenty of experience. Still, for whatever reason, the boss was leery of letting an outsider get his hands on the audio knobs, especially when it came to controlling his walk-on music. Hearing for the first time that someone named George Gigicos, whom he had never met, would be in charge, Trump scanned the lobby, looking hard for a familiar face. He spotted an older gentleman near the wall, who, as Corey recalls, appeared to be no younger than ninety. (And this was in good light.)

"Johnny!" Trump yelled. "Come over here, Johnny!"

The man looked confused but came over anyway. Trump and Corey stood waiting for him.

"My name's Fred, sir," he said. "I was—"

"Are you working tomorrow, Johnny?" Trump said.

Fred, it turned out, had been working in a couch-size fire control room on the main floor of Trump Tower since shortly after they broke ground on the building.

"Yes, Mr. Trump," he said. "I'm working tomorrow."

"All right, Johnny. Then you're in charge of the music."

Tread lightly, Corey thought. "But, sir," Corey said. "We've got George, sir."

"I don't want George!" Trump yelled, pointing at Fred. "I want Johnny!"

"My name's Fred, sir."

"Whatever!" Trump said, now joking with the guy.

Corey kept trying. "Sir," he said. "I know George is going to get this right. He's done this stuff for the pope! Can we please put George in charge of the music?"

Trump thought for a second and, despite the fact that he didn't know George, said, "I have no faith in this guy, Corey."

Just as an aside, George ended up heading the advance team for the campaign, a job that was like no other in political history before. He would book and stage events in venues like airplane hangars and football stadiums all over the country at a rate that would increase to six a day toward the end. Later, he would work for President Trump in the White House.

In the days before the announcement, Corey pounded Red Bulls and, along with George, worked about thirty hours straight to get the event staged.

At around two a.m. on the morning of the event, someone noticed that the lanyards for the invites and press, some five hundred passes, had the date "June 16, 2016," printed on them, which would have been fine if the event was going to take place the next year. It was a disaster. Corey knew that both the press and the boss would kill him, with the boss being the worst of the two. He sent his most trusted staffer, Joy Lutes, out to find an all-night printing store. She had never been to New York City before but somehow found one open in Harlem and returned with the revised passes at five a.m.

At about six thirty, Corey ran home to shower and change into a suit.

When Corey first took the job with Trump, the plan was to stay in New York during the week and fly home to New Hampshire on the weekends. The thought of renting an apartment in Manhattan was out of the question for him. Far too expensive. But he figured he could work something out with his new boss. After all, Trump owned hotels and buildings all over town, right?

That first day, Corey approached Rhona Graff, whose office is right next to Trump's, and inquired about staying in a room in one of the Trump properties. As Corey remembered it, she recommended the Trump SoHo, but she also let him know that he would have to pay for the room. Corey was pretty sure it would be a campaign expense but went to Trump a little later in the day to talk about it.

"Why would you want to stay at one of my hotels when I can get you a place for free?" he asked.

Mr. Trump owned several beautiful four-story town houses on East Sixty-First Street in Manhattan and kept an apartment on the second floor of one of them for friends and visitors. He had invited the family of the ex-NFL star Jim Kelly to stay there while the quarterback was at Lenox Hill Hospital in Manhattan, battling for his life in a fight against cancer in his jaw.

That first night he stayed in the apartment, Corey received a lesson in Manhattan hospitality.

Keith Schiller gave him the keys, and Corey had written the address down. But when he showed up at the building and tried to get in, the key didn't work. He called Keith.

"Just buzz the woman who lives in the first-floor apartment," Keith told him. "She'll let you in."

Corey did as instructed and buzzed the first-floor apartment. The woman who answered the buzzer told him in no uncertain terms that if he didn't stop trying to get into her building, she would call the cops. Corey was at the right building number, but on the wrong block—he had written down Sixty-Third Street instead of Sixty-First.

When he finally got into the right apartment, it was like walking onto a movie set. He would have the same reaction later when he saw Mar-a-Lago for the first time. The apartment was like a mini version of Trump's Palm Beach club—lots of gold leaf and old oak. Corey would end up staying at the apartment for his entire eighteen-month tenure as Trump's campaign manager and even longer. Throughout that time, he never once used the living room, never turned on the cable TV, and brought every bit of his clothing with him when he went home for the weekend. He was so afraid of ruining something that all he did in the apartment was sleep and shower, which he did before heading back to Trump Tower on the morning of the announcement.

Corey had volunteers rush around and hand out MAKE AMERICA GREAT AGAIN T-shirts to the building's workers. By eleven, he had enough people lining the balcony, some wearing MAGA T-shirts.

Mr. Trump and Melania took the elevator down to the lobby level and then stepped out from behind a curtain. Then, with Neil Young's "Rockin' in the Free World" blaring from the speakers, expertly cued by George (whom the boss had allowed, begrudgingly, to take a shot at handling the audio), Donald Trump, in a dark blue suit, a white shirt, and a red tie, with his beautiful wife, Melania, wearing a pearl-white dress preceding him, took the now-famous ride down the escalator.

It would be the last time any part of his campaign moved in a downward direction for a while.

For two days leading up to the announcement, Corey and George had partly sequestered themselves in a Midtown hotel to write the announcement speech. They were able to file the speech down to a manageable seven and a half minutes. Corey even released it to all of the press, so that they would have the text in advance.

He shouldn't have bothered.

In his office just before the announcement, Trump gave a quick look at the sheet of paper Corey handed him, folded it up, and put it in his breast pocket, never to look at it again. Then, in front of the microphone on the stage inside the dried-out waterfall, with hundreds of members of the media present, the boss delivered what is arguably the most memorable announcement speech of any candidate for office in history. It was a forty-five-minute freestyle soliloquy that included these thirty words: "When Mexico sends its people, they're not sending their best," he said. "They're sending people that have lots of problems . . . they're bringing drugs, they're bringing crime; they're rapists. And some, I assume, are good people."

It's funny. The media's reaction to those remarks was at first a flat nothing.

When people asked Corey or Hope Hicks how the speech went, all he had to say was, "Great, just as we planned."

Sometimes, however, the spark nearly goes out before the forest catches on fire.

Right after the announcement, team Trump, which included Dan, Hope, George, Keith, Corey, and Donald Trump, boarded Trump Force One at La Guardia. The 757 climbed, banked, and headed west toward Des Moines, Iowa. Kevin Chmielewski had gotten Hoyt Sherman Place ready for the candidate. The boss delivered virtually the same message as he had at Trump Tower, with similar words. In the theater, his speech was wildly received. Among the press, there wasn't so much as a ripple.

On the way out of the theater, the boss asked Corey why he thought it would be so hard for him to win in Iowa. "They love me here," he said.

The next day, Trump and his whole team were in New Hampshire, where they announced in a college basketball arena.

The plan was to then head to the third of the first three primary states, South Carolina.

We wouldn't make that trip until two weeks later.

There is nothing that can change a campaign more quickly than a national tragedy.

While the team was still in New Hampshire, a racist maniac named Dylann Roof walked into a historic black church in downtown Charleston and murdered nine people in cold blood.

On the boss's insistence, we canceled all planned trips to South Carolina for three weeks. Some things should be and are above politics.

But not everyone stayed so quiet about it. Just a few days after the tragedy happened, we learned that Hillary Clinton had gone on *Ralston Live* and tried to push some of the blame for Roof's actions onto Trump.

"A recent entry into the Republican race," Hillary said, "said some very inflammatory things about Mexicans. And decent people need to stand up against that. Things like that can trigger an unstable person."

The negative fallout was immediate. News headlines blared reports of a mass exodus from all things Trump: Macy's dropped the Trump clothing line, NBC said that Trump would never host *The Apprentice* again. Stars, producers, and sponsors jumped from the Miss Universe contest as if it were a jet ski heading for a jetty. Even Neil Young, who had once been friendly with Trump, the boss, told the campaign that it could no longer use his music.

But lost in the clamor was a popular uprising that had gone all but unnoticed by the Left and the media, who were, of course, the microphone of the Left.

Clinton had called out Trump's thirty words in the hope of destroying him politically. But all she did was open the eyes of a huge swath of Republicans who hadn't yet thought of voting for Donald Trump. And those who already wanted to vote for him now wanted to do so even more.

Sometime after the tragedy, the phone rang in Rhona Graff's office. The voice belonged to Pam Gross, a friend of Rhona's, who handled booking for *CNN Tonight*, anchored by Don Lemon. We would come to deal with her quite a bit by the end of the campaign.

"We need Mr. Trump on tonight," Pam said. "Will he be available?"

It's hard to remember exactly how this went, since the same scenario would play out so many times, but Corey seems to remember Trump yelling from his office when he heard about the offer, barely looking up from the newspaper on his desk.

"Tell her I'll do a phoner!"

If you get out the map, Trump Tower is about eight blocks from Don Lemon's studio. Seriously, if we'd cracked a window in Trump's office, the boss could probably have hit a three wood halfway there.

Now, if this were Ted Cruz? Ben Carson? Even Hillary Clinton?

Click. No thanks.

There was a long pause on the other end of the line.

News networks do not take call-ins from political candidates. Audio alone doesn't work well on television, and phone reception can be spotty or cut out altogether, which the boss would use to his advantage. Easy as they are to set up, phone interviews make for a real lack of control on the network's end. Plus, the host usually looks like an idiot—looking at nothing, waiting for answers to come down from the ceiling. So, for years, there was a rule: Unless your candidate is trapped in a mineshaft somewhere, you'd better get him to the studio. If you didn't like that, you could find some other way to get him on television.

But this was Donald Trump, the first Republican front-runner in the history of American politics who brought viewers to the networks, not the other way around. If Trump wanted to send in his comments by carrier pigeon, CNN would schedule a full hour for Jake Tapper to read out his notes.

"Fine," Pam said.

By the end of the interview, the boss had taken all of Don Lemon's jagged questions, flipped them, and doubled down on the points he had made in the first place. He had stats and hard facts in front of him (the kind of thing you can't look at in a studio) and kept slinging them till Don had no choice but to throw in the towel. The team would look back on that night as the evening that Trump picked up a few thousand undecided conservative voters—all because he wouldn't back down.

Lemon disputed the data on which the boss had based his remarks about Mexican rapists in his announcement speech. In Trump's hand was a magazine article with data showing the increase in rapes, which might or might not have cited Mexican illegals as the cause. It didn't matter to the people who listened to Trump whether the boss had gotten the details correct. His words captured the way they felt, and that's all that mattered to them. His was a language the Left couldn't and wouldn't ever understand.

It was a virtuoso performance in total, but it is probably best remembered for a single line the boss said. Two weeks later, the same words would start to appear on lawn signs. After Lemon disputed his rape statistics, the boss said: "Well, somebody's doing the raping, Don."

ABOVE: (*left to right*) Jan 24, 2015. Corey, Dave, Donald Trump at Iowa
Freedom Summit hosted by Citizens United and Congressman Steve King.

BELOW: (*left to right*) Capt. John Duncan, Stephen Miller, Michael Glassner,
Eli Miller, Ben Miller, Corey, Steven Mnuchin, Donald Trump, Keith Schiller,
Dan Scavino, George Gigicos, Hope Hicks on Trump Force One.

ABOVE: Donald Trump with local law enforcement in front of Trump Force One.

RIGHT: Corey after Donald Trump kicked him off the plane with instructions: "Go win Iowa for me."

BELOW: (*left to right*) Steve Bannon, Dave, Reince Priebus, Donald Trump, Hope Hicks, Dan Scavino and Stephen Miller at Mar-a-Lago the night of Electoral College victory certification.

ABOVE: (*left to right*) Mayor Rudy Giuliani and Donald Trump with New York City Firefighters on anniversary of 9/11.

RIGHT: (*left to right*) Hope Hicks, Stephen Miller, Michael Glassner, Corey, George Gigicos and Dan Scavino near Trump residence in Beverly Hills the day Donald Trump reached the delegate count to become the presumptive GOP nominee for president.

RIGHT BELOW: Rally crowd in Dallas, American Airlines Center. Sept. 14, 2015.

ABOVE: (*left to right*) Donald Trump Jr., Mayor Rudy Giuliani, Sen. Bob Dole, Governor Mike Pence at Republican National Convention.

BELOW: Griffin Bossie and Don King at Republican National Convention.

ABOVE: (*left to right*) Mayor Rudy Giuliani, Sen. Jeff Sessions, Hope Hicks, George Gigicos, John McEntee (standing) and Corey backstage at the presidential debate held at Washington University in St. Louis, Oct. 9, 2016.

RIGHT: (*left to right* Gov. Scott Walker, Sen. Marco Rubio, Donald Trump, Gov. Jeb Bush, Gov. John Kasich, Dr. Ben Carson, Sen. Ted Cruz, Sen. Rand Paul, Mike Huckabee (center, facing away) and Gov. Chris Christie (center) in elevator before first primary debate in Cleveland.

BELOW: Guests of President Trump, Corey, Dave, and their families at the Easter Egg Roll on the South Lawn of White House. April 17, 2017.

ABOVE: Donald and Melania Trump voting on Election Day at public school in Manhattan.

BELOW: (*left to right*) John McEntee (standing) Bill Stepien (seated), Jeff DeWit (standing), Stephen Miller (seated), Hope Hicks, Sean Spicer, Eric Trump, Dave, Steve Bannon, Jared Kushner and Brian Jack on election night in Trump Tower.

ABOVE: (*left to right*) Jason Miller, Steve Bannon, Dave, Jared Kushner, Eric Trump, Kellyanne Conway, Stephen Miller, Donald Trump Jr., Hope Hicks, Brad Parscale, Reince Priebus on election night right after Donald J. Trump is elected president.

BELOW: (*left to right*) Corey, Jeff DeWit, Dave at the Inaugural.

ABOVE LEFT: Corey and President Donald J. Trump in Oval Office.

ABOVE RIGHT: Dave and President Donald J. Trump in Oval Office.

BELOW: (*left to right*) Corey, George Gigicos, Dave in front of Air Force One.

CHAPTER 7

UP IN THE AIR

I employ thousands and thousands of Hispanics.
I love the people. The Latinos. I love the people. They're
great; they're workers. They're fantastic people.
But they want . . . legal immigration.
—Donald J. Trump, Laredo, Texas, July 23, 2015

EVERYONE KNOWS what the media said about the boss's campaign after he announced his candidacy. Every time he said anything not politically correct, they declared his campaign over. But after weeks of having those thirty-six words from his announcement speech knowingly misrepresented by the media as racist, the boss accepted an invitation to travel to Laredo, Texas, and meet with its border patrol officers and local officials.

The media tried to downplay the warm reception that Mr. Trump got from just about everyone involved, including the mayor of Laredo, a Democrat. The border patrol, the local government, and much of the population knew there was a problem with border security, and they were glad someone had finally dared to propose real solutions. Border security and immigration were Donald Trump's campaign issues.

There was an awfully small group of Latino protesters there when we arrived. But, unfortunately, they were protesting a lie the media told them. They had been told Donald Trump called all Mexicans or all Mexican immigrants rapists, murderers, and so forth. But go back and read those thirty-six words again. He didn't even call all illegal immigrants rapists or murderers. He distinctly said he assumed some were good people.

So if the boss is a racist, why did he say, "They're not sending their best?" If he believed all Mexicans were the same, based on their race, that wouldn't make much sense. Neither would his statements about some of them being criminals and some being good people.

Those thirty-six words were as close to the opposite of racism as any words could be.

So, no matter how hard the media tried to spin the story on his trip, it was a total success. The people there saw through the smoke CNN and others were blowing, just as the boss figured they would. We rolled into town to cheering crowds and appreciation from everyone we met with.

Come to think of it, we rolled into just about every place we visited the same way. Donald Trump knew how to roll—and fly.

When Donald Trump listed the aircraft he had during Corey's job interview, Corey shrugged it off as a random boast. But Trump wasn't boasting. He was pointing out the military equipment he had for the war ahead. A candidate with a jet has a formidable advantage over rivals without one. A candidate with an air force was going to be tough to beat.

And we're not talking cargo planes here.

Trump Force One is a 24-karat-plated, plush-leather-adorned, first-class aircraft complete with a master bedroom, dining room, galley, big-screen TV, and concert-level sound system. The Rolls Royce engines on the 757 can blow the wings off most commercial airliners. It has every amenity you can imagine. And though the jet was the crown jewel of the fleet, there were also other gems, including the Cessna Citation X, the fastest corporate jet available, and the multitude of helicopters.

When you flew with Trump, you flew first class times ten.

Except, that is, when it came time to eat.

The first time Dave told his wife Susan that he was going to be on Trump Force One, she asked him to take some photos of what they served him to eat on the plane. She had read somewhere that Mr. Trump had a personal chef who traveled with him. When dinner came on the flight, Dave pulled out his BlackBerry and snapped a picture of the bag of McDonald's hamburgers and unopened package of Oreo cookies and emailed it to Susan.

On Trump Force One there were four major food groups: McDonald's, Kentucky Fried Chicken, pizza, and Diet Coke. There were also ancillary groups, including Vienna Fingers and the ubiquitous Oreo, before the boycott (after it was Hydrox). The reason the package of Oreos was unopened was because Mr. Trump would never eat from a previously opened package. If you've seen the Seinfeld episode in which George double-dips his chip, you have a pretty good idea of the boss's reasoning. Packages of cookies, along with small airliner-size bags of pretzels and potato chips, filled the plane's cupboards. An army might march on its stomach, but Trump's team flew on junk food. And those snacks would have to sustain us during long flights and even longer days.

The candidate would hardly ever eat lunch and would eat dinner only after he finished the last event of the day. We'd be in the jet or on the road from seven or eight a.m., make however many scheduled stops we had, and after the last one, perhaps around nine p.m., Mr. Trump would clap his hands and say,

"Let's eat!" And the food needed to be hot and ready for him. Some of the time, especially when he was pleased with his performance at a rally or event, he'd say, "Do you think I deserve a malted today? I think I deserve one." Trump, a city kid, grew up drinking malteds, so that's what he always called a milkshake. Whatever you want to call it, it better be there and it better still be thick.

The orchestrating and timing of Mr. Trump's meals was as important as any other aspect of his march to the presidency.

In the beginning weeks of the campaign, with just the core five—Hope, Keith, Dan Scavino, George Gigicos, and Corey— the job of getting Mr. Trump his dinner fell to Corey and Keith, and the task needed teamwork and coordination to accomplish. There were variables to take into account. For instance, we didn't know how long the candidate would spend working the rope line. He could shake hands for ten minutes or half an hour. We had to take into consideration traffic patterns, last-minute chats with VIPs, and other unexpected diversions. There were lots of moving parts. At the end of the day, however, the boss's meal had to arrive on time.

As soon as Mr. Trump came off the stage, Corey would peel off in a car to the local McDonald's while Keith kept him apprised of the candidate's progress.

In no time, they had it down to a science, with Corey arriving at the jet's steps just as Mr. Trump would climb out of the car on the tarmac.

As the events started to get bigger, and Corey had to let others take over the meal run, it became more challenging. Corey hired Michael Glassner in July 2015. He had been Sarah Palin's top adviser in 2008. Later, Corey would promote Glassner to deputy campaign manager. Michael's first job on the campaign, however, was taking over Corey's duty as the food runner.

One time in Chicago, when our motorcade blew through red lights with a police escort, the boss's dinner—two Big Macs, two Fillet-O-Fish, and a chocolate malted—sat in bumper-to-bumper traffic. In times like that, the "run" would become like a scene out of *Fast and Furious*: burning rubber, up on two wheels, donuts. Well, close to that.

And, if you were late, you got no mercy.

We were on the road one time in South Carolina when the boss decided he was ready for dinner. Sam Nunberg was in the follow-up SUV when Keith and Corey went in to get the food. Sam went in also, leaving just Hope and the boss in the car. A few minutes later, Corey came out with the bag that contained dinner for himself, Hope, Keith, and the boss's meal in a separate bag. But Sam had decided he wanted a special order: no pickles, extra onion, hold the lettuce, along those lines. Mr. Trump was sitting with the bag on his lap. We had the SUV's door open for Sam like it was a getaway car. Two minutes went by. Three minutes passed by.

"Keith, go get him, would ya?" he said.

When Keith returned without him, the boss had had enough. "Leave him," he said with absolute finality. "Let's go."

Roger that.

Corey turned and looked out of the back window to see Sam, empty-handed, waving and running after the SUVs. The lesson here is that there is only one boss, and when he is ready to go, you go. Period.

When traveling in the air with the boss, you also learned pretty quickly to like Elton John. Donald Trump *really* likes Elton John. Anthony "the Mooch" Scaramucci got in all sorts of hot water—which is not at all an unfamiliar position for him—when he told an interviewer that Elton John would play at President Trump's inaugural. It had been wishful thinking on Mooch's part, probably because he'd been on the plane when the boss had "Tiny Dancer" or "Rocket Man" playing as loud as the concert-level speakers could bring it.

We're telling you, when the boss cranks up Elton, you can't hear yourself think. The music is loud enough to rattle your brain.

Still, suffering through a brain-rattling "Don't Go Breaking My Heart" is far more preferable than the boss going off over something on Fox News, CNN, or MSNBC—and yes, we would even watch MSNBC, perhaps just to hear what the liberals were saying about him.

In all the time Corey flew with him, some thousand hours plus, he saw Mr. Trump close his eyes maybe five times. And by "close his eyes," he means for three minutes, tops. Donald Trump is an absolute machine. He is the single hardest-working person we have ever seen. You could count the number of times on one hand when, once in a blue moon, when it was a long flight, like coming back from Vegas to New York, he might go into his room and come out thirty minutes later. We'd think at first, *Finally! Now we can watch something other than CNN or Fox.* And then the TV would start changing channels, because the remote he had changed the channels on all the TVs on the plane. It got to the point where he was getting so much airtime not even the boss could take it.

"Too much Trump for Trump," he said one day.

During that flight, instead of news, we watched a film, *Deliverance*. It would be Hope's first and last time she watched the movie.

Speaking of Hope, the last thing we'll tell you about life on Trump Force One is the steamer. Mr. Trump was a stickler when it came to how he looked onstage and at events. He had a steamer on board that would take the wrinkles out of his suits. When we landed, it was Hope's job to steam him.

"Get the machine!" he'd yell. And Hope would take out the steamer and start steaming Mr. Trump's suit, while he was wearing it! She'd steam the jacket first and then sit in a chair in front of him and steam his pants.

One time, Hope forgot to bring the steamer on the jet.

"I don't think we have time, sir," she said when he yelled for the machine. "We'll just get you pressed at the hotel."

But Mr. Trump insisted. When Hope finally admitted she'd forgotten the steamer, he blew his top.

"Goddammit, Hope! How the hell could you forget the machine?"

"Sir, couldn't we have it pressed at the hotel?"

"I want it now!"

It was a mistake she would never make again.

By July 2015, it was pretty obvious, to us at least, that the Trump campaign was going to be like no other campaign in history. The rally in Phoenix on July 11 nearly caused a full-out stampede, and *Politico* called it the start of "Trumpmania." Things quickly got even crazier.

On July 15, Hope, Keith, Corey, and some security flew on the Citation with the boss to Laconia, New Hampshire, for an event at a VFW hall. As the plane was landing, Corey checked his phone. There were fifteen voice mails, all from the same number: the Laconia Police Department. As the plane taxied in, Corey called the number.

"We have a serious situation," an officer said.

All Corey cared about was that people had shown up at the event. That wasn't the problem.

"We can't get you into the venue," the officer said.

The VFW hall had a maximum capacity of three hundred and fifty. There were at least a thousand people outside the hall, literally standing on the roof of the building to get a glimpse of Donald J. Trump. The traffic was backed up for three miles leading to the venue, and as our small motorcade pulled up, people started chasing the cars to touch the car Mr. Trump was in. That day was the first time the Trump campaign needed a police escort, a practice that would become standard operating procedure.

The temperature in the hall neared ninety-five degrees.

When we tried to leave, the police had to lead us through the crowd, and people were shaking the SUVs. It looked like a riot scene from a movie. We had advance guys running alongside the SUV to keep the people away. People just wanted to be near Mr. Trump.

Mr. Trump was scheduled to do Bill O'Reilly's show that night. Originally, we planned to tape *The O'Reilly Factor* from New York after the New Hampshire event. However, the event went long, so we decided to have Mr. Trump phone in from the small regional airport in Laconia. People knew we were heading to the airport, just a short distance from the VFW hall, and they started pouring in to watch Mr. Trump take off. However, what they saw instead was the team and Mr. Trump watching O'Reilly from the airport lounge. The hundreds of people waiting for a glimpse of the boss in the parking lot weren't starstruck *Apprentice* fans standing there. These were sophisticated political people, grassroots activists, and local political ops. The camera crew had a TV monitor set up. A thousand people stood watching Trump as he watched TV. Those of us on the inside of the campaign knew then that what *we* were watching was lightning in a bottle.

It was at this time that Mr. Trump hit first place in the national polls. The numbers had gone from a low single-digit joke to nearly unanimous front-runner in less than a month—something never done before. And when Donald Trump was in first place, there was no looking back. People were begging for something different. They had something different in Trump.

On Saturday, July 18, in an interview with Frank Luntz at the Family Leadership Summit, a conservative Christian conference, Donald Trump showed just how different a candidate he was going to be. Earlier in the week, John McCain had said that Trump was "firing up the crazies" at the Phoenix rally. The boss shot back with some words of his own, defending the people who came to see him. Luntz asked Mr. Trump how he could say disparaging things to a war hero.

"He's not a war hero," the boss said.

Corey, Chuck Laudner, and Hope had watched the interview on a small monitor in the green room of the venue.

"What the hell did he just say?" Corey asked. He didn't have to wait long for an answer.

"He's a 'war hero' because he was captured," Trump said. "I like people that weren't captured."

Corey went into full crisis mode. In the greenroom after the interview, he told the boss that they needed to have a press conference right away so he could walk back his remarks.

"You want a press conference," Mr. Trump asked. "Let's have a press conference."

In what sounded more like a street fight than a press conference, Donald Trump stood his ground. He put his comments in the context of McCain's poor record helping veterans and the absolute disgrace of our Veterans Administration. Mr. Trump and reporter Stephen Hayes got into a screaming match that lasted three whole minutes.

Corey's first thought was that the campaign was over. He called Alison after the presser to tell her he would soon be on his way home. But his second overriding feeling was that of pure awe. He had never seen a candidate have such courage in his convictions. No matter how hard the press pushed him, Trump wasn't backing down from his words.

By the time they got back to the airplane, the story had exploded. In the coming hours and days, just about every other candidate and talking head piled on. Governors Rick Perry and Scott Walker denounced Trump. Lindsey Graham told him he was fired. Cable news was outraged. So was nearly every pundit and op-ed writer in the country and around the world. Sean Hannity told him to apologize. So did Steve Bannon. But the boss never wavered.

Hope, Corey, and the boss flew to Newark and then drove to Bedminster, New Jersey, where Trump owns a golf club and home. There his wife, Melania, met him at the door. She had TiVoed all the news shows covering the uproar.

"You were absolutely right," she said to her husband. "John McCain has not done enough for the veterans."

Corey and Hope looked at each other in disbelief.

The next day, the highly respected journalist and author Sharyl Attkisson took the boss's side, saying his words were taken out of context and the media's reaction to them was part of a larger smear campaign. Chuck Laudner then set up a hotline for veterans to get help.

By Wednesday of the following week, the flaming controversy was only embers.

Corey had said to Hope during the height of the blowback that if the boss survived this he would be president of the United States. Trump not only survived, but his poll numbers continued to skyrocket. Corey knew then what much of the mainstream media would deny until Election Day: that Donald Trump was going to be tough to beat. He wasn't afraid to say and do things that he believed in, no matter how politically incorrect they might seem. And by doing that, his actions and words spoke to people like no other politician's.

Even though we were officially in the race, and despite the fact that we were leading most of the polls, pundits and opinion writers still thought of the Trump campaign as a sideshow. Later, the CNN host Michael Smerconish would call the boss "the George Costanza of the 2016 field." But we were all business and were about to show it. All presidential candidates are required to file a personal financial disclosure (PFD) statement with the Federal Election Commission. You're given thirty days from the day you announce to do so. The liberal media was still branding the boss as a flash-in-the-pan candidate and saying that he was using the campaign as a way to bolster his businesses. They didn't believe he'd ever file the PDF. Around that time, Ted Cruz came to visit the boss at Trump Tower. Trump asked him if he had filed his disclosure.

"I asked for an extension," the senator said.

"See, Corey; we can get an extension."

But Corey knew that the media would kill Trump if he asked for more time. They'd say the boss didn't have the money he purports to have. They'd say he was hiding some shady deals. Corey knew he had to file on time.

The campaign knew it would be the largest single filing of any PFD in the history of candidates and that it would take a lot of hard work to put it together accurately. With the oversight of Don McGahn, we assigned one accountant to the task; the young accountant worked night and day, a finger-bleeding kind of effort. Much to the disappointment of the pundits who were waiting to swoop down on us like vultures, we filed the disclosure in twenty-nine days—one day early. The message the early filing sent was clear: Trump, a man with over six hundred businesses, got things done, while your average politician had to ask for extensions. The disclosure also allowed us to flaunt a number with a nice ring to it: $10,000,000,000. Donald Trump's net worth was ten billion dollars. How about them apples?

The trip to Laredo came later in the month. Stephen Miller, who had been the communications director for Jeff Sessions in the US Senate before joining our team, was the one who initially helped us draft our immigration policy. We also have to give much credit to Ann Coulter, who was a significant influence and held us accountable for our immigration policy. Miller became our top policy guy, and it was Miller who gave us the contact information for officials in the border patrol union. The local union boss invited Mr. Trump to Laredo to see the border for himself. We knew the trip was going to be a big deal, and we knew the press would go wild over it, but we didn't realize just how big of a deal it would be.

When we said earlier that we rolled into town, we mean we rolled. A presidential motorcycle brigade escorted our motorcade of several SUVs with blacked-out windows and two full-scale coach buses carrying credentialed media. At least twenty police cruisers trailed us. Our convoy included multiple unmarked cars and light armor-plated vehicles with military weapons. They closed the border for a full hour during Mr. Trump's visit. They had snipers on the roofs of nearby buildings. And this was all for Donald Trump, who at the time held an official position no higher than John Q. Citizen.

Mr. Trump spent much of the time in Laredo talking to border agents.

"We can't do our jobs," they told him.

"You elect me," the boss said, "and I'll take your handcuffs off."

The trip was also right in Ted Cruz's backyard. The senator was scheduled to join us on the trip, but at the last minute his team pulled out of the event, citing important issues in Washington. Good thing. The boss sucked up all the oxygen this side of the Rio Grande. There was such a feeding frenzy among the press, an overzealous cameraman split Corey's head open with his Nikon.

Over and over again at rallies across the country, Donald Trump's biggest applause line was, "Oh, we're gonna build a wall." The line had been trial tested in front of hundreds of thousands of people. We knew it was an issue as hot as the Laredo sun. The border visit was one of the great photo ops in political history. One hundred and twenty credential media broadcast, published, posted, and tweeted indelible images of a man determined to keep our borders safe. But as politically historic as the trip was, maybe the most lasting symbol was something that the boss wore on his head. On that day, a white MAKE AMERICA GREAT hat became one of the great iconic politcal symbols.

The hat, of course, would become a sensation and one of our biggest early fund-raising tools. No marketing firm, no poll testing. For our first buy, Mr. Trump told Amanda Miller to call his merchandise guy and order a thousand. By September, the *New York Times* was calling it "the must-have accessory of the summer." By April the following spring, the campaign had sold

500,000. And there were five times as many knockoffs sold (ours were American made). The boss signed thousands of them. Even the knockoffs. Corey told CNN that the hat was disruptive technology. "People who weren't involved in politics, that didn't have a political background, wanted to show their support for something different and their way to do that was to buy hats," he said. At rallies, hats formed a red, white, and ultimately camouflage sea of change and helped signify that we were no longer just a campaign, but a movement.

If we didn't know by then that Donald Trump had become a political supernova, we would become irrevocably convinced by August. George suggested we hold a rally in Mobile, Alabama, where he lived. Though the campaign didn't have any staff then in Alabama, our advance man had plenty of friends and relatives who could lend a hand. He also knew someone in the mayor's office, whom he called to see if a small, 2,500-seat theater was available. It was, and they sent George the contract that afternoon. By Tuesday, 10,000 people had RSVP'ed to attend the event. By Wednesday, it was 16,000. George called his friend in the mayor's office back and booked a civic center that sat 10,000. But by Thursday, the RSVPs had swelled to 40,000. They moved the event to Ladd-Peebles Stadium, a football stadium, and people waited in a driving rainstorm to get in. As the weather cleared, Captain John did a flyover and tipped the 757's wing, as George announced Mr. Trump's arrival to the wildly cheering crowd of over 35,000.

Incredibly, the same scenario would happen time after time. If you look at photographs from any one of those rallies, you'll notice something else, besides the hats and T-shirts with slogans, that they all had in common. Everyone seems to be holding up a cell phone and recording the event. Those videos then got emailed, shared, posted, and then eventually seen by the attendees' entire online communities. Donald Trump's reach was rally attendance times X.

O ur lead in the polls grew in early August. Trump zoomed ahead of Jeb Bush and his $150 million campaign like he was Wile E. Coyote and we were the Road Runner. *Beep. Beep.* We had gone by the rest of the field so fast the RNC had whiplash. The pundits chalked it up to it being summertime. No one's paying attention to the race, they said. Nate Silver's *FiveThirtyEight* blog compared our poll numbers with the August numbers of primary candidates who ended up losing the nomination such as Joe Lieberman in 2003, Rudy Giuliani and Hillary Clinton in 2007, and Rick Perry in 2011.

Donald Trump, however, was no Joe Lieberman.

On August 6, the boss participated in his first debate: the *Washington Post*/Fox News Republican primary debate held at Quicken Loans Arena in Cleveland. It was the first of six primary debates leading up to the Iowa caucuses.

No one watching knew what to expect from Donald Trump and, frankly, neither did we. Our debate preps amounted to conversations at Trump Tower on potential topics, a discussion on the airplane, and a final debate "prep" in the SUV on the way to the event. And sometimes debate prep gave way to more important things. In Cleveland, the band Aerosmith, which was performing in the area, reached out to Don McGahn and asked if they could say hello to Mr. Trump. They came over to the boss's suite just before the debate that night. Mr. Trump spent "debate time" talking with the band, who offered their support to his campaign.

Donald Trump is the best game day player that politics has ever seen. He didn't need prep; he'd been preparing for this his whole life. He knew what had happened to Romney. They had poured so much stuff into his head that he couldn't talk when it came time to. Trump knew he could handle himself in front of the camera better than any of the other candidates. He played the game like he had nothing to lose, so he was loose and spontaneous.

Because of his standing in the national polls, Mr. Trump was placed at the center of the stage behind the most prominent podium. We also knew that he would receive most of the questions and be given the most opportunity to speak, because people weren't tuning into the presidential debate to watch Marco Rubio or Jeb Bush; they were tuning in to see Donald J. Trump.

From the first debate on, Donald Trump decimated the field of primary candidates. There were seventeen candidates in Cleveland in August (two tiers), and only four (Cruz, John Kasich, Rubio, and Trump) by the March CNN debate in Miami. The combination of Trump's stage savvy and street smarts was devastating. Although the mainstream media and other haters give him little credit for his intellect, Donald Trump has more than a fundamental grasp on a surprising number of fields, including Jungian psychology. One of his favorite books is *Memory, Dreams, Reflections*, Jung's autobiography. Steve Bannon insists that Trump came up with the idea for the names Lyin' Ted, Little Marco, Low-Energy Jeb, and, later, Crooked Hillary, from his knowledge of Jungian archetypes.

When Megyn Kelly sandbagged him with her first question about things he'd said about women during his life, the boss turned what should have been a devastating problem into a rousing rallying cry for the country. Instead of wasting our time being politically correct, he challenged us to be smarter in trade and energy production. The Rosie O'Donnell line was for laughs. Following the laughs, however, the boss showed himself as a serious candidate. The crowd ate it up.

Donald Trump knows how to ride a popular wave. His assault on political correctness resonated with people across the country. We took advantage of that connection whenever we could. We began posting videos for his Facebook followers. In one, the boss looked directly into the camera and told the viewer that he didn't have time to be politically correct. The video went viral. Whether it was Rosie O'Donnell's weight, or a federal judge, or any of the reporters following the campaign, no one was off-limits. And only Donald Trump could get away with what he got away with.

And because of his honesty, he was the draw. When he decided to boycott the next Fox debate in Des Moines, in protest of the way the network and their star anchor had treated him in the first debate, the ratings dropped 40 percent. Trump came up with the idea of having a fund-raiser for veterans on the same night. We held it less than a ten-minute drive from the Iowa Events Center, where the debate was held. Still Fox News, and Roger Ailes specifically, begged us to come. They were even okay with us getting there at the last second. They promised to move the other candidates so Mr. Trump would have the center podium if and when he showed up. We didn't take them up on the offer, and the press we generated overshadowed the coverage of the debate. And Donald Trump raised $6 million for vets in the process.

Yes, in one way, the primary debates were a reality show, and Donald Trump drove the ratings. But they were also a serious platform from which he delivered his ideas to make America great again: to clean up Washington's corruption and special interests; to protect American workers; to restore border security and the rule of law; to appoint a justice to fill the enormous hole left by the death of Antonin Scalia; to provide a tax code that helped keep hard-earned money in the pockets of the middle class. No doubt the boss was fun to watch onstage, but he was also the most authentic candidate. He rekindled a dream for millions of Americans—and that's why they elected him president.

In the middle of August, we headed to a must-stop event for every presidential candidate, the Iowa State Fair. There the boss pulled off one of the great campaign PR maneuvers of all time. Chuck Laudner actually came up with the idea. He'd heard about Mr. Trump giving helicopter rides to Dave's kids in New Hampshire, and he asked the boss if he would do the same at the fair. Of course, he didn't care that it was a three-day helicopter trip, that the Sikorsky, which had a three-hundred-mile range, would have to refuel four times each way. Nor did he care that it would be a huge insurance liability. But neither did Mr. Trump.

"Don't worry about it," the boss said about the cost. "Let's do it."

As it turned out, the media coverage we received was worth a hundred times the outlay. A photo of the Sikorsky with TRUMP emblazoned on its side ran in newspapers and on television news segments across the country. Martha Raddatz of ABC News elbowed her way onto the first trip on the helicopter with Mr. Trump and the children so she could use the footage for ABC's Sunday news show. One of the kids on the ride asked Mr. Trump if he was Batman. Perfect!

You couldn't pay for better PR.

* * *

On December 2, 2015, Rizwan Farook and Tashfeen Malik, a married Muslim couple living in Redlands, California, walked into a state-run San Bernardino center that provided services for the disabled and shot and killed fourteen people, wounding twenty-two others. Five days later, on the anniversary of the attack on Pearl Harbor, the Trump campaign issued a statement that called for the ban of all Muslims entering the United States. Later that day, at a rally in Mount Pleasant, South Carolina aboard the USS *Wisconsin,* the boss reiterated his stance. As was the case with the uproar over his comments about John McCain, the reaction to and condemnation of the proposed ban in the press and by the other candidates was fast and furious. Jeb Bush called Trump "unhinged." Governor Christie said the plan was ridiculous, and Senator Lindsey Graham said it was "downright dangerous" to the United States. Two days after we released the statement, a Bloomberg poll showed 65 percent of Republican voters were for a Muslim ban, and nearly 40 percent said they were now more likely to vote for Trump because he had proposed it.

We started talking about the Muslim ban right after San Bernardino. There wasn't a person on the Trump team who was against releasing the statement. And yet, according to those who are supposed to know about these things, Donald Trump was a dangerous ideologue and his campaign didn't know what it was doing.

For us, the decision was simple. We wanted none of the other candidates to move to the right of us on immigration. From the overwhelmingly positive reaction we received at rallies to the boss's hard-line immigration stance, we knew he had struck a chord with a large number of voters. What we couldn't believe was how tone-deaf all the other candidates and the mainstream media seemed to be.

A lot of comparisons have been made between Brexit, Britain's June 2016 withdrawal from the European Union, and the Trump campaign. Indeed, we shared the same major issues: immigration and trade. But we also shared a passion that, as strong and significant as it was, was nearly invisible to the establishment. The boss became friendly with Nigel Farage of the UK Independence Party, who, like Trump, was the leader of a movement many underestimated.

By Christmas, the Iowa and New Hampshire primaries were approaching fast. Though the boss, of course, wanted to win them both, he wanted to win Iowa big-league. One reason he wanted to win the caucuses was because so many people had told him that he couldn't. But maybe the main reason he wanted to win the caucuses is because he wanted to beat Ted Cruz.

In one way, the battle for the Iowa caucuses turned out to be a land war against an air campaign. Having the Citation X was a huge advantage because we could hit multiple media markets outside Iowa: the Nebraska media market, the Wisconsin media market, and the southern Iowa media market. Sometimes we'd be in the air for only fifteen, twenty minutes. It would take other candidates hours to drive the same distance. We would do three events in a day while they would only do one or two, tops. Chuck Lauder put together the strategy. He'd tell us where we should go and when to be there, both from a timing perspective and an optics perspective. We'd do a big rally and then a small hall, and then a small hall and a big rally. There are certain boxes that every candidate has to check in Iowa. It was the model Governor Bradstad used to be successful.

But Ted Cruz had been in Iowa for months. He had so many volunteers that his campaign rented a college dorm in Des

Moines to house them. We couldn't field a baseball team with the full-time people we had on the ground. Though we ruled the air, there's something to be said for good old retail politics— hitting the mom-and-pop stores, having breakfast in the local diner. It was a classic race between the tortoise and the hare. Cruz was giving us all we could handle and more.

It wasn't like Cruz was the only one in the race. Dr. Ben Carson started out as a real threat. Marco Rubio had a significant presence, and Jeb overwhelmingly outspent our campaign (later, after losing big there, he denied putting any effort into Iowa). There was also Huckabee and Santorum, both of whom commanded a strong following among religious conservatives. Santorum had won the caucuses there in 2012 and Huckabee in 2008.

As the voting drew near, the boss put a lot of pressure on Corey. It was Donald Trump's first election of any kind as a candidate, and he saw it as do or die. Winning Iowa isn't always an indicator that you'll be the nominee. In 2008, when McCain was the Republicans' choice at the convention, Mike Huckabee had swamped him in Iowa. But you couldn't tell Trump that. One day in January, he ordered Corey off the jet in the middle of a blizzard with the instructions, "Go win Iowa for me."

Six months earlier, the idea that Donald Trump would even be competitive in the caucuses was a fantasy. "You could have won a hundred million dollars betting that he would finish in the top three," Corey said. Perhaps, if everything had broken Donald Trump's way that day, he might have pulled off the victory. But everything didn't break his way.

A caucus system is very different from a primary. Voters go to a given location at a given time, where they listen to candidates or representatives of the candidates. Then they cast votes for a delegate of the candidate of their choice. For a campaign, it requires an enormous amount of organizational skill. You need to have all seven hundred of the caucus locations covered. You need speakers or at least reps in all of those places, and you have to have campaign literature at all of those places. Trump visited the largest sites, in Ames and other areas, while his surrogates covered as many of the smaller venues as they could. At the time, our surrogates numbered eight or nine. They included the candidate's grown children, Donald Jr., Eric, and Ivanka, and his son-in-law Jared. Our limited number was a recipe for disaster.

Though the small number of campaign representatives would indeed prove problematic, it was perhaps unrealistic expectations, mostly from family members, that would lead to the beginning of the end of Corey's time as Donald Trump's campaign manager.

Corey was in the SUV with Keith, Hope, and the candidate on caucus day when the call came. When Trump hung up the phone, he looked at Corey.

"You don't know what you're doing," he said to him. "This team is completely lost."

It had been Ivanka on the phone. She and Jared had arrived as surrogates at a precinct caucus to find it without any Trump campaign staff or even literature. Nothing makes the boss angrier than when someone embarrasses his children. As far as Trump was concerned, the screwup at the voting location was inexcusable and a permanent mark against Corey. Though the mix-up was more the state director's fault than his, Corey was the campaign manager and ultimately bore the responsibility for all aspects of the campaign in Iowa. Plus, for most of the time, he was seated right next to Trump, so he was an easy target.

In retrospect, the campaign's performance in Iowa was pretty remarkable given the size of and inexperience of the team. We had set a goal of 45,000 votes, which we achieved with room to spare. Of course, we thought that 45,000 would be enough to win. In 2016, however, the Iowa caucuses drew a record-breaking number of voters—in no small measure because Donald Trump was in the race. And had it not been for a robocall blast by Cruz's campaign the day of the voting containing the erroneous message that Ben Carson had dropped out of the race, Trump might have won. There was also the not-so-little matter of the boss skipping the Fox News debate in Des Moines the week before the caucuses because of the Megyn Kelly issue, which, though his base supported the move, might have hurt him in Iowa. Still, he finished second, falling short by just a little over six thousand votes. Any other candidate would have had plenty of positives to take from the effort. Marco Rubio took third, and his campaign was ecstatic. But for Donald Trump, second place was the same as coming in last. And in the boss's eyes, losing Iowa was a significant strike against Corey.

The week following the Iowa caucuses was a low point in the campaign. Mr. Trump wouldn't let go of the loss and took every opportunity to remind audiences how Cruz had cheated. In close quarters, he took the opportunity to chastise Corey and anyone else on his team who crossed his path. Trump was in a miserable mood, and his temperament started to have a discernible negative effect on his numbers. The New Hampshire primary was only a week away, on November 9, and Corey was concerned his attitude would turn voters off. Then Jeff Roe, Ted Cruz's campaign manager, called, and the concern increased to real worry.

"Your candidate is dropping like a rock," Roe told Corey. "Your favorable rating is dropping through the floor."

Why, you ask, was Ted Cruz's guy so concerned about the health of our campaign? Well, the Cruz camp had made a strategic decision to run against Donald Trump at the end of the campaign, when most of the other primary candidates would be out of the race, and not compete in New Hampshire. He also knew the Trump campaign did not use polling (hard to believe for a candidate who just missed winning the Iowa caucus) and so Corey didn't have the data he had.

"You're down nine points in the last three days," Roe said. "And if you don't do something soon, you could lose New Hampshire, and John Kasich will catch you."

On the Thursday before the Tuesday primary, Corey called Ed Rollins. Like many in politics, Corey has great respect for Rollins. Rollins had run Ronald Reagan's presidential reelection campaign. Without looking at any data, Rollins estimated that Trump's "fave/unfave" number had dropped 10 points.

"You're on the cusp of losing this thing," he told Corey.

Corey was not traveling with the candidate when he called Rollins. Although the boss spent most of his time in the Granite State that week with Corey, Trump also did events in South Carolina and Little Rock, Arkansas without him. After talking with Rollins, and while the boss was on the road, Corey called Ivanka, Don Jr., and Eric.

"Guys," he said on the teleconference. "If your father doesn't change his negative ways, he's going to lose New Hampshire. And if he loses New Hampshire he'll lose South Carolina. If he loses South Carolina, your father will be a very wealthy person who once ran for president of the United States."

That afternoon, Mr. Trump walked into the campaign office in Manchester for lunch. He greeted the volunteers who were busy making phone calls for him. Trump's volunteers received very little credit in the press, but there wasn't a more enthusiastic or dedicated group among the campaigns in the 2016 cycle, or any other cycle for that matter. Corey was in the small office he had taken over since his arrival in New Hampshire. On his desk sat a bag from McDonald's for the boss. When Trump walked in, Corey got right to the point.

"Sir, we need to talk," he said.

Corey remembers the moment as the frankest conversation he had had with his boss—just campaign manager to candidate. He told Trump of the Roe and Rollins telephone calls. He informed the boss of anecdotal evidence he'd gathered. Corey knew the New Hampshire voter.

"If you don't start talking about what your positive vision is for the country and stop complaining about Ted Cruz, you're going to lose," he said frankly.

The candidate listened quietly as he ate his hamburger. When he finished, he stood up and walked out of the room. That day he had an event at the Manchester Police Department and had to be there for the afternoon shift change. Along with Chief Nick Willard and much of the department's rank and file, waiting for him at the police headquarters was an officer who had recently been shot in the line of duty. The hospital gave the injured cop a temporary pass to leave because he wanted to see Trump. The bond between law enforcement and Donald Trump is one of the strongest among his base. And the admiration goes both ways.

The cameras that day didn't capture the true emotion of the event. It's very seldom you see the boss emotional. As he shook the wounded man's hand, however, you could see the gratitude in his expression.

When the boss left the police headquarters, he went to Theo's Pizza Restaurant on Elm Street in Manchester for a CNN town hall meeting. Most people see Donald Trump only when the camera lights are on him. In Theo's, he was gracious and friendly. He worked the room and shook every hand. When the lights went on, Anderson Cooper pressed him about the feud with Cruz. "Who cares," the boss said. "This is the place I'm focused on." He then laid out his vision for America, and from that moment forward he didn't mention Iowa to Corey again. Not once.

The celebration for Trump's New Hampshire primary election win took place at "the Yard," the same location as the 2014 Freedom Summit, where Mr. Trump first met Corey. It was not a coincidence. Corey made sure of it. We knew we were going to win that night. The New Hampshire primary ended in a landslide victory for Trump. In the hold room, before he went onstage, someone took a photo of the campaign team—Corey, Hope, George, Michael, and Dan Scavino—with our arms around each other's shoulders. The whole team knew that Corey's job depended on a win, and they hadn't let him down.

New Hampshire has always been a better indicator of who will be the Republican nominee than Iowa. We could feel the confidence building, and Corey could feel the candidate's confidence in him growing too. We had a chip on our shoulder. Mr. Trump won the New Hampshire primary by nineteen points. It was our first win against the establishment and for the American people. The feeling was righteous. We wanted more.

The misfit toys were becoming Transformers.

CHAPTER 8

THE DELEGATE HUNTER

Listen to me, never rat on your friends and
always keep your mouth shut.
—Jimmy Conway, *Goodfellas*

IT WAS an unusually warm March evening when the Chicago
Police Department came up to our hotel room bringing news
of a major protest taking place around the venue of our rally
that night. We were in the presidential suite of the Trump
International Hotel, right on Wabash Avenue, along the banks
of the Chicago River. Most nights, you would get a great view of
the city from any window in the tower, all sleek, gray metal and
clear panes of glass.

Corey was looking a few blocks in the other direction, where a crowd of a few hundred had gathered around the University of Illinois Pavilion. We were scheduled to begin there at eight o'clock, and about eleven thousand people—not all our friends, as it would turn out—stood inside waiting for Trump. On the television in the hotel suite, Corey could see the crowd inside getting restless. It was close to showtime, and it was getting clearer and clearer as the hours went by that there was trouble brewing.

Chicago's interim police superintendent, John Escalante, said things were getting out of hand. And they were only going to get worse.

He was right. Footage was playing nonstop on every major network. MSNBC was carrying images of people getting unruly inside the pavilion; CNN had these wide aerial shots of mobs bumping up against the barricade outside. It all looked much worse on camera than it did from the window, but still, at first glance, you'd think you were watching dispatches from a riot rather than a rally. We worked closely with the United States Secret Service, our on-the-ground police contact, Keith Schiller, and, of course, Mr. Trump before he decided to cancel the event. Corey picked up the phone and called Bobby Peede, our lead advance man for the Chicago event, and told him to say the following: "For the safety of all the tens of thousands of people who have gathered in and around the arena, tonight's rally will be postponed until another date. Thank you very much for your attendance, and please go in peace."

Yeah, right.

Half the crowd started cheering and jumping around, while the other half hung their heads. A good number of people did manage to go home without incident, but the ones who stayed wanted trouble. Anti-Trump protesters started smacking down signs and pulling the hats off people's heads. Some of the Trump supporters got just as angry and fought back. Before long, CNN was running an endless B-roll of fistfights and hair-pulling in the arena, cut together with shots of protesters knocking down the barricades. Pundits talked over the footage like the world was ending. They had footage of police on horseback trying to hold the crowds back, small fires burning in garbage cans, guys in masks throwing bricks in the streets.

Remember the word "optics" from a few chapters back? These are the bad kind.

The view from the hotel window was getting worse, and the television—with Trump flipping, as he always did, between the same three news stations—showed us only bad things. We were stuck in a room a few miles away from any action, and there was no way we could leave. Mr. Trump would never be intimidated or driven out of town, especially not by people who think they can just shut down speeches by people they don't agree with. What kind of message would that send? Corey and Hope started thinking about how to spin this for the next morning.

Then, before anyone even knew what was happening, Trump had the receiver of the hotel phone in his hand. He was dialing CNN.

"This is Donald Trump," he said. And just like that, as he always does, he took control of the situation.

He was on the air with Don Lemon again before the crowds had even dispersed, offering a view of his rallies that you could get only from his place on the stage. The boss blamed CNN, and rightfully so, for twisting the narrative and shifting the perspective to make his fans look bad, and he swatted down anything that Lemon threw at him. When Lemon accused the boss of inciting violence against innocent protesters, the boss came right back at him.

"You know it's not true when you say that statement, Don," he said. "You know it's not true. [The protesters] will stand up and they'll start swinging at people."

It was evident to anyone watching that Trump wouldn't be intimidated or cowed by a few thugs, and certainly not by Don Lemon. By the end of the night, he had spoken with five anchors on five different live broadcasts, reaching millions of people, all for the price of a phone bill from a hotel that he ultimately owned anyway. The expression is "earned media," which is a fancy way of saying free media. Donald Trump is the undisputed, undefeated heavyweight champ of earned media. According to mediaQuant, an outfit that figures how much it cost each candidate if he or she had to pay for the coverage he or she was getting, Donald Trump's earned media was near $2 billion, with a "b," at this point in the campaign. He had earned $400 million in February 2016 alone. To put it in other terms, he had more free coverage on television, radio, newspapers, Facebook, Twitter, and Reddit than all sixteen other Republican candidates and Hillary Clinton combined. And he had spent only about $10 million on ads at that point, which was $4 million less than Governor Kasich had.

We'll admit that it was fun to watch. These were the pundits—geniuses—who said that Trump could never be a serious candidate in the first place. They'd been telling viewers for months that he was going to treat the whole campaign as a game show, maybe stay in long enough to promote a new product or give his brand a few minutes of free air.

This was March 11, 2016. And our boss was not any daytime host, and his campaign was not a game show. He was on a path to be the president of the United States.

* * *

In like a lion, out like a lamb, they say of March. There were no lambs to be found in our campaign, except maybe a sacrificial one. The month began with Super Tuesday, when we took seven of the eleven voting states. Two days later, Mitt Romney added his name to a growing list of establishment Republicans against Trump by calling the boss a con man in a delivered speech. Then we had to cancel the Chicago rally. The next afternoon in Dayton, a nutjob jumped the barrier and tried to get to our candidate. Secret Service officers rushed the boss from the stage. On March 29, the Jupiter, Florida Police Department processed Corey for simple battery "in that he did intentionally touch Michelle Fields," as the official report said. Watch the video, Corey says. About five million people have. But it was a new addition on the twenty-eighth that would be the most significant event for Corey and the campaign.

Not that he had the time to realize it.

To give you an idea of what our campaign schedule looked like then, consider this: From March 21 to March 29, nine days, Trump Force One flew from Atlanta to Elko, Nevada, from Elko to Las Vegas, from Las Vegas to Reno to Virginia Beach, from Virginia Beach to Houston for the CNN debate, from Houston to Fort Worth, from Fort Worth to Oklahoma City, from Oklahoma City to Bentonville, Arkansas, from Bentonville to Millington, Tennessee, on to Alabama, Virginia, and back to Georgia. In eight days. Thirteen flights, nearly 8,500 miles. With two pilots. Not two sets of pilots. Two pilots, Captain John Duncan, who joined the Trump world in 1989, and copilot Peter Harron. From the beginning of the campaign until Election Day, our two amazing pilots, John and Pete, and our campaign team, along with our flight attendant, Stacy, flew to 45 states, visiting

203 cities and flying 370,725 miles during 722 flight segments. The 757 used 988,991 gallons of jet fuel. Corey once figured out that during his time as campaign manager, he sat next to Donald Trump on the 757 for a total of 1,000 hours. That's over forty-six days spent in an airplane. Sitting next to your boss. And in that period you get to know someone. It was during that time that Corey saw the side of Mr. Trump few would get to see. The funny, magnanimous, gracious, loyal person who wanted only to change America for the better.

As tough as the boss could be—and he could be tough—a bond developed between those of us on those flights that was akin to family; in particular, a bond between the boss, Hope, Corey, and Keith. Trump called Hope and Corey, "Hopester" and "Cor." When they would RON (remain overnight) in Mar-a-Lago, Mr. Trump would insist they sit with him for dinner. He loved being around "the kids" because they shared his experience of the campaign and they understood his thoughts and feelings about it. But mostly he loved being with them because he liked them, and he knew they liked him. Yes, the campaign was business. And in business the boss could get angry. But he would never sacrifice friendship for business. The friendship between the boss and Corey and Hope—and Keith too—was strong. At dinner, the boss would be charming and entertaining. He would regale them with stories from his amazing life, the people he'd met and the places he'd gone. It's hard for us to say this without sounding corny. But Mr. Trump, at his core, is a good man. When George Gigicos had to miss his little girls' ballet recitals because of the campaign, the boss recorded a video message for them:

"Girls, your father loves you. We're running for president. If it's okay with you, I'll steal your father for the day. He's a very talented guy, and I need him. Thank you, girls." There is so much hate and misunderstanding that people rarely get the chance to see the man for who he is. We have. And we consider ourselves lucky.

B ut business was business. And by the spring of 2016, Corey's days as campaign manager were numbered. Though the boss never talked about it, he didn't forget the loss to Ted Cruz in Iowa, or the embarrassment Ivanka and Jared had suffered at the caucus site. And though the incident with Michelle Fields wasn't the reason for the fallout between him and the boss, the negative attention didn't help Corey's cause. It especially didn't help his relationship with the boss's children. Though none of those things was solely responsible for Corey's being fired, combined, they set the stage. The last act for Corey began at a dinner at Mar-a-Lago on March 28.

Corey knew the name Paul Manafort; you couldn't work in Washington, DC and not know the name. The political consulting and lobbying firm Black, Manafort, Stone, and Kelly had been a power broker in town since Ronald Reagan was first elected president. Our hero, Lee Atwater, had joined the firm as a partner in 1984. The Stone in the name is Roger Stone. And the Manafort is Paul.

Though he knew the name, Corey knew nothing of the man. He wasn't alone. Not a lot of people working in politics under fifty knew Paul Manafort. His last foray into a political campaign was Bob Dole's campaign, and there he had been an "informal" adviser. You'd have to go back to 1980 and the relatively small role he played as "southern coordinator" for Reagan to find any real on-the-front-lines campaign experience.

So when the boss asked to set up a meeting for him with Manafort, Corey had to think for a second before the name made sense to him. It was Tom Barrack, the CEO of the investment firm Colony Capital and a friend of the boss's for thirty years, who recommended Manafort. Corey made the call, and a dinner was set up for the following week at Mar-a-Lago.

The first thing the boss said when he met Paul was, "Wow, you're a good-looking guy," the same words he'd said when he first met Corey. Significantly older than Corey, by about thirty years, Manafort had had some work done to secure his youthful appearance. By then, Corey, with Hope and others, had had dinner with the boss at Mar-a-Lago at least fifty times. "Come on, kids, let's eat," Mr. Trump would say. They always sat outside, where Mr. Trump would interact with his guests. Throughout the meal, members of the club and guests would come over to say hello. But with Manafort, the boss wanted to sit inside by the fireplace, for privacy.

Later that night, the campaign flew back to New York. On Monday, in Trump Tower, Corey received a call from a reporter asking if Mr. Trump had had dinner with Paul Manafort at Mar-a-Lago the night before. Corey went into Hope's office and asked her if she'd spoken to a reporter about Manafort. She hadn't. Then he went up to the twenty-sixth floor and asked the boss if he had. Sometimes Mr. Trump would just talk to a reporter, but this time he hadn't said a word.

Corey knew from that moment on that Manafort was a leaker. Corey could also tell good people from bad, and he could tell right away that Paul was a bad guy. And somewhere in his soul, he knew that the addition of Manafort to the team was not going to turn out well. Especially for him. It is now clearer than ever that Paul was trouble. It is reported that the FBI had wiretapped Paul before and after he was at the campaign.

* * *

Barrack told Trump to bring Paul on as a "delegate hunter." At the time, a narrative had appeared, one that was blown completely out of proportion, that the boss was in jeopardy of losing the Republican nomination. The narrative revolved around the number of delegates he had.

To explain the delegate-selection process, which varies from state to state, would take up its own chapter in Louisiana, for example, half the delegates are awarded to the winner of the primary, and half are set by an election in the state House. But simply put, to win the nomination a candidate had to reach 1,237 delegates. Despite the primary victory routs, the campaign hadn't secured the delegates needed to prevent a contested convention. But what hurt Corey was the perception in the press—and within the family—that the Cruz campaign knew how to game the delegate system and Corey didn't. At that time, all in, the Trump campaign numbered about forty people. To put that in context, Hillary's campaign had eight hundred in the Brooklyn office alone. The Cruz campaign was also much bigger and more sophisticated, with people like Ken Cuccinelli, who is smart and was dedicated to do one thing: seat delegates. Trump was watching MSNBC, CNN, and Fox News all day, and two of the three were telling everyone in America that he still could lose and not be the Republican nominee. That narrative became very troubling because he'd never been in a political campaign before, and quickly it became the dominant thought in his brain. They kept telling him he could still lose. So Paul, who had last hunted delegates for Gerald Ford in 1976, was brought in.

Almost immediately, Corey began to feel marginalized. Dave had been telling him to start looking for people to help take some of the work off his plate. Figure out one problem and solve it, Dave said. Corey didn't have the time to take the advice.

Maybe it's best for Corey himself to tell you what happened next:

Working eighteen to twenty hours a day for months on end takes a toll on a person's health. We'd been pushing so hard there was no time for me to work out, eat well, or even sleep. It was just planning the events and then going to the events. The first thing that happened during this time is that I caught pneumonia, or at least something close to pneumonia.

So, in the first week of April, I'm sick as a dog. I mean, deathly ill. And you can't get sick around the boss; heck, he gets freaked out when people sneeze around him. And I'm way past the sneezing stage. So I'm basically relegated away from him. On the second of April, we fly to Wisconsin to do several events leading up to the state's primary on the fifth. On Sunday the third, I wake up in Green Bay and can barely get out of bed. Somehow, I do the Green Bay event, pounding Monsters and Red Bulls, and then go to Milwaukee for a town hall with Greta Van Susteren. The next day we fly to La Crosse and do a town hall there, and then one in Superior, and then fly back to Milwaukee for a town hall with Sean Hannity. It's a killer schedule under any circumstances, but it's unbearable when you're sick. But I know we're in trouble in Wisconsin. The Speaker of the House, Paul Ryan, is killing us, and Governor Scott Walker is far from being on the Trump train. Mr. Trump, however, thinks he can win. So we spend all day traveling and doing events.

Meanwhile, Manafort is back at Trump Tower, in his apartment, 43G, making charts—he was big on charts—or sitting in the conference room with the Trump kids, and going out to the

Hamptons on the weekends. And I'm on the road. I'm not sitting in my house in New Hampshire, which I hadn't been to in two months. I'm in cars. I'm in planes. I'm in cities, because that's where the campaign is. That's where decisions are being made, on the plane, in the cars, because that's how the boss is. He makes decisions on the move.

I think it was on the flight from La Crosse, Wisconsin, to Superior, Wisconsin, that Monday morning when I went to the back of the plane and put my head down. It's a twenty, thirty-minute flight. I fell asleep. And the boss looked back at me and said, "Corey, if you can't take it, we'll get somebody else."

"I just don't feel well, Mr. Trump."

I'd been running hard, insanely hard. From January 2015 to April 2016 nonstop. Almost no days off. And it's real work. Don't get me wrong. I'm not complaining. Managing the boss's campaign was the best eighteen months of my professional life. But that doesn't mean it wasn't hard. It was. And there was an enormous amount of stress.

By this time in the campaign, and really by just before the election victory in New Hampshire, the Trump family is involved, big-league. Dave told me to get somebody to help. Lots of people were calling me telling me they wanted to help, but none of them were willing to move to New York. Others offered to be "professional consultants," people who wanted to get paid a lot but weren't willing to show up every day. I relied on my deputy, Michael Glassner, to staff our state offices and find talent. But he wasn't able to do that and travel, where we needed him more. I literally didn't have the time to interview anyone. I was stressed about everything.

We lose the primary in Wisconsin, which I knew we were going to do. The boss does Fox & Friends *the morning after and we get on the plane and head back to New York. On the twenty-fifth floor of the Trump Tower the family's offices and conference room, there's rumbling that Corey can't run this campaign anymore. It's beyond him. He should have never lost Wisconsin.*

"Look," I told them, "we should have never won Wisconsin." Doesn't matter what I say. Minds are already made up.

We head into the Acela primaries: New York, Connecticut, Pennsylvania. And Paul asks for and receives operational control for all campaign issues. They tell me I can fly around in the plane with the candidate, do all the events, and work twenty hours a day, but you don't have any say anymore.

We do a massive event out in Bethpage on Long Island, ten, twelve thousand people. I'm in the motorcade, and I can feel something's not right. The boss is not happy that we lost Wisconsin. The family's not happy with me. They haven't been happy with me since Judge Gonzalo Curiel and the Trump University case. They think I should have kept their father from making the comments he did. Right. Like that could ever happen.

Meanwhile, the delegate fight is going on. The boss was asking me questions like, "How come I win Louisiana but don't win all the delegates?" Paul is telling Trump that he came on board too late to have made a difference in Louisiana. It's all Corey's fault, he said. During that first dinner at Mar-a-Lago, I thought Manafort was the cavalry coming to help. I didn't think he was coming to stick a shiv in my back—but that's what dishonest people do.

We're in Rochester, Albany, and then Utica. Then we shoot over to Pittsburgh because Pennsylvania's coming up. From Pittsburgh, we go to Hartford. Then we're back campaigning hard in New York with Carl Paladino. We're doing event after event all over the state: Rochester, Albany, Buffalo. Radio interviews. Small conference rooms. Television interviews. We take a side trip to Indiana to meet with Mike Pence and then on to Maryland. Back to New York, the Bill O'Reilly interview. The Today Show *with the family. And back to Pennsylvania. Then onto Delaware.*

For the trip to Delaware, we take the Trump helicopter. On board are Mr. Trump, Hope, Keith, one Secret Service agent, and myself.

By now, Paul Manafort is firmly ingrained and has made strategic alliances with family members. He flies to Florida in April and attends a meeting with members of the RNC. There he tells them that everything Trump has said up to now is a ruse, that he is going to show them the real Donald Trump from now on. Paul is going to change Donald Trump. While we're in the air, somebody, I think it was Ann Coulter, tweets out a quote from Paul saying that Trump shouldn't be on television anymore, that he shouldn't do the Sunday shows. And from now on I—meaning Paul—will do all shows. Because he's the fucking expert, right? Not Trump, who had already turned the whole primary race on its head. So, we're in the helicopter and Hope says to him: "I turned down all the Sunday show requests."

"What?!" the boss screams. "Without asking me?"

"Yes, sir," Hope says, "Paul said he doesn't want you on TV."

Mr. Trump goes fucking ballistic. We're over the metropolitan area, so you can get cell service if you fly at a low altitude.

"Lower it!" he yells to the pilot. "I have to make a call."

So he gets Paul on the phone, "Did you say I shouldn't be on TV on Sunday??" And Paul's like . . . he could barely hear him because of the helicopter motor. But Mr. Trump is like, "I'll go on TV anytime I goddamn fucking want and you won't say another fucking word about me! Tone it down? I wanna turn it up! I don't wanna tone anything down! I played along with your delegate charts, but I have had enough."

We land the whirlybird at the West Side heliport and get into the car. I'm in the back of the car, Trump's in the back passenger seat. He gets Paul on the phone and completely decimates him again verbally. Rips his fucking head off. I wish I'd recorded it, because it was one of the greatest takedowns in the history of the world. The greatest.

"You're a political pro? Let me tell you something. I'm a pro at life. I've been around a time or two. I know guys like you, with your hair and your skin . . ."

And, wait, it gets even better. Part three came when we got back to Trump Tower. A complete annihilation. And Paul's saying, "I didn't mean that, sir."

I had worked for Mr. Trump for fifteen months, and he had never spoken to me like that. He had ripped my face off, sure, but never for disrespecting him. I never pretended to be smarter than the boss, because I'm not. But Paul did, and he isn't.

Though I felt vindicated, the feeling didn't last long. I immediately got a phone call from Jared telling me that I wasn't a team player and that I'd thrown Paul under the bus. After his call with the boss, Paul had called Jared and complained about me for what he'd said in Florida. Talk about a little baby. At this time, I believed the family thought I wasn't a team player and that I was trying to sabotage Paul's relationship with their father. They didn't realize it was the other way around. I knew right then that my job had an expiration date.

The boss begins to give policy speeches—one a week—to show that he's got gravitas and credentials, and so he can learn the issue, which he ended up knowing cold. He does a foreign policy speech at the Mayflower Hotel. And that's where I get the call from the reporter who tells me that three sources inside the campaign say I'm going to be fired for embezzling money, that there's an internal investigation going on. After the speech, we go out to Indiana to do an event. Paul doesn't come with us. Later it would be reported that Paul stayed behind to meet with the Russian ambassador, I think. We are out there for a couple of days, and then we go out to California. I tell the reporter his sources are liars. I've spent thousands of hours with Trump, I say. And he knows I'm a loyal guy, and that I'd never steal his money. And he knows that Allen Weisselberg, the chief financial officer of the Trump Organization, knows of every dime that leaves the building. And Allen knows that I don't even have access to write myself a check, that's not how it works. There are controls in place, and procedures. The real story, I say, is that people inside the campaign are trying to get rid of me. Trying to get the boss to fire me so they can have access to the campaign's money and allow their friends and the political hacks who never supported Trump in the first place to get rich off him.

What Paul wanted was to be in charge. He wanted the title, but he wanted it not to help Trump win the election. He wanted the title for Paul. And he got it.

What's the old saying? Be careful what you wish for? The day Paul sent out the press release announcing that he's the campaign chairman has to be one of the worst of his life. Because now the spotlight is directly on him, and Paul never looked good under the lights—I think it's all the Botox.

Now it's May.

I might be loyal, but I'm not stupid. I know I'm in trouble with the boss. One day we were in Texas—Jared, Brad Parscale, Steven Mnuchin, Eli Miller, the boss, and me. The conversation escapes me, but at some point, Mr. Trump looked at Brad.

"Who tells you what to do?" he asked. He had put Brad in a tight spot. Though I was the campaign manager still, Jared was

much more involved in the digital part of the campaign, which was very important.

"I have a lot of bosses," Brad said, trying to sidestep the answer. But there is no sidestepping Trump. He asks you a question, he'll sit back and stare at you until you give him a real answer. Which is what he did with Brad.

"I guess it's Jared," Brad said finally. "He knows how to work people better."

"You don't have to listen to Corey anymore," Mr. Trump said. "He's no longer your boss."

The cut was deep, but it was only one of a thousand.

The Indiana primary is on the third of May. We go out with Bobby Knight and Lou Holtz, and we win Indiana, then Nebraska, then West Virginia. Still, every Tuesday feels to me like a game of "Is Corey going to survive?" If we win, Corey stays. If we lose, it's "See? We told you so."

June brings primaries in California, Montana, New Jersey, New Mexico, and South Dakota. We win some of those. Candidate Trump won thirty-eight times, by all accounts a record for any candidate in a contested primary season in the history of modern politics. But by Father's Day, I know it doesn't matter anymore. Soon, I'll be going home.

On June 20, Corey walked into his office on the fifth floor of Trump Tower at six a.m. just like he did every morning that he was in New York. His habit was to watch the morning shows: *Morning Joe*, *New Day* on CNN, and *Fox & Friends*, which he did. He then made a couple of conference calls and called a staff meeting. It was a Monday, which meant the 9:30 a.m. "family meeting" on the twenty-fifth floor. Every week, the senior staff would brief Mr. Trump's grown children and son-in-law on the happenings of the campaign. Along with Donald Jr., Ivanka, Eric, and Jared Kushner, those meetings usually included Hope Hicks, Paul Manafort, Rick Gates (who was Paul's partner in crime), and Corey.

When Corey walked into his office, Don Jr. asked if they could talk privately. They walked the fifteen steps down the hall to a conference room, in which sat Matt Calamari and Michael Cohen.

With Matt and Michael sitting there, it should have been obvious to him what was about to happen. Still, when Don Jr. started reciting the exit lines, he was stunned.

"Things aren't working out, Corey," he said. "There have been complaints from the staff, and you've become a distraction."

Corey pushed back some and asked for specifics, which Don Jr. didn't offer. All the younger Trump said was that Corey was terminated effective immediately. Those words felt like a punch in the stomach. For the last eighteen months, he'd given everything to the campaign and Mr. Trump. He'd worked eighteen-hour days, seven days a week. He was practically a stranger to his wife and children, missing birthdays, recitals, and sporting events. He'd worked for nearly two weeks when he should have been in the hospital. He hadn't been to a Red Sox game in over a year. And he did a great job. He was the person who helped Donald Trump from the beginning develop and execute the strategy to win thirty-eight primaries and caucuses, and helped Mr. Trump receive more votes than any GOP candidate in history, all on a shoestring budget when every political pundit in the country, and members of his own family, said it couldn't be done. Yes, he was acutely aware that none of that success would have happened if not for Donald Trump. But, with absolute certainty, he believed that Donald Trump couldn't have found a better campaign manager than him.

Corey's thoughts went back to the night when Mr. Trump invited Ivanka and Jared, along with Melania, Barron, Tiffany, and Melania's parents onstage. The rally was in Myrtle Beach, South Carolina, at the end of November 2015. Jared wore one of those black puffy vests and was the last to come onto the stage to join his wife and the others. He looked reluctant to do so. It was the first time any of Mr. Trump's family had been involved in the campaign. By then, Corey had been on the road with the candidate for six straight months and had run the campaign for eleven.

Back at Trump Tower, swept up in the emotion of the moment, and with thoughts ricocheting around his brain, Corey didn't at first pay attention to his phone pinging from inside his pocket. The campaign had already sent out the press release of his firing. It was sent before they even told him he was being fired. Paul Manafort had hit the send button, culminating his rise to the top of the Trump campaign—a rise that would last a mere eight weeks and one day, until it was reported that he'd received millions of dollars from Russians in an "off the books" ledger.

Matt Calamari escorted Corey down to his office to pick up some personal effects. "Whoa, is dat your computer?" He then walked him out of the building.

Out on the sidewalk, Corey didn't know what to do. He began to walk to the apartment on Sixty-First Street. On the way, he took out his phone and saw that he had hundreds of media requests. He was breaking news on every major network. He scrolled to the boss's number, tapped it.

"Hey, Cor, what's up," Mr. Trump said.

"Sir. I couldn't have worked any harder for you, and I'm sorry if I disappointed you, I don't know what else I could have done," Corey said.

"Yeah, they've been killing us," the boss said. "They've been killing us, and they hate you, and they hate me."

* * *

Back in the brownstone apartment, Corey took off his suit and put on a pair of jeans and a T-shirt. *Fuck it*, he thought, *I'm going to New Hampshire*. Then Governor Rick Scott called. Then Chris Christie.

"Need any help?" the governor of New Jersey asked.

Corey likes and respects Governor Chris.

"Nah, I'm all set."

"You know I'm never going to be vice president now," the governor said. One of Corey's jobs on the campaign had been overseeing the vice president selection list.

The governor suggested that Corey make a statement. He took the advice and called Christie Bear, a CNN booker.

"Hey Christie, is Dana Bash around? I'd like to come over and talk with her."

"We'll have a car there in three minutes," the booker said.

The producer did it one better: she made it from CNN's studio in Columbus Circle to Sixty-First and Lexington Avenue in heels in less time than it took Corey to put his suit and tie back on.

It was quite the "get" for Dana Bash and CNN, and the studio was buzzing by the time Corey arrived, mostly because people thought that he would turn on his ex-boss. After all, Trump had unceremoniously dumped him, hadn't he? But those who expected him to settle a score didn't know Corey Lewandowski. They didn't know he was an altar boy so long that he was still one when he was driving to mass during the last years he served. They didn't know his idol growing up was his grandfather, a union printer for forty-two years. They didn't know he grew up poor in Lowell, where loyalty meant more than money. They didn't know that he'd worked every job he ever had like his life depended on it. What they got that day on CNN is what Corey was and still is: a man devoted to Donald Trump, even after the candidate's family fired him.

His appearance was so heartfelt and faithful, Trump called immediately afterward and told him how proud he was of him.

There are those who will argue that firing Corey was the right move at the time. Plenty would say that. The mainstream press was saying he wasn't qualified for the job even as his candidate won state primary after state primary. He won more primary votes than any Republican candidate in history, including Ronald Reagan and Dwight D. Eisenhower. And as the boss liked to say, Ike won World War II! Yes, Corey did have a candidate like no other, a political phenomenon who seemed to defy the laws of gravity and certainly of convention. "It was 99 percent Trump and 1 percent campaign," Corey said often. But another campaign manager would've tried to make the candidate into something he wasn't.

In hindsight, Corey still doesn't know if the day he was fired was the worst or the best of his life. Dave had some experience with getting fired, which he shared with his friend. When Newt Gingrich was House Speaker, he fired Dave as the chief investigator on the House's government reform and oversight committee. Dave had felt the same way Corey did when it happened. But things worked out just fine. And he assured Corey they would for him too.

Corey has certainly had opportunities since then that he couldn't have imagined.

And he can't remember whether it was that very day, perhaps when he was packing his bag, or whether the thought came to him days later. But at some point, he had the overwhelming feeling that though his role might have changed, his objective stayed the same.

He was going to do everything he could to get Donald J. Trump elected president of the United States. And that was the fundamental difference between the Trump campaign's former manager and the "chairman" who was now in control.

CHAPTER 9

THURSTON HOWELL III

To all the politicians, donors, and special interests, hear these words from me today: There is only one core issue in the immigration debate and it is this: the well-being of the American people. Nothing even comes a close second."
—DONALD J. TRUMP, AUGUST 31, 2016

ALL AMERICANS ever hear about from the fake news media is the plight of people who entered this country illegally. They're told how hard they work, how dangerous the journey was, how they face challenges most Americans who were born here or entered legally don't. It doesn't occur to people who buy this to consider there are many more people born in this country or who immigrated legally who face all the same challenges. Lower-income Americans are struggling and uncontrolled borders are making it harder on them, not easier.

Listening to the media, you would think that immigration has no effect on the existing US population. But it does. And while the boss certainly has sympathy for people in countries without the opportunities the United States might offer them, that sympathy doesn't outweigh his equal sympathy and first duty to the people already living in this country. That's what putting "America first" means.

But America First is contrary to the special interests of a lot of deep-pocketed multibillion-dollar multinational corporations that owe their first allegiance to their stockholders. And if they can drive their labor costs down with workers taking advantage of porous borders, they are all too happy to do so. That's just one reason you saw most of the corporate money go to Hillary Clinton during the campaign.

The other special interest opposed to America First is the Democratic Party. It's no secret that immigrants—legal and illegal—overwhelmingly vote Democrat. So the Democratic Party is always pushing for lax immigration rules and enforcement, and for amnesty for those who come here illegally. Then they argue for a "path to citizenship" for illegals, hoping to acquire millions of new Democratic voters by ignoring our laws.

This is the party that holds itself up as the champion of low- and middle-income earners.

Remember what the boss said way back in 1988 about getting the best response from taxi drivers and workers? That's because he really cares about those people, and they know it. You can't fake that, not with them. Everyday people are too street-smart. If you really care about the people who drive the taxis, pour the concrete, wire your dishwasher, or cut your lawn, then you must care about immigration.

At one time, US immigration policy was based on the same principle as that of virtually every other nation: to admit only people who will be a net positive for the country as a whole.

So, the boss is tough on immigration enforcement when it comes to our borders. But immigration into the campaign during the last few months before the election was another story altogether.

The boss was furious. On the table in front of him in the residence in Trump Tower was that day's copy of the *New York Times*. It was Saturday, August 13. Mr. Trump took his flip phone out of his pocket and scrolled to Corey's number.

"Who do you think leaked it?"

"Well, there were only five people at the meeting, and one of them was you," Corey said. "If you fire any one of the other four, you have a 25 percent chance to be right."

The *Times's* reporters Alexander Burns and Maggie Haberman wrote the story. They led it with a secret meeting at Trump Tower. Ivanka, Jared, Chris Christie, Jason Miller, and Paul Manafort were in the room, according to "unnamed sources." Those sources said that the meeting's participants pled with Trump to change his ways, to use the teleprompter, and stay on message.

The rest of the story chronicled the chaos in the campaign and the plunging poll numbers.

With eighty-six days left to Election Day, the Trump campaign was down double digits to Hillary in national polls, and the numbers were even worse in key battleground states. There was no floor. A trapdoor could open at any moment, and Trump could drop to numbers not seen since Michael Dukakis.

"What do you think I should do?" Trump asked his former campaign manager.

* * *

At the time, Dave, Susan, and their kids were on vacation in Disney World. Maggie, their youngest, was five going on six, and Lily was ten—perfect ages for Disney. And there was plenty to do there for Griffin and Isabella too: Space Mountain, watching the nighttime light shows, and doing Epcot.

Dave had earned the time off. Not only was he running Citizens United, but he was also heading up an anti-Clinton super PAC funded by the billionaire Bob Mercer and his daughter Rebekah. He had taken the job when Kellyanne had left the super PAC to join the Trump campaign.

By then, Kellyanne was Dave's only real connection to the campaign. When Don Jr. fired Corey, Dave's influence on the campaign became limited.

If we had any doubts we were on the outs, that notion was confirmed at the Republican convention. Paul Manafort had almost entirely sealed us off. Hope, Dan Scavino, George, and other members of the campaign team wouldn't even want to be seen talking to either of us for fear of reprisal from Paul. And Paul went out of his way to make life difficult for us, especially for Corey. With space in Cleveland at a premium, he had promised Corey he'd save a room for him at the Westin, where the campaign was staying. When Corey got to the front desk with his bags, the clerk told him there was no reservation under his name. Corey ended up staying at one of those suite hotels a half hour out of town with his CNN colleagues. And Dave stayed with the Maryland delegation in Independence, Ohio, twenty minutes from the convention center. Even our access in the convention hall was limited. We were issued only floor credentials. Dave brought Susan and the four kids but couldn't get tickets for them. A couple of times, we tried to visit the candidate's family box at Quicken Loans Arena. One time, we waved up to Michael

Glassner, Corey's former deputy. But instead of him inviting us up, Glassner came down to the floor. Don McGahn, however, came over and in the middle of the convention floor gave us big hugs and thanked us for all the work we put into the campaign. It was a sign of true class.

We wouldn't have been at the convention at all had we not been elected chairman of our respective delegations: Dave from Maryland, Corey from New Hampshire. At the time, Trump's delegate count had started to become a big issue (and the reason for Paul's hiring). We knew that by being elected chairmen of our delegations, we would have control over who was on the rules committee from our states, which would have been important had the convention been contested.

Though we continued to do our best for the campaign, we couldn't have felt any more detached from it. Corey had spent eighteen months at the candidate's side. As an outside campaign adviser, Dave weighed in with Corey regularly. He had talked to the team and the candidate often. But now it was as though that hadn't happened at all.

At one point, Mike Pence walked by with his wife, Karen, daughter, Charlotte, and the team of Nick Ayers and Marc Short. Dave had known Pence since he was a congressman, and Charlotte had interned at Citizens United years before. Corey, meanwhile, had headed up the original VP selection committee.

"What are you guys doing back here?" Pence asked. The vice presidential nominee was as surprised at where we were standing in the convention hall as we were.

Still, Corey stood straight and proud in front of the microphone and announced the delegate count for New Hampshire.

"Eleven votes for my friend, the next president of the United States, Donald J. Trump."

Dave stood next to Diana Waterman, a breast cancer survivor and state party chair, as she read the Maryland roll call.

The morning the *New York Times* story was published, Rebekah Mercer called Steve Bannon. All the way back to the New Hampshire Freedom Summit, Bannon was convinced that Trump would be the nominee and would win the presidency. "It's 100 percent," he'd tell anyone who would listen. He practically bet the future of the Breitbart website by backing Trump.

"The conservatives hated us, *National Review*, they all hated us," he said.

But the way Manafort was running the campaign sickened him. He couldn't shake the thought of Trump's new campaign chairman on *Meet the Press* the week before. Bannon hated the Sunday shows; he never watched them and tuned in only to see what Manafort was all about. He didn't know the guy at all, only having talked to him once on the phone at Breitbart, and thought he was a stiff. The image of Manafort wearing yachting blue filled the screen above a banner that read, "From Southampton, New York." Bannon was incensed. "This is a populist, nationalist campaign?" he screamed at the TV. "And the guy's on from the Hamptons?" And if that wasn't enough, he thought Manafort was terrible on air—he had no energy whatsoever, and didn't know the issues.

He can't find his own ass with both hands, Bannon thought.

On the phone, Rebekah told him that major Republican donors had begun to jump ship, and that was before the *New York Times* article. Things were going to get worse, Rebekah told him.

They would. There was already talk of the party cutting Trump loose. Mitch McConnell was going to focus on the Senate,

Paul Ryan on the House. Super PAC money would be redirected to down-ballot races. The way things were going, Trump could lose by twenty, twenty-five points. But Bannon still believed in Trump and his message.

"I think I can help," he said.

Five minutes later, Bob Mercer was on the phone. Mercer is the quietest man in the world. He's a mathematician. He'll listen to you all day. He'll whistle once in a while. But he's not a big talker.

Bannon told him his ideas, which included promoting Kellyanne, who was working for Trump on women's empowerment issues, to campaign manager. "We'll put her on TV, she can be the face of the campaign," he said.

"That sounds like a terrific idea," he said to Bannon.

It was a sentence that spoke volumes.

Later that day, Rebekah and Bob Mercer arrived at Woody Johnson's beachfront estate to see the usual deep-pocketed suspects Carl Icahn, Peter Kalikow, Lew Eisenberg, Steven Mnuchin, and Anthony Scaramucci. There was only one person they wanted to speak with, however, and that person was Donald Trump. Rebekah had the *Times* article in her hand.

"It's embarrassing," the candidate said to them.

Rebekah came right to the point.

"You have to hire Steve Bannon and Kellyanne Conway," she said.

The next morning was Sunday, August 14. Bannon was at the front desk at Trump Tower telling the doorman that he had an eight o'clock appointment with Trump.

"When's the last time you talked to him?" the doorman asked.

"Last night."

"He doesn't live here on the weekends. He's in New Jersey."

What did Bannon know? He figured a guy named Trump lived in Trump Tower all the time. Bannon dialed his number.

"Where are you?" Trump asked.

"Trump Tower."

The miscommunication didn't seem to faze the candidate; he was eager to talk. They did for two hours.

"I'm going out to play golf," Trump said finally. "Come out later, and we'll have lunch."

"Where are you?" Bannon asked.

"Bedminster!"

Bannon, who wouldn't know Bedminster from Westminster, had to ask where it was.

"You have to get off on Rattlesnake Road," Trump began, "then take a left at the small church; you'll see a stone house on your right . . ."

By the time Trump mentioned the stone house, Bannon had made up his mind to take an Uber.

What he thought was going to be a one-on-one lunch turned out to be something entirely different. Bannon arrived at Bedminster to find a table set for eight in a glass gazebo overlooking the first tee.

While Bannon was standing there contemplating his situation, Roger Ailes, with an accordion file under his arm, walked in the door.

"What the hell are you doing here?" he growled to Bannon.

"I'm having lunch with Trump."

"This isn't lunch. It's debate prep. He shouldn't be out here dicking around with lunch. He's got to get his mind right for the debate."

With that, Rudy Giuliani and Chris Christie walked in. Then Mr. Trump. Right off the golf course.

"Where's the hot dogs and hamburgers?" he asked.

After several rounds of burgers, the "debate prep" portion of the program finally started and consisted almost entirely of Roger Ailes telling war stories of prepping Ronald Reagan and George H. W. for debates. He said nothing of any substance that might help Trump in September against Hillary.

Bannon was beside himself. He'd come all the way out to God-knew-where New Jersey for a cookout and war stories.

Then, just when things couldn't get any stranger, Paul Manafort appeared, dressed in boat shoes, white capri pants with string ties, and a blue blazer complete with a crest on the breast pocket.

Thurston Howell III, Bannon thought.

Somehow, Manafort's lieutenant, Rick Gates, had gotten wind of the meeting at Bedminster and had called Paul. Manafort dropped whatever he had been doing, perhaps out on a three-hour cruise, and drove from Southampton to Trump's golf club in New Jersey. It's at least a three-hour ride.

With Manafort's arrival, the meeting went from theater of the absurd to a scene out of *The Godfather*.

"Trump was hot enough to fuck," Bannon remembered.

"You think I'm a baby, Paul?" the boss began.

Giuliani and Bannon both tried to calm Trump down to no avail.

"Am I a baby, Paul? You think you're so fucking smart! Like you're a genius! Well, you suck on TV."

By the time the boss finished, Manafort looked like a crushed blue beer can. Even Bannon felt sorry for him.

The boss is one of those people who can be hot as an August afternoon at one moment, then turn a switch and be as calm as a spring evening the next. With his fury spent, he stood and clapped his hands.

"I'm going for ice cream," he said.

Bannon sat there for a full few minutes wondering what the fuck had just happened.

Later, however, real business took place. Mr. Trump called Bannon that evening.

"Look, no doubt you can win," Bannon said to the candidate on the phone "You just need to get organized. Get some pollsters. Tony Fabrizio."

"Fine, let's do it," the boss said.

"And you have to get Bossie," Bannon said.

Bannon began working for Trump that very night. On Sunday night, even Trump Tower was relatively empty. He made his way to the fourteenth floor and took a desk that belonged to Dan Scavino. Scavino wouldn't miss it, the staffers there told him. He was always in the air with the candidate. Just as Bannon was settling in, his phone rang. Paul Manafort thanked him for trying to calm Trump down at the luncheon and then asked if they could meet.

"Sure, where are you?" Steve asked.

"Trump Tower," Manafort said.

Well, that's convenient, Steve thought.

"I'm in 43G," he said.

The apartment, like all the apartments in Trump Tower, was beautiful, with a drop-dead view. On the couch lounged a woman wearing a white muumuu. Manafort wanted Steve to look at a transcript of a story, yet another one, that a *New York Times* reporter had sent to him. Bannon read the first three paragraphs and then looked up him.

"Twelve-point-seven-million-dollar payment from Ukraine?"

The woman in the muumuu sat bolt upright. "Paul?" she said.

"How much of this is true?" Bannon asked.

"It's all lies," Manafort said. "My lawyers are fighting it."

The muumuu-clad woman was now on her feet, her arms folded.

"Paul, twelve million?"

"When are they going to run it?" Bannon asked.

"They're threatening to publish tomorrow."

"Does Trump know about this?"

"What's to know, it's all lies."

"But if it's in the paper someone has to give Trump a heads-up, because if it's in the paper, it's reality."

"Paul?" she asked imploringly.

"It was a long time ago," he said to her. "I had expenses."

Bannon knew what he had in his hand. It was an explosive, page one story. And even if the story wasn't true, it was in the fucking *New York Times*. At the very least it would leave a mark.

J ust as Steve had thought, the story ran the next day, August 15, page one, above the fold.

"I've got a crook running my campaign," Trump said when he read it.

Paul's propensity to operate in dark corners had perhaps showed itself early in his tenure on the campaign. On the day Corey was fired, amid the craziness, Paul went to Jeff DeWit, the campaign's chief operating officer, and asked for a $5 million check to be cut for a media buy that sounded vague at best.

DeWit said he would issue the check only after he received a memo from Allen Weisselberg with Donald Trump's "D" signed on it. That was the last DeWit heard about the check or the buy.

Then there was the strange and murky case of Left Hand Enterprises LLC. In May 2016, after Manafort joined the campaign, and before they fired Corey, the campaign operated on two separate budgets. Corey oversaw the funds in one, and Manafort managed the other. Soon after the campaign hired Manafort, his budget quickly cut successive checks totaling over $700,000 to a newly formed Delaware company that was supposed to provide direct mail to Nebraska and Indiana. Whether or not the mailing found its way to those states, or to any other location, is still up for debate. What is known is that Left Hand LLC had a mailing address at a farm in Virginia that just happened to be the voting residence of Manafort's former business partner.

The complete story of the Left Hand incident has never been fully resolved. But the amount of $700,000 for a mailing that no one knows for sure ever happened is something that a guy with the initials DJT will not soon forget.

Trump told Bannon to fire Manafort right away. Steve argued that firing his campaign chairman would cause a shit storm of bad press. Instead he argued that Trump should take away his authority and give him a new title, which is what happened. When the campaign announced the new team, Bannon had the title of campaign CEO, Kellyanne Conway was the campaign manager, and Manafort remained the campaign chairman.

The kill shot for Paul came on Thursday the eighteenth, when Trump was about to go onstage at a rally in Charlotte, North Carolina. A friend showed him a printout of an AP story written by Jeff Horwitz and Chad Day. Based on emails that the AP had obtained, the story described Manafort running "a covert Washington lobbying operation on behalf of Ukraine's ruling political party, attempting to sway American public opinion in favor of the country's pro-Russian government." It also said that Manafort and his deputy, Rick Gates, had "never disclosed their work as foreign agents as required under federal law."

"Tell Jared to fire him," Trump said.

The next morning at a breakfast meeting in Trump Tower, Jared asked Manafort to resign. At first, Paul balked. He was worried about the perception of being forced out of the campaign right after the Ukraine stories broke.

"It will make me look guilty," he said.

Jared told him there wasn't much that could be done. A press release was going out in sixty seconds.

Steve Bannon would prove to be a significant change for the campaign, and the promotion of Kellyanne Conway was equally important. A few days after she took over as campaign manager, Kellyanne was in Mr. Trump's office on the twenty-sixth floor of the tower. That day, the boss happened to be in a surly mood. He was shooting a Facebook ad and didn't like the way it was going. He had asked Kellyanne to look over the script, which she did.

"It's not in your voice," she said.

The boss asked the other staffers to leave. He wanted to talk to Kellyanne privately.

"You're running against the single most joyless candidate in politics," she said. "And it's starting to feel that way around here."

Mr. Trump said he missed the days when it was only a few of them—Corey, Hope, Keith, Scavino, and the rest. He said he had more fun then, because he talked to the people who came to see him.

"Well, let's see if we can replicate that for the general election campaign," she said.

Kellyanne had known the boss from back in the 2000s, when she owned a condo in one of his buildings. She sat on the condo board and was surprised and impressed that a man who owned eighteen buildings in New York City and dozens more around the world would find the time to show up at a condo board meeting, but he did. She also knew something about his allure as a politician. She had run Dave's poll in 2013 when Mr. Trump was considering running for governor of New York. Corey had tried to hire her early in the campaign.

"Do you do any polling?" she had asked.

The answer was no, so she didn't come aboard then. But even in those early days, she was impressed with the moxie the candidate showed, and his fervent and consistent resistance to naysayers and haters. Mr. Trump, which out of deference she always called him, was one of the few politicians who could go off script and stay on message.

Though she was called the "face of the campaign" and was a ubiquitous Trump presence on TV, Kellyanne was much more than that. She navigated the campaign through some very sticky moments. She brought to her job as spokesperson for Mr. Trump a depth of political knowledge that was deeper than most, probably all, who interviewed her. Even Rachel Maddow, MSNBC's big Kahuna, couldn't outduel Kellyanne.

One of Kellyanne's biggest assets was her understanding of Mr. Trump and the brilliance of how he delivered his populist message. She would use the example of him talking to a stadium filled with people at one of his rallies.

"China is killing us," he'd say.

Though some did, plenty of those who came to see him didn't know the nuances of our trade deficit with the People's Republic. But they did know that everything they bought seemed to be made in China. So the message resonated. The message was also defendable in the same simple terms.

With Mr. Trump, changes in staff wasn't as important as it would be with a traditional candidate. Still, with Bannon and Kellyanne, the Trump campaign had traded up considerably from Manafort and Gates. All they needed was one more piece to complete the puzzle.

Dave was pulling into his driveway in Maryland when his BlackBerry buzzed. The caller ID read DONALD TRUMP. In Disney World, and on the drive home, he'd received calls from Corey, Kellyanne, and Bannon. It was a full-court press trying to get him to come on board as deputy campaign manager. Corey told him he'd been in touch with the boss and the boss wanted him on the team.

Susan and the kids were unpacking the Suburban. The idea was exciting to Dave. Opportunities to help run a presidential campaign are few and far between. But he had a lot going on, and it would be a huge sacrifice. The kids were going back to school. He would miss Griffin's baseball and Isabella's softball seasons. Yes, there were only a couple of months left in the campaign, so it wasn't like he'd be gone forever. But the last two months of a presidential campaign are brutal, a pressure cooker at best, and a trash compactor at worst. Dave knew he could stand the pressure. He thrived on it. He just wondered if his heart could.

Three years earlier, he had been on a hunting trip with Griffin in Alabama. A few days before the trip, he began to feel like he was getting the flu. Griffin was looking forward to the weekend, so he went. Deer hunting is not an activity to do when you're not feeling well: up at four a.m., trudging through the woods, bagging deer. By the time they returned home, Dave felt terrible. Susan took one look at him and demanded he see his doctor. As it happened, his doctor was away. But Dave had a fallback, a cardiologist. The year before, he'd had a mild heart attack. He didn't even know he'd had it until he took a physical for an insurance policy. Dave never smoked and isn't a big drinker. He'll have a beer or a glass of wine now and then. Stress was the culprit.

That Tuesday, he called the cardiologist, who couldn't see him until Friday at four p.m.

By the time he got to see the doctor, Dave had lost a bunch of weight.

Dave described his symptoms: he was having chills and night sweats, and said he'd been sick for about ten days. It was more like two weeks.

His cardiologist instructed him to drive to Washington Hospital Center. He would call and have him admitted.

Dave had been in the fire service for fifteen years. Long enough to know you never check into a hospital on your own on Friday afternoon.

"I'll wait until Monday."

"You might not make it to Monday," the cardiologist said.

Doctors never fully ascertained how Dave contracted the infection that invaded his heart. Once it did, he became septic, and his organs started to fail. And when the infection found its way to his heart, the microbes blew up his mitral valve.

Doctors inserted a PICC line, so Dave was on a twenty-four-hour continual antibiotic IV drip for two and a half months. He carried the portable IV to work in a bandolier, and Isabella, his twelve-year-old daughter, helped him change it every morning.

The IV was just the prelim. The heavyweight fight was the open-heart surgery performed after the infection had cleared. A doctor named Louis Kanda, known as one of the best valve repair surgeons around, performed the operation at Washington Hospital Center. Dave told Kanda that he wanted the valve repaired and not replaced. A pig valve or a mechanical device would most likely have meant blood thinners for the rest of his life. Plus, replacement valves wear out. Dave was forty-seven years old at the time and had no interest in having to do the surgery again, especially after he kissed his wife and children before going in for the operation and the thought came to him that it might have been for the last time.

Dave never dwelled on his heart history, but he'd be lying if he said it wasn't in the back of his mind as he considered the offer from Corey, Kellyanne, and Bannon. But any concern dissipated when he answered the BlackBerry to take Trump's call.

"I didn't think you'd want to," the candidate said. Mr. Trump knew about Dave's health issues and had always expressed concern. "What about Citizens United?" he asked.

"I'll be able to work it out, sir."

"Good, we need you."

Paul Manafort had been in charge of the campaign for eight weeks. In that time, the campaign had gone from a primary juggernaut under Corey to a death spiral. He was brought in as a delegate hunter, but the truth is he did little more than relay information from the RNC, which did all the work collecting delegates. By the time he was fired, many in the press and else-where believed that the race was over for Trump. They also thought that the only reason he brought on Bannon was to burn the house down, an arsonist hired to extract revenge for Trump on a party that had turned its back on him. Inside the campaign, people were seriously concerned.

In any other circumstance, only a miracle could have helped. But in our circumstance, we had Donald Trump.

CHAPTER 10

THE GROUND GAME

Anyone who cannot name our enemy is not fit to
lead this country. Anyone who cannot condemn the
hatred, oppression, and violence of Radical Islam
lacks the moral clarity to serve as our president.
—DONALD J. TRUMP, AUGUST 15, 2016

IT'S HARD TO BELIEVE, but the Obama administration's
approach to defeating radical Islamic terrorism was completely
wrongheaded on every conceivable front. And his secretary of
state, Hillary Clinton, was a key part of his failed approach for
much of Obama's presidency.

Donald Trump is probably best known as the most politically incorrect candidate who ever ran for the presidency.
Millions of people loved him merely for that reason. They were
tired of the PC double-talk from coastal elites and even more
tired of those condescending attitudes. The boss took a flame-
thrower to all of it.

But what a lot of people don't understand is how deeply the
mind-set behind political correctness affected crucial policies
that risked the safety and well-being of everyone in this country.
The reluctance to call radical Islamic terrorism what it is was

rooted in the radical liberal belief that all people on the planet are equal, no matter what they believe, no matter what they do. The PC crowd in both political parties just can't bring themselves to admit that not all belief systems are equal and that not all people who do bad things are simply victims of their environment or some sort of social oppression. Some of them are simply evil people.

That's why Hillary Clinton's State Department thought it perfectly fine to recklessly destroy what stability there was in the Middle East. Support the toppling of dictators, they naively thought, and American-style democratic republics would emerge naturally from the wreckage.

Does that mean we like dictators or don't recognize people's right to freedom in other countries, including those in the Middle East? No. But we do recognize that there are limitations to what America's foreign policy can do. Running around the world trying to make every country equal simply isn't one of them, especially when we're dealing with long-standing tribal conflicts we don't understand. America's foreign policy should be focused on the security of American citizens and peaceful relations with every country with which it is in our interests to have relationships—period. America first!

The boss has taken a lot of heat from the fake news media regarding their absurd conspiracy about collusion with Russia, which we can both tell you firsthand is ridiculous. The whole charade has somewhat muted the boss's wise approach to alliances against radical Islam. Hillary Clinton chose radical Islamic groups as bad as those we are fighting as her allies in the war against ISIS. That resulted in people the Obama administration armed and trained simply taking the weapons and training and joining ISIS not long afterward.

Mr. Trump repeatedly said Russia would be a natural ally against radical Islam. Anyone who can read a map or watches international news headlines can see why. Terrorism is at least as much a problem for them as for us. But Obama and Clinton thought militants carrying "Death to America" banners would make better allies.

And just as their rose-colored view of the world blinded them to the dangers of allying with radical Islamists overseas, it blinded Barack Obama and Hillary Clinton to the dangers of admitting into our country hundreds of thousands of unvetted refugees and immigrants from countries rife with Islamic terrorists. A key plank in Donald Trump's approach to fighting radical Islamic terrorism is to contain the terrorists. ISIS has explicitly said it plans to infiltrate Western countries, including the United States, through immigration. To ignore this threat is tantamount to suicide.

The boss wasn't proposing anything radical. It was just common sense. People coming from hotbeds of terrorism should have to go through extreme vetting, and we shouldn't let a single person enter the country from one of those places unless we are sure we can complete that vetting. Beef up border security operations and give the people who patrol the border what they need to do their jobs properly. We're not talking about a large portion of the federal budget here. We spend a lot more money on things far less important, and some on things that shouldn't be done at all.

Having spent his entire life paying taxes instead of consuming them instilled Donald Trump with the kind of common sense that is completely missing from Washington, DC. But as lousy a job as Hillary Clinton had done fighting radical Islamic terrorism, she was beating the pants off our campaign in August 2016.

* * *

The day after Trump called him, Dave was on a train with Susan to New York to meet with Steve Bannon at Rebekah Mercer's office, just a few blocks from Trump Tower. Bannon was going to go over Dave's role and update him on the state of things within the campaign. After they had covered a few broad topics and logistics, Dave and Bannon went to speak with Kellyanne. Although Dave had a good idea where the campaign stood, Steve and Kellyanne had a whole presentation ready for him—data, poll numbers, predictions. As it turned out, the inside info wasn't any better than what was more widely known.

"There's no floor here," Bannon told him. "It could get really bad."

Hillary was killing them on the ground, especially in the battleground states, where she had three times the number of campaign offices. At the end of August, the Clinton campaign had more than twice the number of field offices in Ohio. They outnumbered Trump's campaign offices 34 to 1 in Florida and 36 to 2 in Pennsylvania—states without which a Trump victory was practically impossible.

There was a total lack of focus of the staff due to Manafort's lack of leadership. Mr. Trump had become frustrated and bemoaned the state of the campaign often and then railed against any attempt to rein him in. He lashed out at Khizr and Ghazala Khan, whose son, an army officer, died a hero in Iraq. He nearly imploded over the avalanche of horrible press that his campaign manager's ties to Russian oligarchs and Ukrainian strongmen brought. Things were going so bad for the boss, his opponent took an extended fund-raising vacation on Nantucket and in the Hamptons during August, less than three months before the election!

And then there was the morale of the team. The campaign staff in the tower was demoralized and in disarray. Paul Manafort had managed like a tyrant, dispatching orders and Rick Gates from 43G. Gates performed as a henchman and a buffer between Paul and the staff.

Paul rarely moved among the troops, instead spending his time huddled with the boss's family or on trips to DC, where he tried to ingratiate himself with the Republican establishment. It was on these trips where he promised "to change Trump."

What polarized the campaign office even further was the sudden drop in temperature when Manafort took over. The staff wasn't used to the cold, sterile inaction that Manafort fostered—he was low energy.

During Corey's reign, the campaign ran on pure emotion, adrenaline, and Red Bull. Close friendships formed, and a team developed. The only name that mattered back then was Donald J. Trump, and they all liked it that way. On Corey's birthday, the team threw him a party at campaign headquarters and presented him with a framed copy of a front-page New York Times profile of him. It's still on the wall in his office at home, beside a small picture of the whole team.

With Manafort, there was no such camaraderie. Not even close.

Dave and Susan went back to DC. On the train, thoughts spun in Dave's mind. He'd need a few days to tie up Citizens United and a few other projects he'd had in the works, including walking away from a new CU production film with Bannon and Phil Robertson of *Duck Dynasty*. Presidential campaigns, he knew, meant a whole lot of crushing stress, late nights, greasy food, and a mind-bending amount of travel—not the kind of thing they prescribe to a guy with health problems. Add that to missing all four kids and the little one's first day of school, and he had a pretty good reason to turn down the job. Maybe he could just keep up his advisory role from afar, he thought. Life was better when you were a nameless team player anyway, moving around on the outside without being noticed much.

He talked about taking the job with Susan, insisting that it'd be a temporary thing, a couple of months, tops.

When he made it back to Trump Tower, Dave decided to keep up the low profile, moving among the campaign staffers without any mention of the role he was taking.

It's not like they didn't know who he was. The year before, in 2015, *Politico* magazine ranked Dave number two in its list of the fifty most influential people in American politics. He'd been the president of Citizens United, a conservative advocacy group with over 500,000 members and supporters, since 2001. During that time, along with producing twenty-five political documentaries, including six feature-length films with Steve Bannon and seven films with Callista and Newt Gingrich, he had authored several books, and been a champion of conservative causes. The campaign staffers were well aware of Dave Bossie, but not of the extent to which he was about to become involved.

Those first two days, he shared an office with Brad Parscale and Rick Gates, who had somehow survived the regime change, even though Trump had instructed several people to fire him multiple times. Survival seemed to be Gates's main talent. On either Dave's first or second day, Mr. Trump came down to the fourteenth floor, saw Gates, and immediately told Dave to fire him. It was not the first or the last time Donald Trump wanted Rick Gates fired. The team was worried about the press that firing Gates would engender. Besides, one of the first things the new deputy realized was how outgunned the campaign was. He needed more bodies, not less. Steve came up with a plan that would move Gates off the campaign but not out of the overall operation by making him the campaign's liaison to the RNC. The plan boomeranged, however. The RNC mistakenly believed that Gates was their liaison to the Trump campaign. So, after just a few days, Gates was clocking in again at Trump Tower— much to the consternation of the candidate. To the senior staff, Gates was a bad penny that kept turning up.

For the new team, however, there were far more important things to worry about.

J ob number one was to try to reestablish an esprit de corps. On September 14, 2016, Dave made one of his first trips with the boss on the campaign trail, to Ohio. They made a stop at the Pro Football Hall of Fame in Canton. Arriving just before the hall closed, they were given a private tour by the organization's president, David Baker. During the visit, Baker gave Mr. Trump a Hall of Fame football. Trump spun it in the air and then lateraled it to Dave.

Dave brought the football back to the office, where he put it on his desk for anyone to toss around. It traveled around the office. Dave would carry it under his arm to the conference room. Staffers would have a catch with it in the middle of the office, firing spirals, or dying ducks, depending on athletic ability. Johnny McEntee would show off his trick shot prowess. But even for those without Johnny's arm or aim, the football became the symbol of teamwork and helped bring energy back to the staff.

The uplifted mood was good, but there were also specific things that needed to be changed. Bannon and Jared asked Dave to take over the strategic scheduling for the campaign, which meant not only building the candidate's day in, day out schedule, but also the schedules of Governor Pence, Ivanka and Jared, Don Jr. and Vanessa, and Eric and Lara. Dave also worked with the indefatigable Anne-Allen Welden to schedule all of the "super surrogates" like the Trump family, Jeff Sessions, Rudy Giuliani, and other governors, senators, and congressmen. Anne-Allen Welden was working out of the DC campaign office with Rick Dearborn. Dave immediately moved the entire DC campaign shop including John Mashburn's policy shop to New York.

Being in charge of Trump's schedule was a surefire way of being the target of his wrath. But Jared explained to Dave it was one of the most important tasks of the entire campaign.

F. Clifton White, the political strategist who wrote *Why Reagan Won: The Conservative Movement 1964–1981*, was another of Dave's political heroes. White was an organizational genius. Dave needed to draw on all of White's knowledge for the Trump campaign's schedule, which had a lot of moving parts. Mr. Trump and Mr. Pence were like opposite hands of a clock. If Mr. Trump was visiting New Hampshire, Governor Pence would be in South Florida. The boss is out West? Then the governor would be on the East Coast. When the candidates traveled west, we'd use time zone changes to our advantage. Ivanka and Jared are modern Orthodox Jews; the couple had a house filled with children and had to be home for Shabbat, which limited their travel on the weekends. Eric and his wife, Lara, played especially well in Southern states, and Lara was a spokesperson for the campaign's "Women's Empowerment Tour." Don Jr. was hugely popular in the gun and hunting states such as Nevada and Colorado. Later on in the campaign, Brad and Jared's arm of the campaign provided digital data the digital team collected to help direct Trump's moves.

Hillary had a team of scheduling experts. Except they forgot where Michigan and Wisconsin were. Her team was sending Hillary and her surrogates to places they should never have been. For a campaign that was supposed to be so sophisticated, they were acting dumb. The team used everything the campaign had to offer and sought input from multiple stakeholders to make sure the schedules were right.

If he had it his way, Dave might still be living in the firehouse, doing the duty he'd been devoted to earlier in his life. And when we say "devoted," we mean he lived in Firehouse Station 15 in Burtonsville, Maryland from 1990 to 2000. He slept in a bunk bed and responded to several hundred emergency calls every year. Those calls ranged from going to house fires to delivering babies to cutting victims from bad car accidents to helping sick people in need of treatment. He stood helpless in front of the Pentagon when American Airlines Flight 77 slammed into the building's western wall. His close friend and partner in the Clinton investigations, Barbara Olson, was on the plane. He was living in the firehouse in the 1990s when he served as the chief investigator for the US House of Representatives Committee on Government Reform and Oversight, in which capacity he led all the Clinton investigations. He lived in the firehouse when he was the investigator for North Carolina senator Lauch Faircloth, a member of the Senate Whitewater committee. He lived in the firehouse almost until the day he married Susan.

Right from the start, we knew the path for a Trump victory went through Florida. It was the base of what we called "the spine": Florida, North Carolina, Ohio, and Iowa. When the new team arrived on the campaign, the Florida operation was lagging. Hillary, as we said, was pressing hard in the state, with over five hundred full-time staffers. The Trump campaign, by contrast, had a small headquarters in Sarasota and a few people who drove from city to city in RVs, knocking on as many doors as they could.

The numbers on the ground were equally embarrassing. The state director was Karen Giorno, who had been at the helm when Mr. Trump destroyed Marco Rubio in the state primary. Karen was a superstar and had Mr. Trump's ear. She also was a terrific person, but Dave wanted to move Karen to a bigger role as the chairwoman of coalitions. And Steve Bannon wanted to make the change in Florida quickly. Bannon began talking with Dave about ideas for a replacement.

Dave had years of experience dealing with Bannon, and his one steadfast rule for managing things with him on the Trump campaign was this: don't solve one problem by creating a bigger one. Luckily, Dave already had a solution, and she was working a few feet from him in Trump Tower.

There aren't a whole lot of people in Florida politics more capable than Susie Wiles. The daughter of the legendary football sportscaster Pat Summerall, Susie is the consummate political pro. Besides other numerous statewide campaigns, she ran Governor Rick Scott's 2010 campaign. Corey had named her cochair of Trump's Florida campaign, and she recently had begun working for us in Trump Tower as the communications coordinator in battleground states.

One night, just as she was settling into her life in New York, Steve and Dave called her into Bannon's office. Together, they told her they needed to make significant changes in Florida and they needed to do it immediately. Otherwise, Florida might fall into the lost-cause category, as would Trump's election chances.

But her arrival didn't change the bad numbers, at least not right away. The team needed additional staff to be successful.

But it was the polls that the boss had noticed.

Sooner or later, everybody who works for Donald Trump will see a side of him that makes you wonder why you took a job with him in the first place. His wrath is never intended as any personal offense, but sometimes it can be hard not to take it that way. The mode that he switches into when things aren't going his way can feel like an all-out assault; it'd break most hardened men and women into little pieces. Around the campaign, we'd call it getting your face ripped off. Being the target of his wrath can make for a pretty jarring experience, especially if you aren't used to it. Corey and Dave both had firsthand experience with this, both had moments where they wanted to parachute off Trump Force One, but it was new to Susie.

She had been in charge in Florida for about a month and the polls had continued to drop, sinking even lower than they'd been when we had declared the state of emergency that brought her back to the state in the first place. Even polls that had historically leaned our way had the boss down three to five points. The "geniuses" on TV and in newspaper columns—most of whom, by the way, still have jobs—were predicting a Hillary landslide, for Florida and the country at large.

To try to stem the tide, Dave and Susie scheduled the candidate for a four-day, seven-city swing across Florida, set to kick off in Miami. That first night, along with Dave and Susie, Mr. Trump had dinner with the usual group, including Keith, Hope, Dan Scavino, and Rudy Giuliani. He knew that he was down in the polls and that Susie, the woman sitting across the table from him, hadn't fixed it yet. There were a lot of phone calls to New York and other campaign offices, tirades against people, both present and not, and a few pointed questions about the failure of the Florida ground team—which had only existed, actually, for a couple of weeks—to get him better numbers. Multiple times, he told Susie that she might not be up for the job. He could not have said anything more hurtful to a pro like Susie Wiles.

The heat she was feeling got so bad that Susie couldn't take it anymore. She turned to Dave and said, "I'm done," got up, and walked away from the table. Dave was sure that she had quit. He ran after her and talked her off the emotional cliff. In the end, she assured him that she wasn't leaving but, she said, she wanted to get back to the office and redouble her efforts.

People say that Donald Trump never apologizes. There is some credence to that. In an interview, Frank Luntz once asked the boss if he ever asks God for forgiveness. "I don't think I do," Mr. Trump said. "I just try to do better."

For example, Corey and Hope were in the car with him on the way to a rally in San Diego in May 2016. A few months before, he'd told Fox News that Judge Curiel was hostile to him because of his positions on immigration. US District Judge Gonzalo Curiel was presiding over the Trump University lawsuit. Then in June on CNN, he said that Curiel's bias against him stemmed from the fact that the judge was Mexican. The blowback was insane, a veritable avalanche of bad press. Reince Priebus told the boss he should apologize. Corey knew better than to do that but pleaded with him in the car to not mention Judge Curiel at the rally. And what happened? He went out onstage and hammered the judge.

"Screw it," he told Corey later. "I feel better, and I'm glad I did it." The same thing happened with Alicia Machado, the Venezuelan Miss Universe. When they came at him, he hit back twice as hard.

But that doesn't mean it's personal. Although apologies are not in his makeup, the boss does know how to make things right, especially with the people who work for him.

When Susie met us at the last stop, the boss couldn't have been more gracious to her. When he got offstage and met her again, they were talking like old friends. "I'm going to call you every day," he said. "I'm going to find out if you have what you need. And if you don't have what you need, I want you to call me. Don't take no from anybody. And if it's slow, or it doesn't come, I want you to call me personally."

It became apparent to Susie only later, after the Florida team cobbled together one of the most successful short-term ground games in the history of American politics, what a turning point that dinner had been. Amid all the tense discussions, she and Dave had put forward several ideas for electoral improvement in Florida, mostly to do with money, mailing, and door knocking. In the days and weeks that followed, Trump had arranged for her to get all the resources she wanted.

Most of the improvements, Susie believed, had to do with wresting control of the campaign away from the Republican National Committee—which still had, remarkably, little faith in our campaign or our candidate—and putting it back into the hands of our own team, made up of people who were loyal to Donald J. Trump.

At the time of the dinner, the Florida GOP was sending out pieces of mail that barely mentioned Donald Trump. It was as if they'd cut their losses and just focused on down-ballot candidates. At the time, hardly anyone in that organization had any faith in Mr. Trump. After the dinner, Susie was given sufficient funds and the authority to design a few new pieces of mail— things that put Trump front and center.

After Susie got all she wanted from him, Trump asked her, point-blank, if she thought he would win the state. Susie emphatically told him she thought he would, a statement that seemed ludicrous at the time to many, even to those who make their living in politics.

The month of August ended with Mr. Trump's trip to Mexico to visit with President Enrique Peña Nieto. The trip was so secretly planned very few people knew it was going to happen. The campaign also thought discretion the better part of valor and used Phil Ruffin's jet instead of flying Trump Force One into Mexico City. In his speech, Mr. Trump praised the Mexican people and their president. He talked about the need for the two countries to work together on the issues of illegal immigration and drug trafficking. It was a big moment. "We just want to give people permission to vote for him," Steve Bannon always said. The Mexican trip was a big step in that direction. And Hillary's lead, which had been well into the double digits when the new team took over the campaign, was now down to five points.

But things were just starting to get interesting.

CHAPTER 11

DIGITAL MADNESS

My Twitter account has become so powerful I can
actually make my enemies tell the truth.
—DONALD J. TRUMP

We are in a competition with the world, and I want
America to win. When I am president, we will.
—DONALD J. TRUMP, AUGUST 8, 2016

AMERICA HAS the largest economy in the world, thanks to its
long traditions of private property, economic freedom, and hard
work. Donald Trump should know; his companies have contrib-
uted more to our GDP than most others. But GDP measures
only what a country is producing right now, not how much it is
growing. And as far as growth is concerned, it's barely 1 percent
in the United States.

As we said before, multinational corporations don't nec-
essarily have a vested interest in any one country. That's why
they're 100 percent behind any public policies that will boost
their revenues or lower their operating costs. NAFTA did both.
It was a win-win for Wall Street and corporate America, but a
lose-lose for most Americans.

Everyone was surprised the boss won Michigan and other Rust Belt states like it, but we weren't. We knew his message was like water to a man dying of thirst in places like Detroit, formerly one of the capitals of American industry, now reduced to a blighted ghost town. These people haven't only seen firsthand the devastation wrought by trade deals like NAFTA, they've lived it.

And it's not just that people in foreign countries will work for less. It's how much doing business in America costs, due to taxes and regulations. Hillary Clinton took for granted that the same tired old Democratic message of more regulation and more "taxes on the rich" was going to give her blue-collar states like Michigan. But once again, it was Donald Trump who understood and truly cared for the people whose jobs had been exported and whose dreams had been downsized.

The Democrats like to talk about how wonderful European socialism is, cherry-picking a few statistics from categories where they can show supposedly better results. But what they don't tell you is that along with their larger welfare states, most of those countries have much less regulated economies. Denmark, for example, scored a 93.9 in the business freedom category in the Heritage Foundation's 2016 Index of Economic Freedom. The United States scored 84.4. The United States has fallen to seventeenth in the world overall on that index. In 1995, we were fourth.

Unlike the self-appointed experts in Washington, the boss doesn't presume to know how to run every single business in the United States. So he made it very simple: for every new regulation enacted, two must be repealed in its place. Most people know when regulations go from the reasonable to the ridiculous. When your goal is to make America competitive, to make America great again, rather than appease lobbyists, it's not hard to figure out which ones should go.

Another inconvenient fact for the Democrats is the US corporate tax rate. They like to demagogue about how the rich don't pay enough taxes, but the United States has the third-highest corporate tax rate in the world. Donald Trump knows you aren't going to put people back to work if all the new business investment is fleeing to countries with lower tax rates. And just like with immigration, he wasn't afraid to tell unemployed blue-collar workers the politically incorrect truth, instead of the class-warfare message they got from Hillary Clinton.

He wasn't afraid to say things many Republicans didn't like either. There would be no more one-sided trade deals that benefited their big-business donors but impoverished middle America. Even NAFTA was going to be renegotiated. The days of free trade for them, currency manipulation and subsidies against us, were over. American workers were no longer going to be asked to compete on a playing field that slanted straight up.

But before any of that could happen, we needed a competitive advantage to overcome the huge special-interest funding advantage that Hillary Clinton enjoyed.

Early on in his time with us on the campaign, Brad Parscale went to Mr. Trump and Jared and made this analogy: Imagine, he said, two television screens. The one on the left is a commercial for a new personal music device. The device is open so you can see its inner workings. It is a marvel of engineering. You can also see how sleek it looks on the outside, and the gold plating where you plug in the headphones.

The scene on the right has only a silhouette of a woman with long, curly hair dancing while listening to the device. The tagline is, "iPod, this is how it's going to make you feel."

Brad was new to politics. He told everyone who would listen that he'd never worked on or even volunteered for a political campaign before. But he had been in the Web design business for many years, and he knew what sold and what didn't.

"The people want to know how it makes them feel," he said. "They want to buy the dance."

If Donald Trump was Twitter, then Hillary Clinton was LinkedIn. Her online presence was filled with long descriptions of stances and policies. Every time she had the chance, she explained who she was. She was the television screen on the left. But people never cared who she was. Voters didn't want a scripted intellectual connection. They wanted a visceral one. That's what Mr. Trump gave them.

He made them dance.

Brad began working for the Trumps back in 2011. A real estate executive who knew Brad's Web design work called and asked if he'd be interested in bidding to build a real estate website for Ivanka and Jared Kushner. He bid low, ten grand, and told them he'd give them the money back if they didn't like his work. He thought that having a Trump contract on his résumé would be good for his business. The Kushners liked the website, and Brad got the job. That one job would lead to many others in the Trump Organization, such as with the Trump Winery and the Eric Trump Foundation.

He would bid low again when Corey called in January 2015 looking for a website for the Donald J. Trump presidential campaign. Brad charged the campaign $1,500, and then worked overnight, hunched over his computer in his living room, on the design.

For the first seven months that Brad worked for the campaign, Corey didn't even know what he looked like. He was just a country voice on the other end of the phone. When he did finally meet him, Corey was like, "Whoa, big fella." Along with being six eight, he had a buzz cut and wore an Amish-style beard. All he was missing was a plaid shirt and a giant ax.

Together, Jared and Brad would run the entire digital operation, gaining voters and donations via the internet. When they started working together, Brad was still pretty much a low-level design guy—at least compared with what he'd become—and Jared was serving as an unofficial adviser to Trump. When the boss needed an opinion or some numbers run, his son-in-law was usually his first phone call.

Jared first traveled with the campaign in November of 2015. It was on a plane ride back from Illinois, almost by accident, that Jared and Brad would first become destined to work together, though neither one knew it.

Jared had come along on the flight hoping that he would be able to get some time with the boss to break down data for him. He did. Then, on the plane ride back, just as they were finishing up, Jared made an offhand comment to his father-in-law.

"You know, I'm not sure you're utilizing your Facebook correctly," he said.

Jared had been noticing a few trends in the way that other campaigns were using Facebook, and saw some potential. If he could learn those techniques, then use them on an online audience that was as dedicated as Trump's, the campaign would go into the primaries with a big advantage.

He offered a few more details, and Trump listened intently. After a few seconds, the boss nodded.

"All right," he said. "Why don't you be in charge of the Facebook? Scavino, you're with Jared now."

Just like that, Jared was involved. With what little experience he had in digital media and data analytics—he didn't even have his own Facebook account—he now had to work with Dan Scavino and find the best way to reach voters through their computer screens.

The first thing he did, as always, was to watch, listen, and learn. One thing about Jared that made him invaluable throughout the entire campaign was his ability, not unlike that of Trump himself, to find the experts on a given topic, make friends with them, and then soak up whatever they had to say. He was a sponge. Before long, he and Dan had done full studies on every other campaign's social media strategies, inventoried their own strengths, and decided what messages would resonate best on the internet. Jared even brought in friends from top marketing firms to give him and Scavino presentations on the microtargeting tools that Facebook offered.

It all sounded good, but nothing that he could look after on a day-to-day level by himself. For that, he'd need to find somebody with enough tech and marketing skills to take over.

It didn't take him long to think of the perfect guy.

Soon Jared was on a conference call with Brad Parscale and Dan, delegating the tasks as best he could. On Brad's recommendation, the new team of three leaned heavily on tweets and Facebook, the social media aspect of the campaign, and on online fund-raising. The advantage there, as with all other aspects of the campaign, was the passion that Trump's supporters had. They were excited, sure, but they also couldn't help sharing their excitement. You couldn't hope for more from a Facebook audience. Donations soon came rolling in at an unprecedented rate.

"People vote with their wallets," Brad would say. By paying close attention to the donations page—Does the Donate button go on the left or right side of the screen? Should it be green or red?—Jared and Brad got a pretty good idea of who their voters were and what they cared about. Trends that showed up in donations would be reflected days, sometimes hours later, in the polls.

Still, in the early days of the primary season, the campaign's digital operation had a small budget. Brad began marketing the candidate with ads on Facebook. We shot many of the videos on Dan Scavino's iPhone. Mr. Trump would just look into the camera and talk off the top of his head about a topic we'd give him.

With the data he collected from Facebook's marketing tools, Brad would target the ads, and we'd watch the traffic spike. Ad targeting also allowed us to hone our message to specific subsets of groups and accumulate data. That information would in turn become our message and policy. When Mr. Trump was out on the stump, he would know what issues the local people cared about. And, along with Trump's established greatest hits—the wall, China, draining the swamp—the digital team would recommend a local issue that pertained directly to the people who were coming to hear him.

Even later, when our video production was much more sophisticated—and Brad's budget was greatly expanded—we were getting much more than our money's worth online. We'd make internet ads for five grand and get six million views. We could get a whole state's voting population to watch a video for twenty-five grand. During the debates, Jared's assistant, Avi Berkowitz, a Harvard Law grad ran what we called *Trump Tower Live*, a live-feed Facebook talk show that we posted pre- and postdebate. The show was a hit. In the days leading up to the election, we called it *Facebook Live*, which made Boris Epshteyn, the campaign adviser, an internet star and made Kellyanne's media profile even more substantial than it already was. The whole business cost us practically nothing. Of course, we had the product that people wanted to see—the one who made them want to dance.

* * *

Though Jared and Brad's partnership began back in November 2015, the digital operation didn't start kicking ass until after the convention. That's when the RNC let us in on a little secret, one they'd been keeping for a while.

Donald Trump, emerging as the clear favorite in a field of sixteen candidates, had a good digital following and a killer Facebook strategy. But if he was going to win, he would need to reach voters of all kinds, and in all places. Luckily, the RNC had spent years working on it.

Not that it had been easy. When Reince Priebus took command of the Republican National Committee in 2011, the organization was in shambles. Its leaders had been focused for years on outdated and expensive forms of campaign messaging like old-fashioned direct mail and television ad campaigns. They knew little about their voters and couldn't collect the donations that were supposed to keep the organization running. Even through the beginning of Reince's tenure, the RNC survived on table scraps from big donors. At the end of the year, after these individuals had given to the senatorial and congressional committees, and to their political action committees and specific congressional campaigns, maybe they would throw the RNC a few thousand bucks. Back then, the RNC, like the party it represented, was reeling.

This new influx of money into politics, in the form of new organizations called super PACs, could exist only after Citizens United won its landmark case before the Supreme Court. Super PACs could take in as much money as they wanted, spend it on whatever political activity they wanted, put up as many ads on television as they could buy in support of whatever candidate they felt like endorsing. It was a kind of freedom that some had never known. For organizations like the RNC, which had become bloated and ineffective, the decision could have been a death knell.

If he wanted the RNC to survive, Reince was going to have to figure out what it could do that nobody else could. The answer, he realized, was collect data. According to the laws of campaign finance, the RNC is allowed to collect data on voters, store it, and then share that data with individual campaigns. No other organization can. Considering all the money that's now allowed in politics, it's one of the most important things—along with a solid ground game and infrastructure—that make the RNC incredibly useful. Reince redefined the mission. Under his watch, the RNC would build the most comprehensive voter file that the country had ever seen, and it would fold it all into a complex digital operation. He'd coordinate the ground game—that's people like door knockers and volunteers in small communities—and work to locate voters who hadn't been engaged in the past few elections. When it came time to name the new digital initiative, which began around 2014, Reince and his team settled on Para Bellum Labs—*para bellum* meaning "prepare for war" in Latin.

So when the 2016 election cycle came, the RNC was ready. All it needed was an army. Whatever campaign emerged from the sixteen-person field of candidates was going to have the entire infrastructure of the RNC at its fingertips. All it would need to do was flip the switch. On the book tour for her lament *What Happened*, Hillary Clinton said the Democratic National Committee's digital operation was bankrupt and inept. "It was on the verge of insolvency. Its data was mediocre to poor, nonexistent, wrong." Conversely, of ours she couldn't have been more complimentary, calling it the foundation of our ultimately successful campaign.

"So Trump becomes the nominee and he is basically handed this tried-and-true, effective foundation," she said.

Though the apparatus the RNC assembled was state-of-the-art, their ability to analyze their data would prove to be something less.

Many within the RNC were surprised that Donald Trump turned out to be their candidate. Even after he became the Republican nominee, some establishment Republicans were putting pressure on the rest of their party to disavow him. Many hoped in private that he would fail.

Part of the reason for the animus was because of a common misconception. When Steve Bannon came aboard, fresh out of the dissident world of Breitbart, some in the party believed that the purpose of the Trump campaign was to blow up the RNC and reestablish it into a Tea Party–like conservative Right. When the campaign hired Cambridge Analytica, the controversial data mining company partly owned by the Mercers and on whose board Steve Bannon sat, that mistrust only deepened. But Dave helped smooth the divide. He served as the national committeeman from Maryland, one of the 168 members of the RNC, and interfaced with the RNC daily. And by late August and early September 2016, Reince and the RNC wanted to elect Trump as president of the United States.

Enter Katie Walsh. Katie had joined the RNC in 2013, just as the Para Bellum system was being implemented, and she knew how to work it. She became the director of all finances for the organization. In 2014, using the newly designed digital tools, the RNC broke the record for the amount of money that it had raised in a single year—about $200 million. When it came time to meld this operation with that of the Republican nominee for president in 2016, she became the conduit between the RNC's and the Trump campaign's digital operations. She would correspond remotely with Brad and his team in Texas, then spend three or four days a week at Trump Tower in New York. During meetings, she was the voice of the RNC and made sure that nobody on our campaign ever felt that the Republican party wasn't behind us one hundred percent.

As the GOP nominee, Mr. Trump relied on the RNC for voter data, ground game, dedicated walkers in major cities—things we hadn't been able to afford. Luckily, the RNC had been building it all for us. All we had to do was figure out how to dovetail what we had—namely, Donald Trump and his legion of loyal supporters, "the Army of Trump"—with the infrastructure that the RNC had spent years building. It was "plug and play."

So we had Brad—who, just like Jared and Corey, has always been great about admitting what he doesn't know and then learning it quickly—sit for hours with Katie. They'd go through the technology that the RNC had built, take it apart, and then put it back together in a form that we could use. Together they figured out how to mobilize an entire ground game.

Maybe Dave said it best. During the postelection conference at Harvard's Kennedy School of Government, a symposium for the campaign managers and senior staff, Hillary's team began boasting about its digital campaign and director. "I hate to break it to you, guys," Dave said. "But Brad and Jared ran the best digital campaign in the history of American politics."

In the last months of the campaign, the data team in Texas had over a hundred people, including data scientists, Web designers, graphic artists, programmers, copywriters, network engineers, "gun-toting elderly call-center volunteers" (as a Bloomberg article called them), and others working for us in the "nerve center" of his San Antonio office. Brad also had help from big tech and social media companies such as Facebook, Google, and Twitter. He figured that since the campaign was spending so much money with these firms—about $50 million each—the least they could do was send someone over to give the campaign a hand setting up and teaching them the platforms. So they did. Whenever the team needed help with Facebook, they would call—who else?—Facebook, and the company would give him all the help he needed.

The logic was simple, and the companies were happy to comply. But it was an idea that Hillary's campaign hadn't thought of, or if they had thought of it, had decided not to implement to the extent our campaign would.

As the digital budget increased, not everybody was confident of the bang it provided for the buck—at least not right away. But winning had a way of making the boss just fine with the way his money was being spent—$100 million by Election Day. Facebook would become our biggest fund-raising tool, bringing in some $250 million in contributions. The base and the supporters would vote with their credit card every day. Ten bucks here, five dollars there. If they liked what they heard or saw, they might give you twenty bucks. For each dollar we spent on ads, we were making around $1.70 back. Most campaigns spend a dollar and make only 70 cents. But our profit was because of Mr. Trump more than anything else. The cash would go up when the candidate did something that captured the public's imagination, such as the time he visited the Mexican president. And the money would predict the polls, which spiked after the Mexican visit. Conversely, if something broke bad, like the *Access Hollywood* tape, the cash flow would dry up, and three days later the polls would take a hit. When all was said and done, everything was Trump driven. And real-time data gave us a leading edge.

By mid-September, with the digital operation in full gear, the boss focused like a laser on Hillary, and, with the Trump road show in overdrive, the polls had us pulling even. In a little over a month, we made up ten points. We also knew from our data research that there were millions of voters who hadn't yet made up their minds, many of them living in battleground states.

CHAPTER 12

THE HIGH ROAD

For centuries, the African American church has been the conscience of our country. It's from the pews and pulpits and Christian teachings of black churches all across this land that the civil rights movement lifted up its soul and lifted up the soul of our nation.

—DONALD J. TRUMP, DETROIT, SEPTEMBER 3, 2016

A FEW WEEKS before the first presidential debate at Hofstra University on Long Island, Mark Cuban, the owner of the Dallas Mavericks who appears on *Shark Tank*, went on Fox Business and said that a Trump victory in November would cause the stock market to crash.

Though much of the animus between the boss and Cuban was just the usual billionaire rivalry—Cuban offering millions if Trump shaved his head, Trump calling Cuban a "dummy"—as the first debate with Hillary Clinton approached, Cuban wasn't always down on the boss.

"I said pay attention to how DJT says things more than what he says," he said. "People hate politicians. Donald fashioned himself a killer of political correctness. A killer of politics as usual. A killer of those both real and imagined who would threaten Americans' future."

When the boss announced his candidacy, Mark thought that he would bring fresh ideas and new perspective to the White House. He touted Mr. Trump's "honesty," and said that he "had the chance to change the business of politics as a result of it." In those early days, Cuban called Mr. Trump regularly to offer advice. The day before the Republican primary debate at the Reagan Library in Simi Valley, California, the campaign held a massive rally at the American Airlines Center in Dallas, Cuban's home court. "We need new ideas. We need candor," Cuban said about Trump's candidacy. "That only comes when the candidate getting all the attention is candid and open."

But as the first general election debate neared, Cuban had a change of mind. Why he began to sour, who knows. Jealousy? There were stories in the newspapers about Cuban considering a presidential run in 2020.

"He's not smart enough to be president," the boss tweeted in February 2016.

A few days before the debate at Hofstra University, Cuban tweeted that Hillary Clinton was saving him a front row seat at Hofstra just to get into Trump's head.

Mr. Trump responded to Cuban with a tweet of his own saying he would get Gennifer Flowers a seat next to him. It was a good comeback, but it was an even better harbinger of things to come. The Hofstra debate would have its soaring moments. It would also loom over maybe the most controversial and audacious weekends ever in politics.

In the two-week span between mid-September 2016 and the Hofstra debate, the Trump campaign held rallies in at least five cities in Florida. On September 16, at a $10,000-a-plate fund-raiser at Cipriani on Wall Street, Hillary called half of our supporters "a basket of deplorables."

Mr. Trump immediately took advantage. In Miami, he told George Gigicos to play the theme from *Les Misérables* as he took the stage. "Welcome to all you deplorables!" the boss said as the crowd went nuts. We went to Hartford, Connecticut, Greensboro, and Cleveland with Don King. A big fight fan, the boss had been friendly with the boxing promoter for many years and was disappointed when he thought Don hadn't come to the convention in July. But King had come to see his friend accept his party's nomination. Dave had run into him there and took a photo of him with Griffin. When he showed the boss the picture, he told Dave to call King, which he did. The next day, Keith Schiller made sure Don King was on the campaign trail with us.

In Philadelphia, the legendary Indiana coach Bobby Knight introduced the candidate, and we played the theme from *Rocky*. We went back to Laconia, New Hampshire, where the press plane was delayed, much to the amusement of candidate and crowd. "They called and asked if we could wait," Mr. Trump told them. "And I said absolutely not."

Around this time, similar to what was done during the primaries, we started to book hangar rallies whenever we could. The campaign was making so many stops, and the motorcades to and from the events took so much time, renting airplane hangars was simply more convenient and a huge time saver. All we had to do was land, pull Trump Force One up to the hangar, walk down the steps, and climb up onto George's stage. Beautiful! We did thirty-five rallies in September, compared to seventeen by Hillary. From October 1 up to and including Election Day we did 143!

We loaded the bosses schedule with rally after rally each drawing 10,000 to 20,000 people. He'd do Virginia, Colorado,

Nevada, and Ohio, all in one day. Days before the election we scheduled a rally in Minneapolis, the Clinton campaign didn't know what we were thinking. But Marc Short had approached Dave with a poll that had us only down five in Minnesota, and the next day Dave saw another poll that had us down only three. After speaking to Steve, Jared and Nick Ayers, Dave scheduled a hanger rally for the boss in Minneapolis and a rally for Governor Pence in Duluth. When we advertised the boss's rally online the response was insane--a thousand RSVP's an hour. The hanger held 12,000 and we could have filled three times that. As it was, 24,000 people showed for the event. We ended up losing the state by only 44,000 votes and that was with Gary Johnson receiving 112,000 votes and Ed McMullen getting 53,000 otherwise we might have pulled something off not seen since Nixon.

Though Donald Trump was a draw, we had to make sure that we got the word out about his events in enough time for people to plan and RSVP. John Pence, the vice president's nephew, was working at an Indiana law firm when he came aboard the campaign. John helped come up with a system we called the "crowd-building process." Once the advance team had booked the event and the rental contract was signed, we'd go live with ads on Facebook. John and the team would create segments by zip codes, and send out email blasts. Later on, we'd buy radio ads and robocalls. And if it was a really big event, we'd have the boss tweet out an RSVP link. In all, we did 276 public events from the convention to the election. That's an average of three a day. And they all had a lot of moving parts. It was a remarkable feat of logistics, and John and the team played a big part in the success.

On September 11, during a visit to the National September 11 Memorial and Museum, Mrs. Clinton wobbled and nearly collapsed getting into her Scooby-Doo van. The health of the candidates had been a huge issue, and the video of her staggering exploded in the media. She took several days off to recover from what her campaign called "pneumonia." Mr. Trump was gracious by wishing her a speedy recovery and return to the campaign. We were gracious—for a little while, that is, as grace has a short shelf life on the campaign trail. The boss taped a segment with Dr. Oz on Wednesday, September 13, in which he presented the results of a recent physical exam he was given by his doctor in New York. The results concluded that Donald Trump was not just a horse; he was a thoroughbred—American Pharaoh, as Corey called him. In all the time we spent together on the campaign trail, we saw no indication of him slowing down, never mind being ill. Not even a sniffle. And it wasn't as if the guy was a health nut. He subsided on Filet-O-Fish and Vienna Fingers. And yet he had the stamina of an ultramarathoner. Amazing. So when he questioned Hillary's strength, and there was all that blowback about him being sexist, all of us on the plane with him knew how wrong that categorization was. Donald Trump questioned everybody's stamina! Because no one could keep up with him!

Though the schedule in late September kept everybody busy, the Hofstra debate was on all our minds. The boss had the momentum and had closed what had ballooned to a sixteen point gap in the polls by mid-August. On the one hand, we were looking forward to the opportunity. But we knew Hillary Clinton was going to be a formidable foe in the debate arena. She had debated at every level she held in politics: senator, secretary of state, presidential candidate. She debated Barack Obama, and more than held her own. Plus, she'd been prepping for months. She took three days off from the campaign trail before the debate and remained sequestered with her team in a hotel in Westchester. The Clinton team built a full-size replica of the debate stage to get her prepared. She enlisted Philippe Reines, a former staffer, to play Donald Trump. Reines was so into the role, he bought a Donald Trump signature collection watch and four podiums for his home and the DC office the Clinton campaign had set him up in. But there was no candidate alive, and probably none who ever lived, who could show up bigger in front of a TV camera than Donald Trump. Still, even though Mr. Trump had blown through sixteen tough, smart debaters in the primaries, he had never debated one-on-one or against a seasoned pro like Hillary Clinton.

The biggest worry was that Hillary would get under the boss's skin and say something to set him off. Television executives expected the largest debate audience ever, over eighty-three million.

We brought a good-size team upstairs to the conference room on the twenty-fifth floor for debate prep. Rudy, Reince, General Michael Flynn, General Keith Kellogg, Stephen Miller, Jason Miller, Kellyanne, Dave, Hope, Governor Christie, Bannon, Jared, Laura Ingraham and her associate, Pat Cipollone, a DC lawyer, all attended. At first, Mr. Trump didn't want a traditional prep. He didn't want to memorize a lot of facts or read the research. And he didn't want a mock setup with someone playing Hillary (for the second and third debate, Governor Christie did play Hillary, but that just happened organically—he was smart and quick with a retort and as informed as the former secretary of state). It was hard enough just keeping Donald Trump in the room for any length of time.

Donald Trump didn't need to prepare for the debate in the same way other candidates had, he had been preparing his whole life. When we were in Philadelphia for a rally, we went to famous Geno's for cheesesteaks. There the usual ravenous press pack attacked him on the concession he had made concerning Obama's birth certificate a few days earlier. For a second, Mr. Trump had the stare, the killer look that always made the team nervous. Instead, he faced the reporters and said, "Jobs. That's what the country needs." He then turned to the counter and ordered a sandwich. In Detroit, he withstood a barrage of insults by protesters and stayed on message to deliver an economic speech.

Though the candidate was focused like a laser, there were still moments for laughs. In Detroit, Mr. Trump made a speech in a traditionally black church, then did an interview with Ben Carson in front of the doctor's childhood home. The video of that interview became an internet sensation. Actually, the candidate and campaign team were already pulling away in our motorcade when the surprising part of the video happened. By the time the motorcade made the quick drive to the airport, the video of the interview had gone viral. Jeremy Diamond, the CNN reporter, asked Dr. Carson what he thought Donald Trump had taken away from his visit to his Detroit neighborhood.

"My luggage!" Carson said, just realizing that he'd left his bags in our SUV. He then ran off camera and after us on live television.

In the weeks leading up to the first debate, Stephen Miller and Jared spent time with the boss crafting solid, nuanced policy speeches—which was all part of the debate prep. Whatever the topic, Jared would be sure to load the speech up with facts, figures, and a few salient points that would play well as sound bites over many weeks. Mr. Trump would then give the speech, and—we kid you not—the material would stay in his head forever. Not a single detail or group of numbers would slip from his memory. Even when they'd made edits to the text, he could always recall both versions of it in seconds.

* * *

On Monday night, September 26, a crowd of two thousand packed the Hofstra auditorium. The debate commission saved some seats for the candidate's families and guests. As promised, Mark Cuban sat in Hillary's section, his large head blocking the view of those unfortunate students seated behind him. "It's as big as a beer keg," Steve Bannon remembered.

When Lester Holt introduced the candidates, the crowd stood, cheered, and shouted. It would become the most-watched presidential debate in history for good reason. The drama of the general election had been building since the conventions. Both of the nominees were "firsts," Hillary as the first woman, Mr. Trump as the first nonpolitician. Both had fervent followers, and the division between the two camps was stark. In Mr. Trump, Hillary's camp saw everything they loathed; and in ours, Hillary stood for all that was corrupt about politics.

The Clinton campaign had been pounding the boss with negative ads calling him a racist, a misogynist, unstable, crass, unsympathetic to those less fortunate, a narcissist, a thief, a cheat, a liar, and just about every other bad thing you could say about someone.

We decided to take the high road. The digital team had done analysis that showed our negative ads hurt us as much as they hurt Hillary. These ads might have made undecided voters less likely to vote for her, but they didn't make any of them want to vote for us. A few weeks before the first debate, we released our first television ad of the general election. Called "The Movement," the two-minute mini-movie was filled with American flags, soaring buildings, and bright, hopeful faces young and not-so-young alike. Even the New York Times described the ad as having "an energetic and uplifting feel."

It also happened to be true. The press and cable news had distorted so much of the story of our campaign and our rallies. Even those who conceded the size of the crowds and some who came to our rallies dismissed Mr. Trump's followers as celebrity hungry, angry, or nuts. They didn't know the feeling in those stadiums. They didn't bother to look into the eyes of his supporters. He was offering them a change they had longed for, a voice that was just like theirs—that of the forgotten man and woman.

For Mr. Trump, the debate started with a microphone problem. Though the national television audience couldn't tell, those of us backstage, in the auditorium, and in the greenroom knew that there was a problem with Mr. Trump's microphone. Whether the volume on the mic had malfunctioned or something more nefarious had happened, the mic problem was a distraction for the boss. When the sound was soft, he tried to compensate by hunching closer to the microphone. Mr. Trump, a television professional, is a marvel with a microphone. When he wants to make an important point, he grabs the microphone with his right hand and leans in closer to make sure what he is about to say is not missed. He plays it like an instrument. When the sound went bad on the road, which it did now and then, Mr. Trump would yell to George right from the stage, "Don't pay the son of a bitch."

Despite the microphone problems at Hofstra, Mr. Trump held his own and had Hillary on the defensive several times. And, in spite of her fixed smile, he was getting to her. As usual, he had some memorable one-liners. For instance, this one that set the cyber world ablaze as it related to hacking: "It also could be somebody sitting on their bed that weighs four hundred pounds, okay? You don't know who broke into DNC," he said.

The phrase "four-hundred-pound hacker" immediately became an internet meme. His "Hillary's got experience, but it's bad experience," delighted his followers too.

When the debate got testy, though, the boss found himself on the defensive. Here is the exact transcript:

CLINTON: And one of the worst things he said was about a woman in a beauty contest. He loves beauty contests, supporting them and hanging around them. And he called this woman "Miss Piggy." Then he called her "Miss Housekeeping," because she was Latina. Donald, she has a name.

TRUMP: Where did you find this? Where did you find this?

CLINTON: Her name is Alicia Machado.

TRUMP: Where did you find this?

CLINTON: And she has become a US citizen, and you can bet—

TRUMP: Oh, really?

CLINTON: —she's going to vote this November.

TRUMP: Okay, good. Let me just tell you—

[*Applause*]

HOLT: Mr. Trump, could we just take ten seconds and then we ask the final question—

TRUMP: You know, Hillary is hitting me with tremendous commercials. Some of it's said in entertainment. Some of it's said—somebody who's been very vicious to me, Rosie O'Donnell, I said very tough things to her, and I think everybody would agree that she deserves it and nobody feels sorry for her.

But you want to know the truth? I was going to say something—

HOLT: Please very quickly.

TRUMP: —extremely rough to Hillary, to her family, and I said to myself, "I can't do it. I just can't do it. It's inappropriate. It's not nice." But she spent hundreds of millions of dollars on negative ads on me, many of which are absolutely untrue. They're untrue. And they're misrepresentations.

And I will tell you this, Lester: It's not nice. And I don't deserve that.

But it's certainly not a nice thing that she's done. It's hundreds of millions of ads. And the only gratifying thing is, I saw the polls come in today, and with all of that money—

HOLT: We have to move on to the final question.

TRUMP: —$200 million is spent, and I'm either winning or tied, and I've spent practically nothing.

The Trump supporters in the room, a hefty number of whom were college students, exploded in applause.

Still, Hillary was leading with her jaw. Perhaps she thought that time had healed old wounds and that the older voter didn't care about her husband's documented history of sexual misconduct. Maybe she was banking on the millennials not being familiar with it. Even if she was correct, which she wasn't, we hadn't forgotten. The discussion whether or not to bring Bill Clinton's past into the debate had come up. The boss didn't want to at first, perhaps because he'd known the Clintons for many years and thought it would be too hurtful. And he'd also heard the voices of those who wanted him to show restraint and look "presidential"—whatever that means.

But Hillary had taken off the gloves with the ads she was running and the Alicia Machado business.

It might have been better had she kept them on. The boss was never one to shy away from a street fight. And Donald Trump is the best counter puncher to ever enter the debate stage.

Though most of the pundits said he lost (they said the same thing in just about every single one of the primary debates too), for Donald Trump, the fight was just beginning.

"Go out and spin," he said backstage. "Remember Lee Atwater, Reagan lost all of his debates!" Jeff Sessions and Don King were two of the surrogates, and he sent them into the media scrum. Kellyanne went out, as did Jason Miller. But they only set the stage for the big entrance. Having the team spin wasn't a new thing for the boss. He did the same after the New Hampshire Freedom Summit, at CPAC, and every one of the primary debates. But now we were in the general. This was for keeps.

One of the many traditions Donald Trump shattered during the campaign was the age-old custom of having only a candidate's surrogates in the spin room after debates. During the primary debates, Mr. Trump looked forward to the lights, boom mics, and crush of reporters afterward. The spin room at Hofstra, however, made the ones during the primaries look like the minor leagues. The room was the size of an airplane hangar, with every inch of it filled with press from all over the world. As the boss walked in, eight minutes after he'd left the debate stage, an electrical charge coursed through the room. Reporters, camera people, and sound people rushed to get near him. The boss was at the top of his game, smiling brightly, complementary to everyone, even Lester Holt, who had badgered him. Melania was at the boss's side.

He did an interview with Hannity as soon as he entered the room.

"All the polls look good," he said over and over.

Bannon asked Hope and Dave to ride in the limo with the boss for the ride back to New York City. Trump wanted everyone to know he'd won the debate, so he had Hope Googling poll after poll, some of which he said he'd won, some of which had him losing. When she would find one, like *Drudge*, which had him winning, she would show it to him. "You see!" he'd yell. "*Drudge* thinks I won." He also had Hope call reporter after reporter to spin a win to them.

When the national polls came out that week, they had us slipping badly, especially in Pennsylvania. The press had us in turmoil again, with "sources" from inside the campaign telling of backstabbing and mass exoduses. Other talking heads screamed that we were in a death spiral, yet again.

The week after the first debate wasn't our best. But we did raise around $18 million in donations, and we were vindicated when the Commission on Presidential Debates conceded that, in fact, the boss's microphone had been defective, though the statement they issued—"Regarding the first debate, there were issues regarding Donald Trump's audio that affected the sound level in the debate hall"—wasn't exactly an apology.

The Alicia Machado issue ran crazy in the press, and the boss didn't help matters any by raining down a small tweet storm. Kellyanne went on TV and withstood the hosts of *The View* ganging up on her and a Megyn Kelly assault. It was during this time that the boss's respect for Kellyanne was forged in steel.

No one on our campaign team was running for the door. We knew this race was far from over. It would take more than just a debate and a few negative headlines to derail us.

It would take something that none of us saw coming.

CHAPTER 13

THE HURRICANE

First of all, I'm going to win. And second, if the Republican
Party is going to run away and I do lose, then I will take you all
down with me. But I'm not going to lose.
—Donald J. Trump, October 7, 2016

BY THURSDAY EVENING on October 6, 2016, a devastating category 4 hurricane had drawn a dead bead on central Florida.
Hurricane Matthew had already killed nearly nine hundred
people in Haiti alone, and storm-hardened Floridians feared the
worst as some two million people evacuated their homes. But on
early Friday morning, just before landfall and unlike Hurricane
Irma the following year, Matthew turned slightly northward and
skirted the Florida coast like a marble following the contour of
a bowl. In the coming days, the hurricane would wreak havoc
on the coasts of South and North Carolina, causing forty-five
deaths, but most meteorologists agreed that Florida and other
southern states had dodged a bullet of catastrophic proportions.

   Though stories of disrupted early voting and the cancella-
tion of campaign ads and events in Florida filled the press, both
inside the Beltway and out, the storm actually had little effect

on the campaign. The boss sent his daughter-in-law Lara, who had been with Ivanka on the Trump Women's Tour, to North Carolina with tens of thousands of dollars' worth of emergency supplies. The campaign spent the night of the sixth in Sandown, New Hampshire, where the candidate did a town hall event hosted by the radio talk show commentator Howie Carr.

But though we were safe from Matthew, we had a storm brewing of our own making.

If the event in Sandown gave the appearance of a warm-up for the following Sunday's town hall–style presidential debate in Saint Louis, it was only coincidental. We didn't want to give the impression that we were worried about how Mr. Trump would perform in that format by holding a warm-up. The truth was, we weren't worried. The boss was terrific interacting with people. He showed those chops in the commander in chief forum, hosted by NBC's Matt Lauer, and held on board the USS *Intrepid* aircraft carrier docked in New York. It was a misconception that Trump didn't have a personal connection with the crowds that came to hear him speak. The only reason we were in New Hampshire was to keep building the momentum. The boss was at his best when he was on the stump in front of a crowd. Besides, the optics were favorable. While we had our sleeves rolled up talking to the American people, Hillary was again bunkered, this time in Whitehaven, the Clinton mansion in Washington, DC, doing debate prep.

The week following the first debate hadn't been nearly as bad as pundits predicted. Governor Pence and his team of Nick Ayers and Marc Short prepared diligently for the vice presidential debate against Senator Tim Kaine at Longwood University in Virginia. Mike Pence was magnificent. The first polls after the presidential debate, released on October 4, showed the spread not changing much at all. In fact, they continued to show that Donald Trump's base was a block of solid granite. By that night in New

Hampshire, we were feeling pretty good about where we stood in the campaign, and looking forward to Sunday in St. Louis.

When you start feeling good about things in a campaign is when you really should start worrying.

Dave was in the twenty-fifth-floor conference room in Trump Tower for debate prep when his BlackBerry buzzed. The text was from Hope. A reporter from the *Washington Post* had contacted her requesting a statement on a story they were about to run. The story concerned a transcript that had surfaced from the television show *Access Hollywood*. The reporter said the audio file would follow. The date was October 7. It was early Friday afternoon. Dave slowly slid his BlackBerry over to Bannon, who was sitting to his left at the large conference table. The Breitbart chief raised his eyebrows as he read the text, then motioned with his head for Dave to follow him out of the room. Outside the doors, Jared joined them. Hope had come up to the floor with a hard copy of the transcript.

The conference room has glass doors that lead out to the hallway. The boss could see the huddle of his senior campaign advisers. They had to decide whether or not to interrupt the prep—no small thing—but quickly decided an interruption was warranted. When they walked back in the room, the boss addressed them directly.

"What's going on?"

When the boss first read the transcript, he wasn't convinced of its authenticity.

"That doesn't sound like something I would say," he said. The reporter had tried several times to send the audio file. When he finally did, the team gathered around the boss as Dave played the video recording on his iPad.

The media's response to the recording was immediate and forceful. The *Washington Post* put the story up online at four o'clock that afternoon. Cable TV had it within minutes. Via Facebook, YouTube, and Twitter, the story traveled through cyberspace at light speed. It seemed that everyone knew about the *Access Hollywood* tape before the evening network news broadcasts.

Quickly, Hope and Jason put together and released a statement. Calling Mr. Trump's off-color remarks "Locker room talk," we kept on the offensive by saying that Bill Clinton had said far worse to the boss on the golf course and ended it with "I apologize if anyone was offended."

CNN's president, Jeff Zucker, called Corey and told him he wanted him on TV to react to the tape. Corey called Jerry Falwell Jr. to solicit his advice on what he should say. Jerry told Corey to remind America what his daddy had said, which was that we weren't voting for a Sunday school teacher, we were voting for the president of the United States. After speaking with Jerry, Corey did a phone interview with CNN and used the words Jerry recommended to defend Mr. Trump.

Tensions were as high as they were at any point during the campaign.

It was wishful thinking on our part to think the statement would be sufficient to stem a tide that was about to overwhelm our campaign.

We spent about an hour in intensive group therapy trying to come up with a media strategy. It wasn't easy. We knew we had to get something out to the press.

The boss knew that the tape was going to hurt us. But he kept a 35,000-foot view of the situation and saw it in the context of a political campaign. He didn't focus on what he'd said. He saw the release of the tape as a political maneuver by the competition. And you couldn't blame him. In the weeks leading up to October 7, the Clinton campaign had pounded us with ads that presented Mr. Trump as antiwoman. In hindsight, the buildup seemed almost like a drumroll to the big crescendo of the *Access Hollywood* tape's release. We knew the other camp certainly wouldn't be above doing something like that, or worse. They had paid over $225,000 for the Alicia Machado information a full year before Mrs. Clinton sprung it on the boss at the first debate. Also, just two days before the first general election debate, someone anonymously sent a copy of a portion of Mr. Trump's taxes to a journalist in an effort to discredit him. There was a pattern to this, and Mr. Trump believed the *Access Hollywood* tape was just more oppo research. He'd take the hit and move on, he thought. But it wouldn't be that simple.

By seven p.m., the story had reached a critical mass. Republican officials couldn't find the exits fast enough. News sites were hunting down candidates or anyone in leadership and posting lists of elected Republican officials who were publicly denouncing Donald Trump. We decided to issue a more forceful statement on camera. The team wrote it and sent it up to the boss, who by this time was in his office on the twenty-sixth floor making calls.

"Well, I'm going to know who my friends are," he said.

As it turned out, there were fewer than he thought.

* * *

We went down to the fifth floor, the cinder block bunker, where Corey had his campaign office and where we had built a studio where Kellyanne, Sean Spicer (who had joined the team), and Dave did TV hits regularly. As we were getting the set ready, the boss told Jason he wanted a teleprompter because of the length of the statement. He had started using one consistently after we hired Gabe Perez (George found Gabe by Googling "teleprompters." He made the device user friendly for the boss, learning just how he liked it positioned. He became a whiz at breaking down and setting up the teleprompter, because he'd fly with us on Trump Force One around the country). But Gabe wasn't on call that night, and the television production crew, Mike and Erik Abate and Ryan Schmidt, had already gone home for the weekend. Luckily, they were still on the road, somewhere in Westchester, when we got in touch with them. While we waited for the crew to return, someone ordered pizza. Everyone stood around in the bunker eating slices. We knew the situation was bad. The tape would have been damaging at any time, Mr. Trump thought, but just as early voting began and only a month before the election? It would be tough to erase the words the boss had said from the minds of 50 percent of the people who'd vote in that short time.

Mr. Trump came down and never sat down. Minutes ticked by like hours in one of the most stress-filled days anyone on staff could recall.

The crew arrived just as we finished the pizza. A little while later, we started shooting. It was nearly nine. We'd told Sean Hannity that we'd have the video ready for his show, which aired at ten. But at ten thirty, we were still reviewing it. When we finally got it done, we called over to Hannity. It was five to eleven. Too late.

We did, however, make the eleven o'clock news block. We had used the backdrop of the Manhattan skyline, and Mr. Trump looked uncomfortable and sounded stilted and canned. Someone, we forget who, called it a "hostage video" and the name stuck.

But it was an apology. And at least it satisfied those close to the boss.

"The words my husband used are unacceptable and offensive to me," Mrs. Trump said in a statement. "This does not represent the man that I know. I hope people will accept his apology, as I have, and focus on the important issues facing our nation and the world." People don't realize that Melania Trump is the rock in the family, and one of the classiest people you'll ever meet. Melania gave us good advice and counsel as the campaign unfolded. She became a huge asset during the campaign and we could not have been successful without her.

On Saturday morning, we had an all-hands-on-deck meeting with senior staff and Mr. Trump in his residence. Sitting around the room in a circle were Steve Bannon, Kellyanne Conway, Hope Hicks, Governor Chris Christie (wearing his trademark New York Giants gear), Mayor Giuliani, and Dave. Whether Reince Priebus was there when the meeting started is a matter of debate. He and Senator Jeff Sessions had gone back to DC after the tape came out the night before. What is certain was the heat the campaign was feeling. The statements already released ranged from Robert De Niro saying he was going to punch Donald Trump in the mouth to Bob and Rebekah Mercer's "America is finally fed up and disgusted with its political elite. Trump is channeling this disgust, and those among the political elite who quake before the boom box of media blather do not appreciate the apocalyptic choice that America faces on November eighth." The Mercers aside, most of the blowback was bad. Very bad. And no one was feeling the pressure of it worse than the RNC chairman. Reince had taken dozens of calls from very influential Republicans, like Speaker Paul Ryan, who weren't nearly as supportive as Bob and Rebekah. There were big donors, state party chairs, members of the house and senate, all calling for Donald Trump to step aside. Reince hadn't gotten a single call backing Trump.

Reince says that there was never a question in his mind whether or not to come back to New York for the meeting.

But according to Bannon, Reince wasn't in the residence when the meeting began, and he had to call him and talk him into coming. According to Steve, that conversation went something like this:

"Where the hell are you?" Steve asked.

"I got off the train in Newark," Priebus said. "I'm going to turn around."

"No you're not," Bannon said.

According to Bannon, Reince wasn't easily swayed. The RNC chair started telling him about the calls he'd been taking for the past twenty-four hours.

"It's horrible. The worst ever. People are dropping like flies," he said.

"Whether this thing ends today or not," Bannon said finally, "you have to do the perp walk."

By the perp walk, he meant the lobby of Trump Tower, which was packed with media. All of us had to walk through the squall. It was Saturday, so people were dressed casually. Rudy was in a suit but had a Yankees jacket over it; but Kellyanne, the savviest with the media of all of us, knew that the lobby was getting worldwide attention. She had her hair done, wore a smart leather jacket, and carried a Chanel bag.

Whether it's Priebus's or Bannon's version that's correct, what everyone agrees on is what Reince said when he arrived at the Trump residence. The boss had gone around the circle and asked for everyone's opinion. In looking back, Reince didn't think people were as blunt as they should have been. For a moment he thought he had stepped into some alternative universe.

When it came his time to talk, he took a deep breath. "With all due respect, sir, you have two choices," Reince began. "One, you lose the biggest electoral landslide in American history and take everybody with you, or, two, you can drop out of the race and let someone else be the nominee."

A tense silence fell over the room. It wasn't like Reince's words were so shocking, however. The same thought was banging around in everybody's head. How could it not be? That's what we do for a living: we think about options and liabilities of candidates. Still, hearing Reince say the words out loud amplified the reality of the situation. To be truthful, there were some there who expressed real doubts about Trump's chances of success. Governor Pence issued a statement that read: "I do not condone his remarks and cannot defend them," the statement read. "We pray for his family and look forward to the opportunity he has to show what is in his heart when he goes before the nation tomorrow night."

But in Donald Trump, there was no such equivocation. Mr. Trump leaned forward in his seat. His jaw was set. He looked directly at Reince.

"First of all," he began, "I'm going to win. And second, if the Republican Party is going to run away from me, then I will take you all down with me. But I'm not going to lose."

Collectively, the people around the room, Chris Christie, Rudy Giuliani, Kellyanne, and Dave, had been through scores of campaigns. But none of us had experienced a similar moment. Even if we didn't share his confidence, there wasn't a person present who didn't admire the guy's balls. Even Reince.

After the meeting broke up, we all discussed the turn of events. A few hours later we would meet again on the twenty-fifth floor for debate prep. The team decided to give an exclusive interview with the boss to David Muir. At first, we believed the ABC News anchor didn't want to do the interview for fear of how the boss would make him look, both on air and afterward on Twitter. Somebody, however (possibly his boss?) talked him into doing the hit. He'd ultimately decided to do the interview but it took Muir and his crew about an hour to get to the lobby of Trump Tower, but by then we'd changed our minds.

Meanwhile, down on Fifth Avenue outside Trump Tower, a crowd began to form. At first, we thought they must be protesters, but then Keith said: "No, they're ours, and there are hundreds of them."

"I'm going down," Mr. Trump said.

Dave called Mark Halberstadt, the Secret Service detail leader. "You're not going to believe this," he said. "But the boss wants to go outside."

Halberstadt told Dave they would need fifteen minutes. What they really needed was another full detail. When the elevator doors opened in the lobby, every camera light flicked on, and a swarm of reporters descended on Trump. Somehow we made it through the crush and out the gold-framed front doors to the chant of "USA, USA." With NYPD circling him, the boss walked straight into the throng, waving, shaking hands, and giving the thumbs-up. The campaign was back.

Just maybe, we thought, things weren't as bad as they looked.

* * *

As with most weekends, we had booked all the Sunday-morning news shows, but after the tape came out, Kellyanne, Governor Christie, and Reince wouldn't do them and you really couldn't blame them.

Still, it would have looked terrible if we didn't do at least one of the shows. Then Mr. Trump's oldest friend in the room stepped up.

"I'll do them, I'll do them all," Rudy Giuliani said.

"The full Ginsburg!" someone replied.

Named after Monica Lewinsky's lawyer, William H. Ginsburg, "the full Ginsburg" is the act of appearing on all five Sunday news programs. Ginsburg pulled off the trick in 1996 during the height of the President Clinton–Monica Lewinsky scandal.

We tipped our hats to America's Mayor. Never mind the stamina, it would take pure courage to run the Sunday-morning gauntlet. But the hero of 9/11 came through while Chuck Todd, Jake Tapper, George Stephanopoulos, Chris Wallace, and John Dickerson took turns pummeling him.

We were sitting in Trump Force One on the tarmac about to go wheels up to the debate in St. Louis when Rudy staggered onto the plane. He looked like he'd been in a cage fight. The campaign staff high-fived him as he walked passed us.

"Way to go, Rudy!" we said.

He made his way to the front and found his usual seat across from Mr. Trump. *Sure, I got beat-up*, he thought, *but it was worth it*. He believed in Trump, and he knew Trump believed in him.

"Man, Rudy, you sucked. You were weak. Low energy," Mr. Trump said to him.

"Well, I—"

"You let them talk to you like you were a baby," Mr. Trump said laughing—which is the way Mr. Trump has been known to be if he is critical of someone but can recognize the humor in a situation as well. While the criticism is real, he appreciates the situation and is the first to recognize the humor in it.

Just about every newspaper in the country—and around the world, for that matter—had the campaign's obituary on its front page. According to news accounts, we were in "crisis mode" and once again they used their favorite parlance, "death spiral." There were reports that a mass exodus was under way in Trump Tower and that even Mike Pence was packing his parachute. Speaker Paul Ryan wouldn't be caught dead being seen with us—he went so far as to disinvite us from an event in Wisconsin—and told his House members to "do what's best for you," which presumably meant keep as far away from Trump as they could. Someone recorded him on a call saying, "Cut Trump loose." News stories told of the coming demise not only of the Trump campaign for president but also the entirety of the Republican Party.

The boss responded to the negative tsunami with, as usual, a Tweet:

"It is so nice that the shackles have been taken off me and I can now fight for America the way I want to."

As Trump Force One streaked westerly thirty thousand feet above the fray, Mr. Trump sat in his seat reading the *New York Times*. Though he truly does think the paper's failing and promotes fake news, he reads it cover to cover regularly and has for most of his adult life. Mr. Trump is a New Yorker to his core.

Born and raised there, he is as tough as concrete. It was either Hope or Corey who once asked him if he ever cried. The question stumped him. He thought for some time before he answered.

"Once, I think," he said. "When I was a baby."

It wasn't the truth. But he never shows weakness.

Yes, he came from a well-off family, but Fred, his father, was a hardworking man. He made his son Donald and his siblings work as soon as they were able. It was Fred who taught him about business and negotiations and how to find opportunity in every situation, even in the direst of circumstances.

The polls that would come out on the following Monday would have us down by double digits again. Been there, done that. Not news for us—it just meant we'd have to work even harder. The boss was about to turn the campaign up to the next level.

CHAPTER 14

THE RACE TO THE BOTTOM

It used to be cars were made in Flint and you couldn't
drink the water in Mexico. Now cars are made in
Mexico, and you can't drink the water in Flint, but
we're going to turn this around.
—Donald J. Trump, September 15, 2016

ON A SNOWY January night in 2002, the New England Patriots played the Oakland Raiders in the divisional round of the AFC playoffs. Tom Brady had just completed his first full regular season as a starter. Trailing by ten points in the fourth quarter, Brady marched the Pats down the field, connecting on nine passes in a row in the frigid conditions. He ran the last six yards himself for the touchdown, narrowing the deficit to three. With time running out, he drove the team into field goal range, and the Patriots' kicker Adam Vinatieri kicked a forty-five-yarder to send the game into overtime. The Pats would get the ball first in the extra period, and the Raiders wouldn't get a chance to run a single offensive play. Brady completed another eight passes in a row to set up the winning field goal.

Two weeks later, Brady would lead the Patriots to a Super Bowl victory over the heavily favored St. Louis Rams. It would be the first of three Super Bowl wins for the Patriots over the next four years.

Ask any of us, Corey, Dave, or Mr. Trump, who the best big-game player in professional football history is, and you'll get the same answer: Tom Brady. There's just no question.

In our opinion, there's no question who the best big-game player is in politics either. Donald J. Trump.

By the second general election debate, held on October 9, 2016 at Washington University in St. Louis, the polls had us down six to seven points on average, and Nate Silver, another real genius, had Hillary with an 86 percent chance of winning the election. Unfortunately for us, those polls had been taken before the release of the *Access Hollywood* tape.

By nearly every measure, with one month to go to the election, in the fourth quarter of the race, we were in deep trouble.

The pressure on Mr. Trump was crushing. Some of the highest-ranking and most influential people in Republican politics were telling him to resign from the race. Smelling blood, the other side went for the kill, sending Michelle Obama to New Hampshire, where she delivered a withering denunciation of the boss that set Twitter and Facebook on fire. Op-eds and editorial pages across the country excoriated him. Even those closest to Mr. Trump offered little support. Any normal candidate would have had trouble showing up at an event in a high school gymnasium, never mind a debate that would be seen by a television audience the size of the Super Bowl's—over eighty million people.

What made his appearance on the stage in St. Louis even more remarkable was his lack of experience with the format in which the debate was to take place. The town hall setting, in which candidates take questions from the audience without a podium to stand behind, makes even the best debaters quake with fear. Once again, Hillary Clinton spent days in preparation. After the *Access Hollywood* tape came out, our prep amounted to a meeting at Bedminster, one session at Trump Tower, and a discussion in the boss's hotel suite in St. Louis led by Reince Priebus. What with all that was going on, it was hard for the staff to focus, but Reince did an outstanding job under difficult circumstances.

Yet in the hours before the debate, and two days after the biggest controversy in political memory, Mr. Trump was as cool as someone getting ready for dinner.

Like we said, Donald J. Trump is the greatest big-game player in American political history. Period. There is no second. None. Not in modern times. No one is even close. If you disagree, show us someone who has never run for office before, and watch him become the leader of the free world in spite of the media, some of the Republican establishment, and the Democratic Party all being against him. We'll argue with you any day of the week.

Of course, before he took the stage in St. Louis to square off against Hillary there was the little matter of settling a score.

We arrived in St. Louis early the afternoon of the debate. The first order of business was to check out the venue. The boss was still smarting from the microphone malfunction at Hofstra. He had already ripped George Gigicos's face off and was no less aggravated when we arrived at the auditorium. The boss's first target there was a young tech guy who happened to be onstage taping wires as we did the walkthrough.

"Was it you in charge of the mic last time?" the boss growled.

The young man didn't know what he was talking about.

"The mic better be working right tonight," he said.

The next targets were Mike McCurry, the former press secretary for Bill Clinton and the current cochair of the Commission on Presidential Debates, and Frank Fahrenkopf, the former chairman of the RNC and McCurry's cochair. They sat in the empty front row of the venue and, when Mr. Trump walked in, they didn't even get up to say hello to him.

"You guys fucked it up last time," the boss said to no one in particular, but McCurry and Fahrenkopf could hear him.

The commission had already issued a weak apology, and neither of them said anything in response to the boss.

After the walk-through, we went back to the hotel to have one final session of debate preparation and to give the boss a little downtime. And that's when the fun began.

Though the boss had brought up the idea in his tweets and press interviews when he said he was going to invite Gennifer Flowers to sit next to Mark Cuban at the debate, pulling the trigger on the scheme in St. Louis was all Steve Bannon's doing.

As executive chairman of Breitbart News, Steve had taken the mantle of his good friend and colleague, the courageous, charismatic, and eponymous founder of the website, Andrew Breitbart, who had died suddenly from a heart attack at age forty-three. Breitbart got his start as a conservative media marksman with Matt Drudge and the *Drudge Report* right around the time of the Monica Lewinsky scandal. He was well versed in the history of Bill Clinton's lurid sexual affairs. And, by association, so was Steve Bannon. So it was of no real surprise that Bannon came up with the idea of bringing the Clinton accusers to St. Louis.

Dave knew the Clinton scandals better than anyone. When he joined the Trump campaign in August, the press wrote about him as little more than a "Clinton antagonist"—someone who would fill his time with opposition research, looking for dirt on the Clintons. Reading the news that month, you'd think he was the Hillary Killer. It wasn't true, of course; he had been hired because he understood the boss, had developed a good sense of how he operated, and he knew how to help run a campaign. But it wasn't an unfair assumption to make.

After serving as the chief congressional investigator in the '90s, looking into campaign-finance abuses by Bill Clinton, he had become an expert on the voluminous lies and misdeeds of the Clinton family. At Citizens United, he chronicled them in books and movies, thinking it important to inform American voters about the danger that Bill and Hillary posed to American politics. The material was easy to come by. His documentary *Hillary: The Movie*, produced in 2008, the film from which his famed *Citizens United* Supreme Court case had arisen, was the latest volume on her. By the time he met Donald Trump, his head was practically an encyclopedia of Clinton scandals, though he felt that his days of tapping into it were behind him. It's an odd feeling to have expended so much film and ink on one person, only to see her keep smashing her way back into the limelight.

Still, no one was more certain than Dave that Hillary's Achilles' heel was her husband's past. For every woman who ever came forward to accuse Bill Clinton of rape or sexual harassment, there was a check to a private detective with a

Hillary connection. It wasn't enough that she made these women pipe down, she dragged them through the mud and shattered their reputations while she was at it.

She was vulnerable, though, when she tried to defend her husband. It was a no-win situation. She would either look like a victim or an accomplice. Neither option was presidential. She had surrogates, good ones like Michelle Obama, to go on the attack, but Michelle Obama wouldn't be on the stage in St. Louis. So the race to the bottom, as Dave called it, began.

For weeks, the press had been hungering for a peek into our debate prep. When Hope and Jason told them that the debate team and candidate would be available for a five-minute photo spray two hours before the prime-time debate, we were assured of a media crush. We also announced it on Facebook. Two hours before the debate, we were in the boss's suite: Jared, Reince, Kellyanne, Rudy, Steve Bannon, Hope, Steve Miller, and Dave. We had let Mr. Trump know what we had planned earlier in the day. At about six o'clock central time, two hours before the debate was to begin, Dave, Hope, and Jason left the suite to go down to the conference room in the hotel to make sure the room was set up right and to see if all the parties invited were accounted for.

The ballroom was set with one long table covered with a green tablecloth, behind which sat four middle-aged women: Juanita Broaddrick, who claimed Bill Clinton raped her in 1978; Kathleen Willey, who accused then-President Clinton of sexually assaulting her in the White House; and Paula Jones, the plaintiff in the 1994 sexual harassment case against Clinton during which Clinton's affair with Monica Lewinsky was uncovered. Clinton settled the case with Jones for $850,000. The fourth woman was

Kathy Shelton. When Shelton was twelve, she told police that a forty-one-year-old man named Tom Taylor had raped her. Hillary Clinton, then Hillary Rodham, was appointed the man's attorney and defended him in court. Ms. Shelton believed that Hillary went out of her way to besmirch her character, calling her "emotionally unstable" and characterizing her as having a tendency to fantasize about older men.

All it took to get these women there were a few phone calls and plane tickets. Paula Jones wore a baseball hat and a sweatshirt. She had just arrived and hadn't had a chance to change. She'd switched flights when she saw Chris Matthews from MSNBC board the plane on which she was originally booked. She didn't want to ruin his surprise.

Dave came back up to the suite and told Steve and Mr. Trump that it was time. We specifically hadn't told Reince about the press conference. We wanted Reince to have plausible deniability. Inside forces applied tremendous pressure on him, and we didn't want to give him more to worry about. On Friday, he'd released a statement that read, referring to the language Trump used in the *Access Hollywood* tape: "No woman should ever be described in these terms or talked about in this manner. Ever." And we'd heard that there was an effort under way to shift the RNC's funds away from the presidential campaign—although that never came to fruition.

As we interrupted debate prep and walked out of the suite, he asked where we were going.

"To see some donors," Dave told him. "We'll be right back."

When we opened the door to the conference room, the press rushed in like water from a broken dam. Though they were asked not to, they began shouting questions about the *Access*

Hollywood tape; that is, until they saw the scene in front of them. The room went from bedlam to almost complete quiet. It stayed like that for a beat or two until one reporter, John Santucci from ABC News, recognized Paul Jones. And at that moment, a collective "Holy shit" hit the proverbial fan. Sopan Deb of CBS News was literally crying when he saw the women seated at the table—he knew this was trouble for Hillary Clinton. Jonathan Lemire from the *Associated Press* and Michael Bender from the *Wall Street Journal* looked as if they were just punched in the face by Mike Tyson.

When the initial shock wore off, a reporter yelled to Mr. Trump if he thought what he said on the *Access Hollywood* tape was appropriate behavior toward women.

"Why don't y'all ask Bill Clinton that," Jones responded. "Why don't y'all go ask Bill Clinton that? Go ahead. Ask Hillary, as well."

As you might remember, the reaction in the press and cyberspace was spectacular. Much of the ink and posts were negative at first.

Politico had this to say: "Ever defiant amidst calls that he surrender the nomination and step aside, Trump is instead engaging in a scorched-earth assault that is only likely to erode further his diminished standing with women voters with potentially devastating consequences for the Republican Party, which is now bracing itself for more sweeping losses down the ballot."

Much was written and said about the nature of our campaign. How low will they go, the pundits asked rhetorically over and over. "When they go low, you go high," Hillary said during the debate. But the truth was, she went as low and we responded to her. And what made her campaign's vicious attacks on the boss even worse was the hypocrisy of them.

We had set up the press conference with two objectives in mind. One was to juxtapose Bill's actions as a sexual predator vs. Trump's locker room talk. On that count, we got almost all we wanted. Although the *Access Hollywood* tape would never fully go away, it was no longer the primary topic of discussion.

The other reason was to get into Hillary's head during the debate.

We put the women in one of the SUVs in the motorcade and drove to the event. Steve told Dave to call George Gigicos to tell the debate commission that they were going to seat Kathy, Paula, Juanita, and Kathleen in the VIP (family) box, which would have been right near Bill Clinton and directly in Hillary's line of sight.

Frank Fahrenkopf and Mike McCurry protested.

"I will get security and yank them out of there," Fahrenkopf said.

"How about if Mr. Trump just walks them to the seats on national TV?" Dave said to George.

In the end, Fahrenkopf and McCurry got their way, and the women sat in the front row of the audience seating. The tone was set. One photograph from that night captured Bill Clinton facing forward but looking sideways at the women.

In the hold room just before the debate started, Corey was waiting to see the boss when the motorcade arrived. Earlier in the day on CNN, Corey had called Reince a weak and feckless leader and demanded the RNC support Mr. Trump. When Reince came into the hold room, he came over to Corey and said, "I don't appreciate you attacking me," to which Corey responded, "support Trump, and we won't have a problem." To which Reince returned a halfhearted "Shut up." Corey elevated it to "Go fuck yourself, Reince." Reince turned around and started walking back toward Corey when Corey stepped forward and said it again to Reince only closer to his face. At that point, Keith Schiller stepped in to cool things down. Tensions were running super high in the hold room. It was a big night, and everyone could feel the pressure. Everyone except Donald J. Trump.

Staff from both camps agreed that the candidates would not shake hands at the start. The mood was ugly on both Hillary's and the boss's part. Mrs. Clinton did bring up the *Access Hollywood* tape, she had to, but her assessment of it was timid:

"What we all saw and heard on Friday was Donald talking about women, what he thinks about women, what he does to women. And he has said that the video doesn't represent who he is, but I believe that it's clear to anyone who heard it that it represents exactly who he is."

This opened the door for the boss to go on a full frontal attack on Bill Clinton. "What he did to women, there's never been anybody in the history of politics in this nation who's been so abusive to women," Trump began. What followed was a greatest hits reel of Clinton's transgressions and the cost of them, including losing his license to practice law, an $850,000 fine, and being impeached.

"I will tell you that when Hillary brings up a point like that," the boss said, "she talks about words that I said eleven years ago, I think it's disgraceful."

Game, set, match.

You could see the fire in the boss's eyes during the St. Louis debate. Donald Trump does not like to lose. Despite what the press had to say about the Trump campaign disbanding and imploding, the look in the boss's eye was enough to keep the team focused and working hard. As you've noticed, throughout this book we've called Mr. Trump "the boss." We did this not only because that's what we truly called him, but also out of respect. As bosses go, Donald Trump is the best. You can't help but feed off the man's energy and his drive to succeed. We knew that if he succeeded, so would we. We knew that because he kept reminding us of it. He brings out the best in his employees: loyalty, willingness to work, belief in his leadership. We weren't alone in thinking of him this way. Look at the people who worked for him for decades in business: Keith Schiller, Rhona Graff, and Matt Calamari, all who interact or interacted with Mr. Trump on a daily basis. Allen Weisselberg started with Mr. Trump's father as an accountant. You have to be a good boss to have that many longtime employees. And to be a boss for that long, you can't let people down.

That's why we knew he wouldn't quit, no matter what the newspapers said. Even after the St. Louis debate, the mainstream media had us packing it in. They said we deserved to lose. Twelve days before the election, a columnist in the *Washington Post* had us running "the worst campaign in history." Dana Milbank from the same newspaper wrote that not only was Donald Trump going to lose the election but also was at risk of losing his business. *Talking Points Memo* wrote that our strategy was "all over the map," and that we were desperate and haphazard. The press said our fund-raising "was out of energy" and that we were doing events in states like Wisconsin that we had no hope of winning. Even a well-known conservative pollster called the Trump campaign "a joke" less than two weeks before Election Day. And perhaps the best source giving us the bad news came from Las Vegas, where bookmakers had Hillary better than a five-to-one favorite to win the election.

* * *

And it was to Vegas where we traveled for the last debate, held at the Thomas & Mack Center on the campus of the University of Nevada, Las Vegas, the home of the college's basketball team, the Runnin' Rebels. We flew in early in the day and checked into the Trump International Hotel Las Vegas.

The press severely outnumbered us in Sin City. According to reports, over five thousand credentialed members of the fourth estate invaded Vegas to cover the debate. Las Vegas, however, has a way of sidetracking even the most dedicated journalist. Fox had a studio on the rooftop of the MGM Grand. At a birthday party for a Fox News anchor, one reporter reportedly ended up in the pool dressed in a suit and tie and with a team of synchronized swimmers.

We also had one of our own get sidetracked.

Jason worked as Ted Cruz's national spokesman up until the time Cruz suspended his campaign. The campaign hired him on June 27, 2016, to help run our communications department. Until his arrival, Hope had handled all the media responsibilities. Jason is one of the best rapid-response professionals in the business. A great guy with a quick smile surrounded by a goatee, he fit right in with the team.

The night before the debate, Miller, who might have had an adult beverage or two, visited the Sapphire Las Vegas strip club, billed as the "largest gentlemen's club in the world." We don't know whose idea it was, but going to a topless bar in Vegas, for even a family man like Jason, is a relatively harmless endeavor. But taking two female junior staffers with him, along with two members of the press, a producer from CNN, and a cameraman from ABC News who, according to Jason, promised that the night would be off the record, was pushing his luck. Still, the story might not have been more than a footnote had it ended there. Not too long ago, the tourist board of Las Vegas ran a series of ads for the city with the tagline "What happens in Vegas, stays in Vegas." Don't believe it.

A few days after his night in Sin City, Jason found his name, along with those of his staffers, Jessica Ditto, the deputy communications director, who had come from the staff of Kentucky governor Matt Bevin, and A. J. Delgado, emboldened in a Page Six article in the *New York Post*, surrounded by a detailed description of the Sapphire rendezvous.

Jason, being a professional communications executive, knew the story was going to run and had called Bannon the day before it did to tender his resignation. What bothered Bannon most about the whole story was that Jason was out fraternizing with the enemy, the dreaded press.

Now, what happens next jumps ahead in the chronology, so bear with us. We figured there was no sense in leaving you in suspense.

Everybody thinks that Anthony Scaramucci, a.k.a. the Mooch, had the shortest tenure as the White House communications director under President Trump. Not even close. He had the post five times longer than Jason.

Jason's tenure lasted exactly two days. He was offered and accepted the position on December 22, 2016, an event that was met with this tweet from Ms. Delgado: "Congratulations to the baby-daddy on being named WH Comms Director!"

According to Page Six, which took a screenshot of a quickly deleted tweet, she also called Jason, "the 2016 version of John Edwards." You might remember the affair the failed Democratic presidential candidate had with a campaign videographer.

Now, Ms. Delgado is a smart woman, a Harvard-educated lawyer, and a savvy media person. And she did good work for us as an outreach coordinator for the Spanish-language media.

She was, however, a bit of a drama queen.

In late October 2016, we stayed overnight in Doral. The Florida staff had set up an event at the Doral with influential Cuban American leaders followed by a second event, a breakfast in Miami for the Cuban American veterans of the failed 1961 Bay of Pigs invasion. A.J. was there as our Hispanic outreach coordinator. The stop was a big success, and the organization endorsed Mr. Trump. After he finished his speech to the group, Mr. Trump did short interviews with three or four reporters. When he came to the last interview, Elvira Salazar, a reporter for a Spanish-language television station, A.J. stepped in between Mr. Trump and the reporter and told the reporter that she couldn't interview the candidate. The boss didn't know what was going on, and neither did Hope or Keith who moved Mr. Trump away. A heated discussion ensued between A.J. and the reporter. Once things went sideways, we didn't do the interview, and instead headed straight to the airplane. When we were in the plane, the Spanish-language reporter called Hope in tears and begged us to come back. Our schedule wouldn't allow us to wait and do the interview, but Hope promised her an interview down the road. Later, when Hope called and asked for an explanation, A.J. told her that reporter was out to trap Mr. Trump. That it was an ambush interview. The answer puzzled Hope, who had set up the meeting originally.

That evening, we were on the jet headed home to New York when the *O'Reilly Factor* came on the big TV. What do you think O'Reilly's first story was? Bill O'Reilly starts the show with, "Donald Trump cancels an interview with a Latina journalist in Florida. We'll try to find out what happened."

"What the fuck?" the boss screamed.

And it got worse. It turned out that the Latina journalist had been completing a favorable video package about Trump that was supposed to have aired on that evening's *O'Reilly Factor*! What could have ended up being a fair and helpful piece just became a huge embarrassment.

After his election, President-elect Trump instructed the team to plan and execute a thank-you tour in key states. It was on December 15 en route to Mobile, Alabama, when the following happened: Jason and A.J. had traveled together on Trump Force One from Mar-a-Lago to Mobile to attend the rally. By this time, A.J. and Hope had been arguing back and forth about the event in Miami with the Latina journalist. A.J. had accused Hope of lying to the boss about the reason she intervened. Instead of attending the rally, A.J. chose to remain on the plane. Jason, who was walking a tightrope between Delgado and the campaign team with whom he worked, was put in a difficult position. When President-elect Trump returned to Trump Force One after the event, he asked A.J., who was still in her seat in the plane, what she thought of his speech. When A.J. told him she hadn't heard it because she hadn't left the plane, the boss didn't know how to respond. So he didn't say anything, and instead sat down in his seat and picked up the *New York Times*. Meanwhile, A.J. turned her ire on Hope, who had just about had it with A.J—Hope had simply done her job with the journalist. So Hope starts to yell back at A.J. All of this is going on as Mr. Trump is trying to read the paper. Finally, in one of the funniest moments on Trump Force One, the boss lowers the paper and yells: "Cat Fight!"

And just as quickly, he went back to reading the newspaper.

* * *

The start time for the Vegas debate was 6:30 p.m., so it was prime time on the East Coast. The local press heralded the matchup as the biggest international event in Vegas's history, and another TV audience of over seventy million was expected. We had the final debate prep in the boss's suite. Before Hofstra, the debate team had included Steve Bannon, Kellyanne, Stephen Miller, Reince, Jared, Generals Keith Kellogg and Michael Flynn (Mr. Trump's foreign policy advisers), Rudy, Governor Christie, Hope, and Dave. By Vegas, we had pared the prep team back to Bannon, Kellyanne, Reince, Rudy, Chris Christie, Jared, and Dave.

After the prep, the candidate and the senior staff made their way downstairs to the venue. Backstage, someone's phone rang. It was Matt Drudge. Someone on the senior team wanted him to talk to Mr. Trump, but no one, except Dave, knew how to pick him out of a crowd. So Dave went out into the arena to find him. On the way back, the two men walked through the bowels of the backstage, a labyrinth of hallways. When Matt and Dave turned a corner, a Secret Service agent stopped them. Now, Dave was wearing a Secret Service hard pin that identified him as being on Trump's staff. The agent told him that it was a lockdown, that a candidate was moving. Dave knew it couldn't have been the boss. And that's when the thought hit him broadside.

For twenty-five years, Dave and Matt had done more damage to the Clinton political machine than perhaps any two other living people. One thing was for sure, they were hated by the Clinton camp. And here they were, just about to come face-to-face with Hillary.

The moment got even more surreal. When Mrs. Clinton turned the corner, Bill was at her side. The couple walked straight to them and turned the corner less than five feet away.

Dave looked at Matt. "Did that just happen?" he asked.

With less than three weeks to go to the election, it would have been safe to say that the Clintons were pretty sure they were about to return to the White House. Just about everything written, spoken, videotaped, and photographed in the media pointed that way. The question in the press wasn't "if" but "by how much." An article in *Fortune* magazine reported the anxiety the Clinton campaign was experiencing, not over whether or not they would win, but rather about the number of electoral votes they would need to establish a clear mandate.

But maybe, just for a second, Hillary's anxiety was over two faces from her past.

Two weeks after the debate, we accompanied the boss to Gettysburg, where he made a speech. In the SUV on the way there he was lamenting the poll numbers he'd seen on one of the Sunday-morning news shows. The *Access Hollywood* tape and the women who had come out of the woodwork afterward to accuse him of sexual impropriety were driving the numbers down.

"Those false accusers are killing us with the women's vote," he said.

"It's not that," Kellyanne said. "It's that you fat-shamed Miss Universe."

"No, it's not. Nobody cares about that."

There was and is a false conception that Mr. Trump is surrounded only by yes-men. It's not true.

"Mr. Trump," Kellyanne said. "Women spend billions of dollars every year trying to lose weight. And guess what? They spend that amount every year because they never get it right."

The candidate looked away. He knew Kellyanne was right. She was a mother of four. A devout Catholic. She was exactly like the women who should be voting for him but weren't. The boss didn't help himself in this regard with his remarks, but he did truly respect and honor women. He was so proud of Ivanka when she made a television ad asking for women to support him.

"The most important job any woman can have is being a mother, and it shouldn't mean taking a pay cut," she had said to the camera.

"And, by the way," Kellyanne said. "Nobody remembers those false accuser's names."

"Well, I can always go back to my old life," he said. "Take a nice long vacation."

"Then we'll just argue for the next seventeen days until the election."

"Why?"

"Because we know you're going to win, and you talk like someone who is going to lose."

Despite what the fake news wrote in the papers and said on television, we were in no death spiral, there was no backstabbing, and the campaign team wasn't breaking apart. In fact, if one of us fell, the rest of us would pick him or her up.

It's hard for us to believe that Hillary's team felt the same way about each other and their candidate. And because they lacked our spirit, we had them right where we wanted them.

CHAPTER 15

FAKE NEWS

Instead of being held accountable, Hillary is running for president in what looks like a rigged election, okay? It looks to me like a rigged election. The election is being rigged by corrupt media, pushing completely false allegations and outright lies, in an effort to elect her president.
—DONALD J. TRUMP, PORTSMOUTH, NEW HAMPSHIRE, OCTOBER 15, 2016

PART OF THE VETTING process for any candidate running for public office is taking fire from the media. And when you're running for president, you expect it's going to be intense. If you can't handle tough questions from reporters and even some unfair reporting, you're probably not cut out to sit in the Oval Office.

But the fake news war waged on Donald Trump was unlike anything anyone has ever seen. Forget the liberal media's usual bias; this was an outright blood feud by traditionally liberal *and* conservative media. The conservative *National Review* published an entire issue attacking the boss. It was unprecedented.

When they weren't publishing the unsubstantiated claims of anyone who had a bone to pick with the boss or who just wanted his or her fifteen minutes of fame, they were blowing anything negative out of all proportion. Meanwhile, nobody was asking

Hillary Clinton anything but softball questions. Here was a former secretary of state who arguably destroyed the Middle East single-handedly, rushing headlong into one regime change after another and learning nothing from the disasters that followed.

When you compare Donald Trump's scandals to Hillary Clinton's, the media's demonization of Trump seems ludicrous. This is a woman who, in addition to her dismal record as secretary of state, had deleted 33,000 emails from the same server she'd used for official State Department business, acid-washed the server, and then destroyed cell phones with hammers to keep their contents from being discovered. There was the Clinton Cash scandal, her receiving debate questions in advance during the primaries, Benghazi—you would think that any one of these would overshadow some locker room talk made by Donald Trump.

They would have, if the media were after the truth, but they weren't. They were after a Hillary Clinton victory and gave the boss the coverage they did only because he was good for ratings. But one thing even Donald Trump's enemies had to admit was that he never backed away from a fight. At times, he seemed to relish them. His supporters couldn't get enough of the boss calling out the corrupt mainstream media for what it was. And for their part, the media never seemed to learn that the more openly biased they were against Donald Trump, the more resolve they gave his base.

As bizarre as the media war against Donald Trump was, the strangest part of it all was where Corey found himself after his job as campaign manager ended: right in the belly of the beast. But nothing ever distracted him from the solitary motivation for everything he did and every word he spoke for the rest of 2016: to see Donald J. Trump elected president of the United States.

* * *

In mid-October, Dave called Corey and asked him to suggest a venue for an event in New Hampshire. The Granite State was bucking a national trend. Whereas Hillary was building leads in just about every battleground state, the race was tightening in New Hampshire—down from double digits in some polls to just three points.

There are few things Corey knows better than the political landscape of New Hampshire. So when he suggested a Toyota dealership for the event, Dave suggested to George that he book it immediately. Though it happened to be a beautiful fall day, the weather had little to do with the size of the crowd that gathered to wait for Trump. The boss's diehards would have come at midnight in a sleet storm.

Colorful, to say the least, some of the Trump faithful wore T-shirts that read: TRUMP 2016: BECAUSE FUCK YOU and HOT CHICKS FOR TRUMP. The boss was in fine form, and he hit his list of policy high notes. When he got to chastising the fomenters of fake news, the dreaded media, the crowd erupted into a spontaneous "CNN sucks" cheer.

Corey had the day off from the cable news network and decided to take a ride to Portsmouth, where the dealership was, to check in on his friends. Not that he was so out of touch with them. In fact, his contact with the campaign, and with Mr. Trump, was drawing the ire of reporters and media watchdogs alike, as it had been from the day he signed on with CNN.

The reason for the displeasure at Corey's position as an on-air political commentator was partly because he was being paid simultaneously by CNN and the Trump campaign. Nearly two years earlier, when Corey had taken the job as Mr. Trump's campaign manager, he had asked for and was given a three-month severance package in his contract. When Don Jr. fired him, his severance was extended to six months, through December 2016.

Considering he was making twenty grand a month as Trump's campaign manager, the parting, at least financially speaking, was a very generous one. Every month, he got a nice check in the mail from the Trump campaign, listed on the Federal Election Commission reports as payments for "strategy consulting." This severance wouldn't have come to light at all had it not been for this odd phrasing on the FEC reports, which journalists pored over like bloodhounds, looking for mistakes. The phrase "strategy consulting" was enough to drum up some talk of impropriety, which caused the first backlash against Corey.

There would be more.

Immediately after his interview with Dana Bash the day the campaign fired him, CNN offered Corey a job, as did other networks. He took CNN's offer. Over the course of the four months he was with the cable news network, the press pummeled him for his views, which he had been hired by the network to articulate. Was he opinionated? You better believe it. So were the network's other hires like the politicos Paul Begala, David Axelrod, and Karl Rove. But on CNN, and on most other news networks, a double standard existed when it came to anything to do with Donald Trump.

Corey wasn't the only one taking the heat. Jeffrey Lord, Scottie Hughes, Andre Bauer, and Kayleigh McEnany, all Trump supporters, were taking their fair share too. Jeff Zucker, the president of CNN, who had hired Corey, was also taking his share of flak. In the eyes of many, Zucker was tainted enough by Trump as it was. He'd been the one, back when he was president of NBC Entertainment in the late '90s, who had first broadcast *The Apprentice*, which turned Trump into a prime-time star. That, combined with Zucker's willingness to carry Trump's rallies in full when no other news organization would, made him an easy target for all these aggrieved, virtue-signaling journalists looking for someone to lash out at. Plus, he did seem to like the people from the Trump campaign. They were interesting, and they made his network more lively than it had been in years.

The reporters under him didn't always agree. Many of them disliked Corey intensely. They had heard some story about how Corey once caught Noah Gray, a producer at CNN, lugging his gear around the floor of a rally instead of staying in the designated press area, and revoked his credentials, and they never forgot it. They would never let go of the Michelle Fields matter, and they certainly would never forgive the boss for the way he talked about them in front of his crowds.

Corey didn't care what they thought. Bold by nature, he was a lightning rod on television, a staunch defender of Donald J. Trump and the movement he led across our great country. He wasn't afraid to speak his mind or advocate for his old team in front of anyone, and he certainly didn't have a problem going toe-to-toe with anyone. That became necessary, considering he would usually be the lone Trump supporter on a panel of three or four people who couldn't stand the boss or him.

Though Corey didn't care what the press thought of him, it mattered to him that he kept the job with CNN. The exposure on television was good for his career, and he got to spend his days talking about the issues that mattered to him. And, let's face facts, it was good for the boss. Plus, the Trump severance wasn't going to last forever. In fact, the campaign eventually paid the balance of what they owed him in a lump sum to help put the controversy to rest.

Though the severance controversy might have been behind him, Corey's tenure with the cable network was still a roller-coaster ride.

* * *

In Portsmouth, New Hampshire, on the day of the event, Corey squeezed through the crowd and walked right through the Secret Service perimeter. He knew all the agents on duty from his days on Trump Force One, when he and the campaign staff would trade their Big Macs and french fries for the store-bought sandwiches and salads that the agents had. He wanted to be backstage, away from the cameras.

Backstage, Corey ran into Steven Mnuchin, who later became Trump's Treasury secretary and who was then the campaign's finance chairman. They watched Trump do his stump speech together, chatting from behind the stage. When Trump had finished speaking and the crowd was all but broken up, Mnuchin asked Corey where he was headed. Corey told him he had the afternoon free.

"Well, why don't you come fly with us?" New Hampshire was the first stop that day. The campaign had events in Maine and New Jersey yet to do.

Before Corey could answer, Mr. Trump walked by.

"Hey, sir," Mnunchin asked, "can we take Corey with us?"

"Absolutely," Mr. Trump said with a smile.

Corey left his car at the dealership and hopped into the boss's SUV, which had been parked in a covered area for security.

Now, most of the ire directed at Jeff Zucker was because of Corey's close relationship to the campaign team and the boss. Most in the media believed the relationship ran contrary to journalistic ethics. "He's a mouthpiece for the campaign," they said.

The media also believed that Corey wasn't worth the damage he was doing to the network's reputation. "Lewandowski is bad television," Callum Borchers from the *Washington Post* wrote. "He remains prone to spouting fiction and doesn't stay on-topic, grinding segments to a halt as CNN hosts have to correct his misinformation or interject to steer the conversation back to the point."

Zucker defended his hiring of Corey and his work on the air. He even had a cartoon that poked fun at the relationship in his office. Drawn by Sean Corcoran soon after the cable news network hired Corey, it depicted caricatures of Zucker and Trump in conversation. The dialogue balloon of Zucker that read, "Another Trump stooge on the payroll, Don Don!" The balloon over the depiction of Trump said, "Big-league move, Zucker." But, behind the scenes, Zucker made it clear to Corey that he couldn't be seen as a formal extension of the Trump campaign.

No matter what anyone said, Corey was good TV. On air, he was high energy and articulate. Plus, he knew his subject better than just about anyone in the world, especially given the direct line that he still had to Trump and people in his circle. When most anchors had a question for Trump, they'd have to speculate or wait until a surrogate could make time to talk to them. Corey, on the other hand, only ever had to answer his phone.

One time on air, Corey was debating Tony Schwartz, the ghostwriter who had helped Mr. Trump write *The Art of the Deal*. Schwartz had been ubiquitous on cable and morning news shows during the campaign, perhaps seeking to use his association with Trump as an opportunity to get his name back into the limelight. Though Corey was holding his own against the ghostwriter, after one commercial break, with a little help, he laid him out cold.

Mr. Trump had been watching the show back at Trump Tower and decided to look through some old papers to see what kind of records he had on the guy. As it turns out, Schwartz had written Trump a letter after he'd finished their book thanking Trump profusely for the opportunity. The letter said nothing but wonderful things about Mr. Trump and the experience. Unlucky for Schwartz, the boss has kept everything that anyone has ever sent him. More remarkably, he remembers where he stores all of it. He had Hope text a picture of the letter to Corey. He also told Corey to ask him how much he made from the book, which was over $1 million in 1987 dollars, and if he'd asked Mr. Trump to write a sequel, which he had.

When the program came back on the air, Corey began shooting the loaded darts.

The ghostwriter, who wouldn't shut up for the first part of the show, suddenly had nothing to say.

But this type of access didn't exactly endear him to his fellow talking heads.

Hiring Corey had placed Zucker in an untenable position. He wanted a good relationship with the Trump campaign—mostly because of the ratings it brought him—but he also wanted to keep whatever was left of his journalistic soul. Like Sergeant Schultz from the old TV show *Hogan's Heroes*, Zucker would rather see nothing when it came to knowing what Corey was up to. Oddly enough, this wasn't a position that he needed to take when it came to the commentators with ties to any other campaigns— Paul Begala and the Clinton super PACs, for instance? No, there was only one campaign that the media didn't want on television: the only one that had any power over them.

Still, with all the heat he'd been taking about the ethics of hiring Corey, the last thing that Zucker wanted to hear was that his new political commentator was catching a ride on Trump Force One.

* * *

The motorcade geared up and headed to the airport, followed by vans filled with reporters. With less than a month to go to the election, the media pool was enormous and from all over the world. The candidate's SUV arrived first, and Corey was in the jet before anybody from the press could see him. He knew he shouldn't be there, but he didn't care.

It was the first time in four months that Corey had boarded the plane that he'd practically lived on for a year and a half. And as he did, it was as though he'd never left.

Mark Halberstadt, the Secret Service detail leader for Trump, greeted him warmly and together they shared a laugh.

"He doesn't know about the dog yet," Mark said.

Corey laughed. Just like during the primaries, during the last months of his campaign, Mr. Trump ordered his advance team to book only hotels that were less than six months old. He didn't care if it was a Motel 6 or a Four Seasons, just as long as it was brand-new. He didn't like the dust. And if you sneezed around him, he would make you go to the back of the plane.

So they decided not to tell him that part of his Secret Service protection was a sweep of the jet by a bomb-sniffing dog. Mr. Trump would have exploded had he known that some wet-nosed mongrel was all over his beautiful leather seats, never mind the dog hairs that were undoubtedly everywhere.

"You deserve to be here," Mark told Corey.

Before taking the seat that had been his for eighteen months on every flight—the back seat at the table, closest to the exit, near the Secret Service—Corey went up to the cockpit to say hello to Captain John Duncan. On many long flights, Corey would pass the time in the cockpit with the pilots. Captain John always met his passengers at the door and welcomed them aboard. And he always wore a smile and had an easy way about him, even during the most hectic days filled with cross-country trips.

"Good to have you back, Corey," John said.

Of course, the gang of Keith, Hope, and Dan felt the same way as Captain John. Also on the plane were Senator Jeff Sessions, Mayor Giuliani, Eli Miller, and John McEntee. It was nice to be back with his team.

The plane took off and landed in Maine thirty minutes later, and Corey joined the campaign team backstage to stay out of sight. But a reporter from ABC News had seen him in the boss's SUV, despite the fact that Corey had worn a big ski parka and had hunched down into it. The reporter tweeted out the news.

His phone rang just as he was getting back on the plane to head to New Jersey.

"Where are you?" Jeff Zucker asked.

"Well I got good news and bad news, Jeff," Corey said. "The good news is I made my flight. The bad news is, it's on Trump's jet."

"Don't you dare get on that airplane," he said.

On either side of Corey, the engines revved. Captain John was ready for takeoff. Corey said nothing.

"I'm warning you."

The 757 began rolling, gathering speed down the runway.

"If you take that flight, you're gone."

Wheels up.

At the time, the *Access Hollywood* tape was still dominating the news across platforms, even after the press conference with Clinton's accusers. The boss and the campaign were able to tamp the story down somewhat by hammering Bill Clinton every chance they had, but the tape still dominated every other

bit of campaign news. The whole business was like an anvil pulling the numbers down to the bottom of the ocean. The boss was
fuming about it.

On the flight to New Jersey, Corey reached back into his
campaign manager's mind and, with Hope's help, came up with
the idea that he thought would solve everything—both with
Corey's job and the plummeting poll numbers.

"What's up, kids?" Mr. Trump asked as Hope and Corey sat
on either side of him.

Hope, who later became the White House communications
director, always had, and still does, an important role when it
came to making recommendations to the boss. Mr. Trump
trusts her implicitly, as well he should. She has no other agenda
than doing the best job she can for him, and he knows it. When
she pitched our idea to him, he responded immediately.

"I love it," Mr. Trump said. "Get it done."

For many campaign watchers, Melania Trump was as myste-
rious as a beautiful actress in a foreign movie. She never wanted
the attention the campaign brought. Instead, she loved her life
as a mom and Mr. Trump's wife. Couldn't blame her. She had a
full, rich life. But when her husband made the final decision to
run for president, a topic they had long discussions about, she
supported him 100 percent. But she also said that her priority
was their son Barron.

As campaign managers, we knew how powerful her presence was. Along with being beautiful and caring, Melania owns
a special allure, an honesty that makes you like her and trust her,
whether you're meeting her in person or watching her on television. Lost in the ridiculous uproar over the similarities of her
and Michelle Obama's speech at the Republican convention, the
cause of which was a speechwriter's mistake, was the effect she
had on the audience both in the arena and around the country.

A successful supermodel, she showed a kind of quiet star power that was both opposite of and complementary to her husband's celebrity.

After the convention speech, she kept a low profile. Melania's privacy made the media froth at the mouth. Just a quote from Melania was a scoop. A one-on-one interview? Just a week removed from the *Access Hollywood* tape? Please. Somebody yell, "Stop the presses!"

That was our idea. We'd get Zucker the most sought-after interview in politics.

Journalistic integrity always has its price. And in this case, the price was an Anderson Cooper exclusive sit-down interview with Melania Trump.

Without exaggeration, the story of the boss's campaign, and now his presidency, has commanded more news coverage for a longer period than any other news story in the history of cable TV. Zucker's timing is sublime. He is the president of a news network during a time when Donald Trump turned the news industry upside down. CNN, specifically, was a dead network before the boss decided to run for president. But since the boss exploded onto the political scene, CNN's ratings increased 50 percent during the day and 70 percent during prime time. For a failing news organization, of which the news industry was then littered, Donald Trump was money. And Zucker realized that before anyone else, undoubtedly because he had been the president of NBC Entertainment and had a front-row seat to watch *The Apprentice* practically salvage the network singlehandedly. Zucker wouldn't have been the president of CNN if it hadn't been for the boss. When it came to Donald Trump, Jeff Zucker had seen the act before, and he liked what he saw.

To his credit, the network exec dedicated time and resources to the story of our campaign when other cable news organizations were just catching on to the Trump phenomenon. And both those who loved and hated the boss would tune in to watch the rallies that CNN televised in full.

Corey stayed on Trump Force One that Saturday until the New Jersey event. Then he hopped a flight to Boston and took an Uber to his car in Portsmouth. That Monday night, Melania did the prime-time interview with Anderson Cooper at Trump Tower. CNN had flown Cooper back from California in a private jet just for the broadcast, and they never told him how it was arranged.

How much the Melania interview affected the sea change that happened over the next few weeks is hard to say. It had to have helped. So did the letter to Congress from FBI director James Comey about the newly discovered emails pertinent to the investigation against Hillary, which would come a week later.

In spite of what's been written and reported ad nauseam, the Jim Comey letter wasn't the reason for the outcome on Election Day. By the end of October, we knew from the data team's numbers that Mr. Trump had already begun to draw even with Mrs. Clinton—and we knew we had the momentum. The Clinton team was so confident (or arrogant) about their certain election victory they failed to poll in the final weeks of the campaign.

It was four in the morning on November 9 when Corey headed back to the George Hotel, where his bag still sat unpacked. He had just resigned from CNN. During a commercial break, Jeff Zucker had told him he needed to be magnanimous and respect his colleagues.

"Bullshit, Jeff," he said. "We won."

When he signed off that morning, he made his departure from the network official and permanent.

In the cab to Reagan National, his thoughts went back to the spring of 2014, and to the Freedom Summit held at "the Yard" in Manchester, New Hampshire. It was there where Dave first introduced Corey to Donald Trump. Earlier in the evening on election night, he'd talked to people in Manchester. He knew the ballroom was filled again, this time with foot soldiers of the Trump campaign who had gathered to watch the results. For Corey, Manchester was the bookend of this most improbable story.

As Donald Trump's campaign manager, Corey had reached a place few in his profession have been. The connection to his political roots in New Hampshire never wavered. He knew that it was the people of New Hampshire, and of Florida's panhandle, of eastern Ohio, Pennsylvania, Montana, and other places like them who were the reason Donald Trump was president.

By eight a.m., Corey was at the front desk of a hotel on the Upper West Side of Manhattan. He hadn't known he was going to New York, so he didn't have a reservation and had to go on Hotels.com. The receptionist informed him that his room wouldn't be ready until four in the afternoon. At that point, he'd been up for forty straight hours. He went to the gym in the hotel's basement to wash up. He was in the small bathroom changing his shirt when his phone rang. It was Donald J. Trump.

"Yes, Mr. President," Corey answered.

"Corrreee!" the new president-elect said.

"Sir? Did you hear what I just said? You're the fucking president of the United States!"

"Can you believe it?"

"No, sir, I can't."

"Me neither. When we started this thing, it was you and me, and an airplane. That's all we had."

"And we had Hope," Corey added, referring to Hope Hicks, the campaign's first communications staffer.

"She had about as much experience as a coffee cup."

"But she's good-looking," Corey said.

"That always helps," he said.

The president-elect told Corey to come over to Trump Tower.

"Corey," he said just before he hung up. "I wouldn't be here without you."

And that was true.

Before anyone else, Corey realized how Donald Trump could pull off the unimaginable. That moment came early in the campaign, when Corey was still in the tiny office on the twenty-fourth floor of Trump Tower that he shared with a couple of interns and Sam Nunberg. On the whiteboard, he wrote a simple reminder to himself and anyone else who had the candidate's ear. Those words stayed on the whiteboard as long as Corey was campaign manager. More than any other strategy, more than Bannon's America First nationalism, more than Jared and Brad's digital campaign, more than Dave's brutal schedule, and more than James Comey's or any other October Surprise, Corey's four-word phrase was the reason Donald Trump won the election:

"Let Trump Be Trump."

Later that afternoon, running on pure adrenaline, Corey stood across the street from Trump Tower. In a sea of people, he looked at a building transformed. Dump trucks from the New York City Department of Sanitation, one abutting the other, formed a ring around the tower. US Army personnel with assault rifles manned metal detectors. The transfer of power had begun. The crowd, protesters mostly, were vile and angry. Corey was too tired to care.

A little less than two years before, he had stood at the very same spot looking up at Trump Tower. That day he was about to interview for a job to manage a campaign he thought would never happen. Now, Donald J. Trump was the president-elect of the United States.

Somehow he made his way past security. The doorman manning the desk in front of the elevator greeted him like the old friend that he was.

Dave was sitting at his desk in what was now the office of the presidential transition and looked up to see Corey in front of him. As they hugged, they both said the same thing at the same time: "Can you believe this?"

For both of us, the 2016 campaign was the ride of a lifetime. And for the most part, all we had to do was to be in the right place at the right time. It wasn't as though we were shocked that Donald Trump was elected president; we'd left everything on the field to help make that happen. Rather, we just couldn't believe our good fortune to have played the small part in it we did.

THE END

THE TRANSITION

You need people with heart. That's probably the one thing you need in government that they don't have in business, not quite as much. You need some, but not a lot.

—DONALD J. TRUMP, ON HIRING A STAFF

A COUPLE of weeks after the election, while Dave sat in the campaign office in Trump Tower with Bannon, Johnny McEntee walked in and told us he was going to order dinner for the boss. It was nearing seven o'clock in the evening. Most of the volunteers and full-time staffers had gone home for the day. The feeling in the room was starkly different from the roller coaster of emotions it held on election night.

"What's for dinner tonight, Johnny?" the president-elect had asked. He'd been taking meetings with potential cabinet secretaries and working the phone since morning, and it was nearly time for him to take his nightly elevator ride up to the residence, where he could watch a little news and have his dinner—then get back on the phone.

"I'll go to the Carnegie," Johnny said. The famous deli, just a few blocks from Trump Tower on Seventh Avenue, had announced that it would soon close its doors for good. Johnny figured he should have one more pastrami on rye from the Carnegie while he still had the chance. They make a nice sandwich.

Dave had never had one of their sandwiches. "I'll have the same as the boss," he said.

Priebus and Bannon had been trying to figure the best way to go about the difficult business of a presidential transition. They had been going through candidates for cabinet positions for a few days, mostly wondering where to start and how to get organized. Bannon was leafing through a book called *The Romney Readiness Project*, that Dave had found in his desk drawer beside a small pile of ketchup packets on his first day working in Trump Tower. It was a comprehensive manual containing suggestions for staff hires and budgetary guidelines, as well as a clear guide to thousands of presidential appointments that the Romney team created to help staff their own White House had they won the 2012 election. Bannon had read through it several times already, and had highlighted a few useful things. If nothing else, the book gave the Trump campaign a blueprint on how to organize itself, and some sense of what to tackle first and how to properly allocate the federal government's funds.

Not many people are aware of this, but the Trump transition didn't have much to work with on its way in, especially when it came to money. By November 2016, the Obama administration had used up about 78 percent of the White House budget for its fiscal year, which begins and ends at the beginning of May. Meaning, the Trump transition didn't have much to work with, and it left us only 22 percent of the budget, or about two and a half months of money, to pay federal salaries and upkeep costs from January 20 until the end of April. That meant, among other things, that we would have to go light on the lower-office appointments, at least for a little while.

On top of that, the details and rituals of the transition itself were all new to the team. During the campaign, for fear of bad juju, we were never allowed to talk about what a Trump White House would look like, never mind a plan for one.

"Remember Romney?" the boss would say. "He was walking around in khakis with his transition team, and what the hell did it get him? I'll tell you what! He lost!"

He had a point. Just as the 2012 campaign was heating up, Mitt Romney had decided he would take two weeks off to focus on the plans that he would implement if—or, in his mind, when— he won. Trump, on the other hand, wouldn't take so much as a minute off to focus on his post-victory plans. And he wouldn't let anyone else who worked for him do it either. In fact, until Chris Christie, who was in charge of the transition team during the campaign, began raising funds, Trump wasn't even aware that he had a full-time, functioning transition team. A federal statute mandates that presidential candidates raise funds to help pay for transition offices and staff should they be elected.

Under Chris Christie, the team made only a few major moves and appointments, one of which was the hiring of Bill Hagerty as director of political appointments. Hagerty, a private-equity investor from Nashville, had done the same job for Mitt Romney's transition team in 2012.

Today Hagerty is the US ambassador to Japan.

About a half hour after he had left, Johnny McEntee walked back into the campaign office.

"Where is the inauguration committee's office?" he asked Bannon.

"I have no earthly idea," Steve said. "I . . . would imagine it's in DC. Why?"

Johnny put the sandwiches down on a desk. "The boss just put me in charge of the inauguration. I need to get on a train to DC."

Dave and Steve looked at each other, and then let out a laugh.

As told, Johnny had brought the sandwich up to the residence. When he got there, Mr. Trump was nowhere to be seen, but the next first lady, Melania, was in the living room with Stephanie Winston Wolkoff, a tall, elegant woman who played an integral role with Mrs. Trump planning the inaugural activities. Mrs. Trump had her phone on speaker and was talking into it about the inaugural.

"Hello, Rick Gates," Melania said to the voice on the phone.

At that precise moment, the president-elect walked into the room.

"Rick Gates!? Where is he?"

"He's on the phone, Donald," Melania said.

"Gates, are you there?"

"Yes, sir."

"What are you doing talking to my wife?"

"I'm in charge of the inaugural, sir."

"Not anymore you're not—you're fired."

Trump looked up and spotted Johnny, wide-eyed in the doorway, holding a bag of pastrami sandwiches.

"Johnny!" he said. "You're in charge of the inaugural now."

When they had gotten control of their laughter, Steve and Dave assured Johnny that he wouldn't be running anything alone in DC. Dave also thought to ask Cassidy, who had been his assistant since just after he joined the campaign, to get a handle on the inaugural organization and report back to the Tower. Cassidy had done an amazing job overseeing logistics and tickets for the three presidential and one vice presidential debates. Together with Tom Barrack, whom Trump named chairman of the inaugural, Cassidy and Boris Epshteyn, communications director for the inaugural, got to work right away. As for Rick Gates, who'd gotten the job via his close personal relationship with Paul Manafort, forged when they worked together in Ukraine, arguably stealing money, and then meeting Tom Barrack? It's really no surprise that he somehow hung onto his job with the transition team.

The transition was a bittersweet time for us. After Election Day, working with Steve and Reince, Dave made several recommendations for all the top jobs and even sat in on some interviews for major cabinet appointments where he gave his counsel during the hiring process. It was a huge honor and an awesome responsibility, and Dave relished the role. The president conducted some of the interviews at Trump Tower but as the Thank You tour wound down, a week before Christmas he moved the interviews to Mar-a-Lago.

Sometimes Dave would also meet the candidates when they arrived at Mr. Trump's private club. They turned the tea room of Mar-a-Lago into a waiting area. Madeleine Westerhout, Katie Walsh, and Dave would keep the candidates entertained until it was time for their interview. Mr. Trump, Jared, Steve, and Reince Priebus would see five to ten candidates a day.

One day in the holding area, Dave got to meet Dr. Toby Cosgrove from the Cleveland Clinic, who was up for VA secretary. Cosgrove was eminently qualified for the position. He had been a US Air Force surgeon during the Vietnam War and was awarded the Bronze Star. And he ran the Cleveland Clinic, a big, sprawling network of hospitals with over fifty thousand employees and an operating revenue of $8 billion. One of the hospitals in his network was the Washington Hospital Center, where surgeons had operated on Dave. While they waited, Dave mentioned his surgery.

"What did you have done?" Cosgrove asked.

"Mitral valve," Dave said.

"Replaced or repaired?"

"Repaired."

Dave then took out his wallet, removed a medical alert card, and handed it to the doctor. Right away, Cosgrove must have seen the details of the procedure in his head. He knew what it had taken Dave a few weeks to find out: that there was a synthetic ring implanted in his heart, helping the mitral valve open and close.

"Oh yeah," Cosgrove said. "I invented that." Dave laughed. What were the chances? They got to talking about other things, then Cosgrove circled back around to the heart surgery.

"By the way," he said, "who operated on you?"

"Dr. Louis Kanda," Dave answered.

"Oh, Louis! I trained him and he's a good friend."

When the president-elect came out to meet Cosgrove, Dave told him that the doctor had trained his heart surgeon. The boss didn't look surprised.

"Who haven't you trained, Cosgrove?" Mr. Trump said with a smile. "He's the best." The president-elect then told them that Cosgrove had been involved in his brother's heart surgery. Cosgrove would end up removing his name from consideration for the cabinet position.

One of Dave's biggest highlights of the transition was planning and attending the president-elect's trip to the annual Army-Navy football game, held that year in Baltimore. Dave brought Griffin. Also attending was Reince and his son, Jack, and Steve Bannon and his daughter, Maureen, a West Point graduate. For the first half, they watched the game from David Urban's suite on the Navy side. One of the things we haven't mentioned about the boss so far in this book is his presence. Any time Donald Trump walks into a room. he owns it. But it was striking to see him have the same effect on a booth filled with three- and four-star generals: the Joint Chiefs of Staff.

"They're like little kids around him," Bannon remembered.

At the half, we visited the television team of Gary Danielson and Verne Lundquist in the booth. As the boss's image was shown on the jumbotron, the stadium, filled with cadets and midshipmen, erupted in cheers, followed by chants of "USA, USA."

That game happened to be Lundquist's last as a college football broadcaster. Danielson mentioned to Mr. Trump that Verne might be looking for work, and seeing as he was of Swedish descent, perhaps the president-elect might consider him for the job as ambassador. Mr. Trump played along.

"Just make sure he's available for the Masters," Danielson said about Verne's annual pilgrimage to Augusta to help call the prestigious golf tourney.

"We have to have him for the Masters, absolutely," the boss answered. "I think Sweden would be very happy." It was just a feel-good moment for everyone and terrific television.

At halftime at the Army-Navy game, it's customary for the commander in chief to switch sides, so after wrapping up the Lundquist interview, we made our way over to Ollie North's box in Army territory for the second half.

"Ah, that was great," Mr. Trump said to Dave on the way.

"Yeah, too bad Verne supported Hillary," Dave answered.

"What?! I wouldn't have done the interview had I known," Mr. Trump said jokingly.

But there were disappointments, too, during the transition, and the sheer number of outsiders who managed to sneak their way into the ranks was perhaps the biggest disappointment. Some of those were people who had never fully supported Donald

Trump when he was a candidate, and many of them had actively worked against him during the campaign. The president-elect always knew who was loyal.

We had dinner at Mar-a-Lago the same night Congress certified the Electoral College results. A famous photo of the team was taken that night to commemorate the evening.

Despite internal competition, Reince had been named White House chief of staff, and he had managed to convince the boss that it was time for him to embrace the Republican establishment and the Priebus team along with it. Paul Ryan and Mitch McConnell each made a few calls on Reince's behalf, telling the president-elect that he would need a Washington insider in the White House if he wanted to move his agenda forward. While Reince was at the RNC, they said, he had put together what amounted to a West Wing staff. He was ready to plug it into the White House. The president-elect, acting in the spirit of unity, decided it was a good move.

To tell you the truth, the establishment/outsider distinction never mattered all that much to Trump. In his mind, people arc placcd into two distinct categories: loyal and disloyal. Once you're in the second category, it's hard to climb your way out.

So when Reince started talking up Sean Spicer, suggesting that he'd be a good fit for White House communications director, and proposed Katie Walsh as Reince's deputy, Trump was leery. He remembered the days before the election when he was told that Spicer and Walsh went to the media and put as much distance between themselves and the candidate as they could.

"He's not loyal," Mr. Trump said about Spicer. Ultimately, Mr. Trump took Reince's advice, and hired Spicer, but he never forgot. "Imagine that somebody would bad-mouth me before the election and then want a job with me after!" the president-elect marveled out loud.

Though Sean Spicer wasn't at the dinner, Katie Walsh was. After Mr. Trump made the remark, she left the celebration. A famous photo was taken of the Trump team the night of the Electoral College certification.

We were glad to see some of the old team getting ready for their new posts in the White House. It was clear from Election Day that Hope Hicks and Keith Schiller would have jobs with the boss in the West Wing,. And the same also went for Dan Scavino and Don McGahn.

We watched as our friend George Gigicos was offered and took the post of White House director of scheduling and advance. We got to see Johnny McEntee become Trump's body man, looking after his schedule and traveling everywhere with the boss. There were spots for Meghan and Cassidy. And it was no surprise that Bannon and Kellyanne would take senior positions in the new administration. The critical post of Attorney General was given to the first United States Senator to endorse Trump, Jeff Sessions.

As for us?

There was much discussion, both privately and in the press, about senior staff positions for each of us in the White House. The prized job of RNC chairman went to Ronna Romney McDaniel, whom neither of us knew very well, and most of the other jobs we could have done were filled, as Reince had promised, with a whole slew of former RNC staffers. Forces were put in place that wanted to make Donald Trump into a Washington DC Republican with a typical establishment staff—that didn't work out very well.

Prior to the inaugural, the boss had called Corey and told him he had a seat on the platform for the swearing-in ceremony. "Just not too close to me," the president-elect said. "They only want good-looking people in the camera shot." Dave had worked with Cassidy on the seating chart and knew he and Corey had seats on the platform.

But when we arrived, we found ourselves, along with Jeff DeWit, in seats next to a college band one level up from the Presidential Platform. It wasn't that bad, but it certainly wasn't where we expected to be seated. We called Kellyanne, and then Bannon, whom we could see down on the platform. Both told us that there were seats for us there, so we moved.

We watched the swearing-in of the forty-fifth president of the United States from a spot few in the world will ever experience.

We never took one moment for granted working for the boss.

IN THE OVAL

Words cannot measure the depth of their devotion, the purity
of their love, or the totality of their courage. We only hope that
every day we can prove worthy not only of their sacrifice and
service but of the sacrifice made by the families and loved
ones they left behind. Special, special people.

—DONALD J. TRUMP, FROM HIS REMARKS AT THE TOMB OF THE
UNKNOWN SOLDIER, ARLINGTON NATIONAL CEMETERY,
MEMORIAL DAY, 2017

BARELY MORE than a month after he took the oath of office,
President Donald Trump was addressing Congress in his first
speech to a joint session. They don't call a president's first one
a "State of the Union address," since it's assumed that a newly
elected president hasn't had time to determine the state of the
union in such a short time.

That might be true for most incoming presidents. After all,
they're usually politicians. But the boss was a different animal
altogether. Not only was he already aware of the state of the

union, but he had also already taken significant action toward improving it, within the limits of the office he was elected to. The very first thing he did as president, on his very first day, was to issue an executive order that effectively relieved Americans of the worst effects of Obamacare. Not only did it direct the IRS to waive penalties on people who didn't carry insurance compliant with the disastrous law, but it also directed other departments in the executive branch to administer the law in the least harmful way to employers and individuals.

In the days and weeks immediately following his inauguration, he wrote orders to require repeal of two regulations for every new one created, to empower border control agents to do their jobs more effectively, and, most controversially, to institute a temporary ban on refugees from certain countries with a high penetration of Islamic terrorism.

We say "most controversially" because that is how the fake news media portrayed it to the American public. Forget that President Obama had for all intents and purposes issued the same order regarding the same seven countries a few years earlier. The reaction to the boss's order foreshadowed the way every attempt of his to keep his campaign promises was going to be treated by the press.

The new president had also issued orders to restore federalism and the rule of law in regulating US waterways, to promote excellence in historically black colleges and universities, to promote energy independence and economic growth, and to do a host of other things. And every order that posed even the slightest threat to the corrupt status quo was misreported, exaggerated, or demonized, to the extent the media were able to do so.

Nevertheless, when the boss walked up to that podium and began to speak that night to the joint session of Congress, it was like election night all over again. Even his critics admitted afterward, in their own left-handed way, that Donald Trump had once again struck a chord. He was, to use the media's worn-out phrase, "presidential." And he once again laid out the legislative agenda that had propelled him into the White House, an agenda he would have to drain the swamp—or wade through it—to achieve.

By that time, we thought our active part in that agenda was over, but the boss had other plans. He knew he was going to need people around him loyal not only to him, but also to the Make America Great Again agenda he'd run on.

President Trump, still "the boss" to us, though we hadn't technically been his employees for a while, reached over to a small wooden box in the corner of the Resolute desk, emblazoned with the letters POTUS, and pressed the little red button on top.

From the adjoining kitchen, a naval steward entered the Oval Office, carrying a tall glass of Diet Coke with ice. For years, Donald Trump has imbibed a steady stream of Diet Coke. He took a sip, then placed the glass in front of him on a coaster. Even with all the pressure that being the leader of the free world brings, he'll never stop being Donald J. Trump. There is something very heartening about that.

"You want?" he asked us. Both of us said, "Yes sir!"

The boss had just returned from his first trip abroad as president of the United States. Among the places he visited were Saudi Arabia, Israel, and the Vatican. By all measures, the trip had been a success. In one nine-day stretch, he had all but erased the Obama-era "lead from behind" doctrine in the minds of the leaders with whom he'd met. And while the whole world watched, he brought back to the American presidency a respect that had been sorely missing for a long time. The trip also had provided a badly needed break for President Trump, who had been under siege by the mainstream media for years, an onslaught that had only intensified with the one-sided coverage of his presidential campaign. These reporters had no interest in covering the new administration or letting things play out; they wanted to bring it down, and they couldn't do it alone.

Someone close to the Oval Office was leaking information, probably multiple people. They were doing it often and with purpose. It was becoming impossible for the senior staff to know who they could trust—even, sometimes, whether they could trust each other. This was in stark contrast to the way things were during the campaign. Steve, Reince, Jared, and the rest of the senior staff had all worked as a team to help get the boss elected.

Finally, the boss got down to it. "I'm not happy with my staff," he said.

"Well, sir, that's why we're here," Corey answered.

"I'm doing a great job, but my staff sucks."

It had been a rainy morning in Windham, New Hampshire, where Corey lives with his wife, Alison, and their four children. He had watched his daughter Abigail's Girl Scout troop march in a Memorial Day parade, which took place inside a local gymnasium. On the campaign trail, he once went seventy-three days straight without going home. He loved seeing his kids every day and made a promise to himself that he would try not to miss any more of their childhoods. It was a promise that would be hard to keep. After the parade, he drove to Logan Airport in Boston and caught a flight to Washington, DC.

Dave also had plans with Susan and the kids to visit Dave's parents for the holiday. Instead, he drove about forty-five minutes into the city from his home in Maryland. When the boss wants to see you, you drop everything and go.

We met at Peet's Coffee at Seventeenth and Pennsylvania. Corey threw his bag into the back seat of Dave's Chevy Suburban, and we walked over to the White House together.

In the West Wing, we met first with Steve Bannon, the chief White House strategist, and Reince Priebus, the White House chief of staff. In his office, Reince and Steve told us what our meeting with the president would be all about. We had a pretty good idea why President Trump wanted to see us. We had met with him together many times since the inaugural and separately on a few other occasions. We knew he relied on us to carry his message on television. We also knew that he trusted us. Multiple times during his trip abroad, and even during the plane ride home, the boss talked about bringing us in to restore order to the West Wing. He wanted to put together the team that had won him the white house.

Reince and Bannon told us that the president wanted Dave to be deputy chief of staff, with broad authority over a vast portfolio. He would report only to Priebus and the president. Corey, per their plans, was going to oversee political operations, presidential appointments, and the RNC, as well as the campaign's handling of Russian meddling in the 2016 election. He would be at the same level as Jared, a senior adviser.

"It's all buttoned-up," Reince said. "A done deal."

It was an incredible opportunity. Like a kid in Little League who dreams of playing in the World Series, just about everyone who goes into politics imagines himself or herself working in the White House someday.

Still, here's the thing we know about our president: from his first official day in politics, which at this writing is still only a little more than two years ago, people have tried to make him into something he's not. Donald Trump is not, nor will he ever be, a part of the establishment. He's not, nor will he ever be, a politician in the traditional sense of that word. And he is not someone who goes back on his word.

For Donald Trump, loyalty is the currency of the realm, and nothing hurts him deeper than when someone he trusts is disloyal.

Back in the Oval Office, Dave told the steward to make sure his Coke was a regular. As Donald Trump's deputy campaign manager, Dave was served a dozen Diet Cokes since their first meeting in 2010, which he doesn't drink, because the boss had ordered them for him. When the steward handed us the Cokes, we realized there was no place to set the glasses down. We weren't going to put them on the Resolute desk, which was a present from Queen Victoria and had first appeared in the Oval Office when Rutherford B. Hayes was president. And we were not about to put the glasses on Ronald Reagan's rug, which President Trump brought back to the Oval when the staff asked him for his furniture preferences in January. So we sat there holding the Cokes in our laps like schoolboys holding flowers.

Even when you don't have a beverage sweating onto your pants, sitting in the Oval Office with the leader of the free world is intimidating. It can make you feel overwhelmed. The view through the window alone, of the famous rose garden in full bloom, is enough to stop even powerful men in their tracks. For us, however, that feeling disappeared quickly, and it was as though no time had passed.

The three of us, and the rest of the core campaign staff, had forged the closest of relationships. And, as a candidate, the president thrived in that chummy, devoted atmosphere. It's the reason that he wanted to spend so much time among the folks when the rallies were over, why he insisted on visiting the smallest corners of every battleground state while Hillary was giving speeches to bankers and vacationing in the Hamptons.

Corey told the president that we had seen Priebus and Bannon and that they had told us about the new roles—Corey as a senior adviser, Dave as Deputy Chief of Staff—that Trump supposedly had in store for us.

"Yeah," the president said. "I don't like that idea."

We looked at each other.

While working on Donald Trump's campaign, there were more *What the fuck just happened?* moments than we can count. And now another one had just happened.

The president leveled Dave with a stare.

"Who's the leak?" he asked.

The two of us exchanged nervous glances.

"I don't know, sir," Dave said. "I don't work here so I don't know, but I assume there's an internal . . ."

He didn't wait for Dave to finish. "Corey, who's the leak?" he said.

"Mr. President," Corey said. "It's probably some low-level communications person trying to gain access and power."

The president looked at Corey with his head tilted slightly, another patented expression. This one's the don't-bullshit-me look.

"I know," the president said. "I think I know. I know. I *know* who the leak is." The president then said to the two of us, "I don't want either of you in here now, because if this place isn't working better in the next four to five weeks, I'm firing everyone. Reince can go to Greece."

In that moment we realized that the rumor we had heard about Reince becoming the ambassador to Greece came from the West Wing.

Corey took the opportunity to tell the President about Tiger Woods, who had been arrested the night before for driving under the influence. He showed the president Wood's mug shot on his phone.

"It was the back surgery," the president said. "I knew he shouldn't have had it." He explained how easy it is for people to get addicted to painkillers after surgery, which is what he believed had happened to Woods. "He's a nice guy, and was on top of the world," the president said, shaking his head as he looked at the mug shot again.

Just then, the chief of staff walked into the Oval Office.

With the Resolute Desk blocking the president's view, Dave tried tapping Reince on the knee to get his attention. Priebus didn't get the hint.

"So, Mr. President, we're all set. Corey is going to come in and run the Russia investigation, and Dave is going to be deputy chief of staff."

President Trump leaned back in his chair. "Reince, we're all friends here," he began. "But if this place isn't working better in the next four weeks, I'm going to make some changes around here and the first change is you."

"But I thought we had a plan," the chief of staff said.

At that moment, Hope and Kellyanne walked into the Oval and the meeting was over.

We walked back to the chief of staff's office, where Bannon was waiting. The four of us reviewed the meeting and we informed Steve that the president had named him as one of the suspected leakers. We also told them to quickly get the building buttoned up or Reince will be enjoying Greece soon.

"Fuck," Bannon said. "I thought you two were my ticket out."

"Wait, what?" Dave said. "You were going to leave just as we came in to help you?"

"Good plan, right?" Bannon said. "I was punching out. I've gotta get out of here."

After our surreal meeting in the Oval, we walked out the front gate of the White House, past the media tents and back to Peet's, where we climbed into Dave's truck. Corey had booked a room in a nearby Marriott. By the time we pulled in front of the hotel, our visit to the West Wing was already taking a viral spin around the twitterverse. A CNN producer had spied us walking from the West Wing of the White House and sent out a tweet. We were "in suits," the tweet emphasized, the inference being that we had come dressed to meet with the president.

In the hotel, we took the elevator up to the concierge level, where they offered a nice antipasto bar for guests. Dave was on the phone with his wife when Reince called him. By the time he clicked off with Susan, the White House chief of staff had already hung up and was ringing Corey. Dave told Corey not to answer his phone when he saw it was Reince. Corey answered anyway. He then watched as Corey listened and started shaking his head.

"He just talked to the boss, he wants us back in," Corey mouthed.

The best explanation we could come up with was that Hope Hicks and Kellyanne, who had come into the Oval just as the president brought the meeting to a close, had talked him back into bringing us on board again. We were still parsing the likelihood of that scenario when Kellyanne Conway, followed by her Secret Service detail as well as by a few admirers and onlookers, walked into the lounge. She had called Corey while we were on our way to the hotel and asked where we were headed and said she wanted to meet us for a drink.

We pushed a couple of tables together. For a moment, it was like being on the campaign trail again. The hotel was full for the holiday weekend and the lounge started to get busy. Since his time as the campaign manager, and afterward working for CNN, Corey had raised his profile quite a bit. People recognized him all the time. Dave, too, had done a lot of TV for Fox and other channels. But compared with Kellyanne, we were B-list for sure. In between people asking her to pose for selfies, she was putting the full-court press on us to come back and join the team in the White House. Flattering as it was, we couldn't take it for long. Trump had said no, and that was enough for us.

"We heard what the president wants with our own ears," Dave told her.

"Well, if you're not coming back, then stay out of the building," she said.

The sun was already starting to set when Dave pulled out of the hotel parking lot in his Chevy Suburban. Susan had told him that she and the kids would wait for him for dinner. Hot dogs and hamburgers, the perfect Memorial Day meal, was on the menu. He let out a deep breath. He couldn't wait to fire up the grill. A job in the White House would have meant twenty-hour days and seven-day weeks. He would have taken the position had the president asked. But on Sixteenth Street heading home, he was glad that he hadn't.

After another drink with Kellyanne, Corey, too, called it a night and headed up to his room. We were fine with whatever role the president wanted us to play. In Donald Trump's army, there were no more loyal soldiers.

We couldn't stay out of the way; the president wouldn't let us. Kellyanne knew that as well as we did. In the coming months, we would watch as the fundamental flaw in the Trump White House made it shake and crumble, until the whole thing split in two with the American people watching. First out of the White House was General Mike Flynn, followed by Katie Walsh and shortly thereafter Sean Spicer. They were followed closely by Reince Priebus. Sebastian Gorka has left, George Sifakis, is out and even our close friend Keith Schiller has left government service.

We watched Anthony Scaramucci flame out. We were in Steve's apartment when Mooch's first tweet hit the fan.

Bannon read it, then looked up from his cell phone. "Is he drinking?" he asked.

We didn't know.

And now Bannon, too, is gone. He walked out of the door to the West Wing with a plan to support the agenda that Trump won on and to pay back all those who opposed him.

Sometimes we think maybe it's better that we stayed on the outside.

And sometimes we think the boss is just waiting for the right time to bring us back.

Whatever happens, things are good for us. Corey opened a strategic consulting business that takes him all over the world. Dave still runs Citizens United and is a top political contributor to Fox News and, as usual, has a thousand irons in the fire.

Both of us are still loyal advocates for the president and staunch supporters of his Make America Great Again agenda, and we promote both as much as we can in the media and other circles. Plus, we got to write this book.

But Dave, for one, sometimes thinks about life after politics. He has a hunting camp in Marengo County, Alabama. Susan grew up in Marengo, and much of her family still lives in Alabama. In the lower western part of the state, the county is in what is known as the Black Belt, a swath of Alabama so rich with vertisol that the topsoil is as black as coal. It is also historically dirt poor. Marengo does, however, have some of the best deer hunting in the state, and Dave and his son Griffin often take advantage. Now, he's not going south just yet. But he'd be lying if he told you that direction is not in the back of his mind.

Not Corey. He still goes a hundred miles an hour and tries to get to the gym often, and there's no stopping in sight. He and Dave both have offices on Pennsylvania Avenue, and he splits his time between the capital during the week and home on weekends. He tries to not miss too many of the parades his kids march in.

It's doubtful, though, he'll run another campaign. Not too long ago, someone asked him if he would.

"I was Donald Trump's campaign manager," he said. "How would anyone ever top that?"

I am asking all citizens to embrace this renewal of the American spirit. I am asking all members of Congress to join me in dreaming big, and bold, and daring things for our country. I am asking everyone watching tonight to seize this moment. Believe in yourselves, believe in your future, and believe, once more, in America.

—DONALD J. TRUMP, SPEECH TO THE JOINT SESSION
OF CONGRESS, FEBRUARY 28, 2017

ACKNOWLEDGMENTS

WE ARE THANKFUL that so many talented and dedicated people worked hard to help elect Donald J. Trump as the forty-fifth president of the United States. We are grateful to the many people who sacrificed and supported us every step of the way. There is no way that this list could ever be completed without missing a few people, so please know as you read this that there are countless other people, from volunteers to state chairmen to elected officials to friends of the Trump family, who proved to be true patriots.

A special thanks goes out to the staff at all the Trump properties, who were so kind to us on so many visits.

To the incredible men and women of the United States Secret Service, specifically Mark Halberstadt and Scott Christensen, our detail leaders. We are grateful to your unwavering commitment to protecting Team Trump.

We also want to recognize the remarkable dedication of Capt. John Duncan and his team who made our air travel possible.

To our editor Kate Hartson and all the people at Hachette, our collaborator Brian McDonald, and our agent Mel Berger at William Morris Endeavor, thank you for helping us make this book a reality.

We also would like to thank all the people who served on advisory boards and as state chairmen and co-chairmen on the campaign. Their services and support were invaluable to our efforts in so many primary states and in the general-election battleground states.

Erik Abate, Mike Abate, Ashton Adams, Mr. and Dr. Sheldon and Miriam Alderson, Joe Alexander, Mike Ambrisini, Alex Angelson, Jennifer Arangio, Auggie Atencio, Nick Ayers, Andy

Badolato, Al Baldasaro, Stephen K. Bannon, Thomas Baptiste, Tom Barrack, Healy Baumgardner, Chess Bedsole, Don Benton, Avi Berkowitz, Jessie Binnall, Josephine Blackwell, David Blair, Dorothy Blumenthal, David Bockorny, Sid Bowdidge, Austin Browning, Mark Burns, Chris Byrne, Matt Calamari, Justin Caporale, Chris Carr, Tony Casler, Aaron Chang, Steven Cheung, Dave Chiokadze, Kevin Chmielewski, Witold Chrabaszcz, Ted Christian, Governor Chris Christie, David Clarke, Jason Chung, Matt Ciepiclowski, Sam Clovis, Alan Cobb, Kellyanne Conway, Ann Coulter, Marshall Critchfield, A.B.Culverhouse, Ed Cox, Tera Dahl, Kamran Daravi, Roma Daravi, Zach Dasher, Tucker Davis, Andy Dean, Rick Dearborn, A.J. Delgato, Vincent DeVito, Jeff Dewit, Diamond and Silk, Jonathan Dimock, Sean Dollman, Annie Donaldson, Kaelen Dorr, Fred Doucette, Cassidy Dumbauld, Captain John Duncan, Jordan Eason, Lew Einsenberg, Boris Ephystein, The Falwell Family, Fletcher Fitzpatrick, Erica Freeman, Robert Gabriel, Lisa Maciejowski Gambuzza, Lou Gargulio, Alan Garten, Daniel Gelbinovich, George Gigicos, Speaker Newt Gingrich, Ben Ginsberg, Karen Giorno, Mayor Rudy Giuliani, Michael Glassner, Rob Gleason, Larry Glick, Tana Goertz, Rhona Graff, Kent Gray, Elizabeth Green, Wells Griffith, Stephanie Grisham, Joe Gruters, Scott Hagerstrom, John Haggerty, Vince Haley, Scott and Robin Hall, Steve Hantler, Sarah Harbison, Samantha Hebert, Hope Hicks, John Hiller, Alex Hinson, Mallory Hunter, Governor Mike Huckabee, Brian Jack, John Jaggers, Suzie Jaworski, Robert Jeffress, Tom Joannou, Darcie Johnston, Josh Jones, Tim Jost, Gen. Keith Kellogg, Jay Krieger, Jared Kushner, Ryan Lambert, Bryan Lanza, Chuck and Stephanie Laudner, David Ledbury, Bruce LeVell, Joy Lutes, Mark Lloyd, Jennifer Locetta, Marc Lotter, Kelly Love, Michael McDonald, Nancy Mace, Bernie Marcus,

Eric Mahroum, Omarosa Manigault, Brian Marriott, Katie Martinez, John Masburn, Dane and Donna Maxwell, John McEntee, Zach McEntee, Geri McDaniel, Don McGahn, Bill McGinley, Governor Henry McMaster, Ed McMullen, Robert Mercer, Rebekah Mercer, Michelle Meadows, Jim Merrill, Molly Michael, Molly Michael, Amanda Miller, Ben Miller, Eli Miller, Matt Miller, Max Miller, Jason Miller, Stephen Miller, Stephanie Milligan, Ashley Mocarski, Hunter Morgan, Darren Morris, Charles Munoz, Mike Murray, Baylor Myers, Laura Nasim, Peter Navarro, Marty Obst, Jason Osborne, Bob Paduchik, Carl Paladino, Matt Palumbo, Bill Palatucci, Brad Parscale, Meghan Patenaude, Lynne Patton, Jamie Peavy, Bobby Peede, Gabe Perez, Brandon Phillips, Katrina Pierson, Josh Pitcock, Megan Powers, Alexandra Preate, Reince Preibus, Pam Pryor, Katie Purucker, Heather Rinkus, Mike Roman, Mike Rubino, Phil Ruffing, John Russell, Will Russell, Hannah Salem, Sarah Huckabee Sanders, Camilo Sandoval, Daniel Sarem, Anthony Scaramucci, Dan Scavino, Darrell Scott, Attorney General Jeff Sessions, Keith Schiller, Ryan Schmidt, Aubrey Shines, Clay Shoemaker, Marc Short, Jason Simmons, Spencer Silverman, Cliff Sims, Jared Smith, McKensie Smith, Sean Spicer, Steve Stepanek, Members of the Strike Force, Andy Surabian, John Sweeney, Robert Swope, Dan Tamburello, Drew Teitelbaum, Danny Tiso, Joe Trillo, Tim Tripepi, Thomas Tservas, Tiffany Trump, Barron Trump, Donald Trump Jr., Venessa Trump, Eric Trump, Lara Trump, Ivanka Trump, Joe Uddo, Tim Unes, David Urban, Katie Walsh, Ray Washburne, Allen Weisselberg, Ben Weiser, Anne-Allen Welden, Kathryn Wellner, Madeleine Westerhaut, Josh Whitehouse, Paula White, Ross Worthington, Caroline Wiles, Susie Wiles, Steve Wynn

INDEX

ABOUT THE AUTHORS

COREY R. LEWANDOWSKI currently serves as president and CEO of Lewandowski Strategic Advisors, LLC. He previously served as the chief political adviser and campaign manager to Donald J. Trump for President. Prior to that, he was an executive for Americans for Prosperity. Lewandowski appears regularly on television and serves as an on-the-record spokesman to major print outlets. He is a contributor to *The Hill* newspaper, serves as senior adviser to America First Policies, President Trump's Super PAC, and was recently named a visiting fellow at Harvard University. Corey previously served as a certified police officer with the state of New Hampshire, where he lives with his wife, Alison, and their four children, Abigail, Alex, Owen, and Reagan.

DAVID N. BOSSIE has served as president of Citizens United and Citizens United Foundation since 2001 and is a Fox News contributor. Beginning in August 2016, Bossie served as deputy campaign manager for Donald J. Trump for President and then as deputy executive director of the Presidential Transition Team. In 2015, Bossie was ranked number two in *Politico*'s top 50 most influential people in American politics. In 2016, he was elected as the Republican national committeeman from Maryland. David, proudly served as a volunteer firefighter for over fifteen years in Maryland where he lives with his wife, Susan and their four children, Isabella, Griffin, Lily and Maggie.